Solutions Manual

for

Investments

Tenth Edition

Zvi Bodie
Boston University

Alex Kane
University of California, San Diego

Alan J. Marcus
Boston College

Prepared by
Marc-Anthony Isaacs

SOLUTIONS MANUAL FOR
INVESTMENTS, TENTH EDITION

Published by McGraw-Hill Education, 2 Penn Plaza, New York, NY 10121. Copyright © 2014 by McGraw-Hill Education. All rights reserved.
Printed in the United States of America. Previous editions © 2011, 2009, 2008 and 2005. No part of this publication may be reproduced or
distributed in any form or by any means, or stored in a database or retrieval system, without the prior written consent of McGraw-Hill Education,
including, but not limited to, in any network or other electronic storage or transmission, or broadcast for distance learning.

Some ancillaries, including electronic and print components, may not be available to customers outside the United States.

This book is printed on acid-free paper.

5 6 7 8 9 10 QVS/QVS 20 19 18 17 16

ISBN: 978-0-07-764191-7
MHID: 0-07-764191-4

www.mhhe.com

Contents

Contents

iv

CHAPTER 1: THE INVESTMENT ENVIRONMENT

PROBLEM SETS

1. While it is ultimately true that real assets determine the material well-being of an economy, financial innovation in the form of bundling and unbundling securities creates opportunities for investors to form more efficient portfolios. Both institutional and individual investors can benefit when financial engineering creates new products that allow them to manage their portfolios of financial assets more efficiently. Bundling and unbundling create financial products with new properties and sensitivities to various sources of risk that allows investors to reduce volatility by hedging particular sources of risk more efficiently.

2. Securitization requires access to a large number of potential investors. To attract these investors, the capital market needs:

   1. a safe system of business laws and low probability of confiscatory taxation/regulation;
   2. a well-developed investment banking industry;
   3. a well-developed system of brokerage and financial transactions; and
   4. well-developed media, particularly financial reporting.

   These characteristics are found in (indeed make for) a well-developed financial market.

3. Securitization leads to disintermediation; that is, securitization provides a means for market participants to bypass intermediaries. For example, mortgage-backed securities channel funds to the housing market without requiring that banks or thrift institutions make loans from their own portfolios. Securitization works well and can benefit many, but only if the market for these securities is highly liquid. As securitization progresses, however, and financial intermediaries lose opportunities, they must increase other revenue-generating activities such as providing short-term liquidity to consumers and small business and financial services.

4. The existence of efficient capital markets and the liquid trading of financial assets make it easy for large firms to raise the capital needed to finance their investments in real assets. If Ford, for example, could not issue stocks or bonds to the general public, it would have a far more difficult time raising capital. Contraction of the supply of financial assets would make financing more difficult, thereby increasing the cost of capital. A higher cost of capital results in less investment and lower real growth.

5.   Even if the firm does not need to issue stock in any particular year, the stock market is still important to the financial manager. The stock price provides important information about how the market values the firm's investment projects. For example, if the stock price rises considerably, managers might conclude that the market believes the firm's future prospects are bright. This might be a useful signal to the firm to proceed with an investment such as an expansion of the firm's business.

     In addition, shares that can be traded in the secondary market are more attractive to initial investors since they know that they will be able to sell their shares. This in turn makes investors more willing to buy shares in a primary offering and thus improves the terms on which firms can raise money in the equity market.

     Remember that stock exchanges like those in New York, London, and Paris are the heart of capitalism, in which firms can raise capital quickly in primary markets because investors know there are liquid secondary markets.

6.   a.   No. The increase in price did not add to the productive capacity of the economy.

        b.   Yes, the value of the equity held in these assets has increased.

        c.   Future homeowners as a whole are worse off, since mortgage liabilities have also increased. In addition, this housing price bubble will eventually burst and society as a whole (and most likely taxpayers) will suffer the damage.

7.   a.   The bank loan is a financial liability for Lanni, and a financial asset for the bank. The cash Lanni receives is a financial asset. The new financial asset created is Lanni's promissory note to repay the loan.

        b.   Lanni transfers financial assets (cash) to the software developers. In return, Lanni receives the completed software package, which is a real asset. No financial assets are created or destroyed; cash is simply transferred from one party to another.

        c.   Lanni exchanges the real asset (the software) for a financial asset, which is 1,500 shares of Microsoft stock. If Microsoft issues new shares in order to pay Lanni, then this would represent the creation of new financial assets.

        d.   By selling its shares in Microsoft, Lanni exchanges one financial asset (1,500 shares of stock) for another ($120,000 in cash). Lanni uses the financial asset of $50,000 in cash to repay the bank and retire its promissory note. The bank must return its financial asset to Lanni. The loan is "destroyed" in the transaction, since it is retired when paid off and no longer exists.

8. a.

Assets		Liabilities & Shareholders' Equity	
Cash	$ 70,000	Bank loan	$ 50,000
Computers	30,000	Shareholders' equity	50,000
Total	$100,000	Total	$100,000

Ratio of real assets to total assets = $30,000/$100,000 = 0.30

   b.

Assets		Liabilities & Shareholders' Equity	
Software product*	$ 70,000	Bank loan	$ 50,000
Computers	30,000	Shareholders' equity	50,000
Total	$100,000	Total	$100,000

*Valued at cost

Ratio of real assets to total assets = $100,000/$100,000 = 1.0

   c.

Assets		Liabilities & Shareholders' Equity	
Microsoft shares	$120,000	Bank loan	$ 50,000
Computers	30,000	Shareholders' equity	100,000
Total	$150,000	Total	$150,000

Ratio of real assets to total assets = $30,000/$150,000 = 0.20

   Conclusion: when the firm starts up and raises working capital, it is characterized by a low ratio of real assets to total assets. When it is in full production, it has a high ratio of real assets to total assets. When the project "shuts down" and the firm sells it off for cash, financial assets once again replace real assets.

9. For commercial banks, the ratio is: $166.1/$13,926.0 = 0.0119

   For nonfinancial firms, the ratio is: $15,320/$30,649 = 0.4999

   The difference should be expected primarily because the bulk of the business of financial institutions is to make loans and the bulk of non-financial corporations is to invest in equipment, manufacturing plants, and property. The loans are financial assets for financial institutions, but the investments of non-financial corporations are real assets.

10.   a. Primary-market transaction in which gold certificates are being offered to public investors for the first time by an underwriting syndicate led by JW Korth Capital.

   b. The certificates are derivative assets because they represent an investment in physical gold, but each investor receives a certificate and no gold. Note that investors can convert the certificate into gold during the four-year period.

   c. Investors who wish to hold gold without the complication, risk, and cost of physical storage.

11.   a.   A fixed salary means that compensation is (at least in the short run) independent of the firm's success. This salary structure does not tie the manager's immediate compensation to the success of the firm, so a manager might not feel too compelled to work hard to maximize firm value. However, the manager might view this as the safest compensation structure and therefore value it more highly.

      b.   A salary that is paid in the form of stock in the firm means that the manager earns the most when the shareholders' wealth is maximized. Five years of vesting helps align the interests of the employee with the long-term performance of the firm. This structure is therefore most likely to align the interests of managers and shareholders. If stock compensation is overdone, however, the manager might view it as overly risky since the manager's career is already linked to the firm, and this undiversified exposure would be exacerbated with a large stock position in the firm.

      c.   A profit-linked salary creates great incentives for managers to contribute to the firm's success. However, a manager whose salary is tied to short-term profits will be risk seeking, especially if these short-term profits determine salary or if the compensation structure does not bear the full cost of the project's risks. Shareholders, in contrast, bear the losses as well as the gains on the project and might be less willing to assume that risk.

12.   Even if an individual shareholder could monitor and improve managers' performance and thereby increase the value of the firm, the payoff would be small, since the ownership share in a large corporation would be very small. For example, if you own $10,000 of Ford stock and can increase the value of the firm by 5%, a very ambitious goal, you benefit by only: $0.05 \times \$10,000 = \$500$. The cost, both personal and financial to an individual investor, is likely to be prohibitive and would typically easily exceed any accrued benefits, in this case $500.

      In contrast, a bank that has a multimillion-dollar loan outstanding to the firm has a big stake in making sure that the firm can repay the loan. It is clearly worthwhile for the bank to spend considerable resources to monitor the firm.

13.   Mutual funds accept funds from small investors and invest, on behalf of these investors, in the domestic and international securities markets.

      Pension funds accept funds and then invest in a wide range of financial securities, on behalf of current and future retirees, thereby channeling funds from one sector of the economy to another.

      Venture capital firms pool the funds of private investors and invest in start-up firms.

      Banks accept deposits from customers and loan those funds to businesses or use the funds to buy securities of large corporations.

14. Treasury bills serve a purpose for investors who prefer a low-risk investment. The lower average rate of return compared to stocks is the price investors pay for predictability of investment performance and portfolio value.

15. With a top-down investing style, you focus on asset allocation or the broad composition of the entire portfolio, which is the major determinant of overall performance. Moreover, top-down management is the natural way to establish a portfolio with a level of risk consistent with your risk tolerance. The disadvantage of an *exclusive* emphasis on top-down issues is that you may forfeit the potential high returns that could result from identifying and concentrating in undervalued securities or sectors of the market.

    With a bottom-up investing style, you try to benefit from identifying undervalued securities. The disadvantage is that investors might tend to overlook the overall composition of your portfolio, which may result in a nondiversified portfolio or a portfolio with a risk level inconsistent with the appropriate level of risk tolerance. In addition, this technique tends to require more active management, thus generating more transaction costs. Finally, the bottom-up analysis may be incorrect, in which case there will be a fruitlessly expended effort and money attempting to beat a simple buy-and-hold strategy.

16. You should be skeptical. If the author actually knows how to achieve such returns, one must question why the author would then be so ready to sell the secret to others. Financial markets are very competitive; one of the implications of this fact is that riches do not come easily. High expected returns require bearing some risk, and obvious bargains are few and far between. Odds are that the only one getting rich from the book is its author.

17. Financial assets provide for a means to acquire real assets as well as an expansion of these real assets. Financial assets provide a measure of liquidity to real assets and allow for investors to more effectively reduce risk through diversification.

18. Allowing traders to share in the profits increases the traders' willingness to assume risk. Traders will share in the upside potential directly in the form of higher compensation but only in the downside indirectly in the form of potential job loss if performance is bad enough. This scenario creates a form of agency conflict known as moral hazard, in which the owners of the financial institution share in both the total profits and losses, while the traders will tend to share more of the gains than the losses.

19. Answers may vary, however, students should touch on the following: increased transparency, regulations to promote capital adequacy by increasing the frequency of gain or loss settlement, incentives to discourage excessive risk taking, and the promotion of more accurate and unbiased risk assessment.

CHAPTER 2: ASSET CLASSES AND FINANCIAL INSTRUMENTS

PROBLEM SETS

1. Preferred stock is like long-term debt in that it typically promises a fixed payment each year. In this way, it is a perpetuity. Preferred stock is also like long-term debt in that it does not give the holder voting rights in the firm.

    Preferred stock is like equity in that the firm is under no contractual obligation to make the preferred stock dividend payments. Failure to make payments does not set off corporate bankruptcy. With respect to the priority of claims to the assets of the firm in the event of corporate bankruptcy, preferred stock has a higher priority than common equity but a lower priority than bonds.

2. Money market securities are called *cash equivalents* because of their high level of liquidity. The prices of money market securities are very stable, and they can be converted to cash (i.e., sold) on very short notice and with very low transaction costs. Examples of money market securities include Treasury bills, commercial paper, and banker's acceptances, each of which is highly marketable and traded in the secondary market.

3. (a) A repurchase agreement is an agreement whereby the seller of a security agrees to "repurchase" it from the buyer on an agreed upon date at an agreed upon price. Repos are typically used by securities dealers as a means for obtaining funds to purchase securities.

4. Spreads between risky commercial paper and risk-free government securities will widen. Deterioration of the economy increases the likelihood of default on commercial paper, making them more risky. Investors will demand a greater premium on all risky debt securities, not just commercial paper.

5.

	Corp. Bonds	Preferred Stock	Common Stock
Voting rights (typically)			Yes
contractual obligation	Yes		
Perpetual payments		Yes	Yes
Accumulated dividends		Yes	
Fixed payments (typically)	Yes	Yes	
Payment preference	First	Second	Third

6. Municipal bond interest is tax-exempt at the federal level and possibly at the state level as well. When facing higher marginal tax rates, a high-income investor would be more inclined to invest in tax-exempt securities.

7. a. You would have to pay the ask price of:

    161.1875% of par value of $1,000 = $1611.875

    b. The coupon rate is 6.25% implying coupon payments of $62.50 annually or, more precisely, $31.25 semiannually.

    c. The yield to maturity on a fixed income security is also known as its required return and is reported by *The Wall Street Journal* and others in the financial press as the ask yield. In this case, the yield to maturity is 2.113%. An investor buying this security today and holding it until it matures will earn an annual return of 2.113%. Students will learn in a later chapter how to compute both the price and the yield to maturity with a financial calculator.

8. Treasury bills are discount securities that mature for $10,000. Therefore, a specific T-bill price is simply the maturity value divided by one plus the semi-annual return:

    $P = \$10,000/1.02 = \$9,803.92$

9. The total before-tax income is $4. After the 70% exclusion for preferred stock dividends, the taxable income is: $0.30 \times \$4 = \$1.20$

    Therefore, taxes are: $0.30 \times \$1.20 = \$0.36$

    After-tax income is: $\$4.00 - \$0.36 = \$3.64$

    Rate of return is: $\$3.64/\$40.00 = 9.10\%$

10. a. You could buy: $\$5,000/\$64.69 = 77.29$ shares. Since it is not possible to trade in fractions of shares, you could buy 77 shares of GD.

    b. Your annual dividend income would be: $77 \times \$2.04 = \$157.08$

    c. The price-to-earnings ratio is 9.31 and the price is $64.69. Therefore:

    $\$64.69/\text{Earnings per share} = 9.3 \Rightarrow \text{Earnings per share} = \$6.96$

    d. General Dynamics closed today at $64.69, which was $0.65 higher than yesterday's price of $64.04

11. a. At $t = 0$, the value of the index is: $(90 + 50 + 100)/3 = 80$

    At $t = 1$, the value of the index is: $(95 + 45 + 110)/3 = 83.333$

    The rate of return is: $(83.333/80) - 1 = 4.17\%$

b. In the absence of a split, Stock C would sell for 110, so the value of the index would be: 250/3 = 83.333 with a divisor of 3.

After the split, stock C sells for 55. Therefore, we need to find the divisor (d) such that: 83.333 = (95 + 45 + 55)/d ⇒ d = 2.340. The divisor fell, which is always the case after one of the firms in an index splits its shares.

c. The return is zero. The index remains unchanged because the return for each stock separately equals zero.

12. a. Total market value at $t = 0$ is: ($9,000 + $10,000 + $20,000) = $39,000

Total market value at $t = 1$ is: ($9,500 + $9,000 + $22,000) = $40,500
Rate of return = ($40,500/$39,000) – 1 = 3.85%

b. The return on each stock is as follows:

$$r_A = (95/90) - 1 = 0.0556$$
$$r_B = (45/50) - 1 = -0.10$$
$$r_C = (110/100) - 1 = 0.10$$

The equally weighted average is:

[0.0556 + (–0.10) + 0.10]/3 = 0.0185 = 1.85%

13. The after-tax yield on the corporate bonds is: $0.09 \times (1 - 0.30) = 0.063 = 6.30\%$
Therefore, municipals must offer a yield to maturity of at least 6.30%.

14. Equation (2.2) shows that the equivalent taxable yield is: $r = r_m /(1 - t)$, so simply substitute each tax rate in the denominator to obtain the following:

a. 4.00%

b. 4.44%

c. 5.00%

d. 5.71%

15. In an equally weighted index fund, each stock is given equal weight regardless of its market capitalization. Smaller cap stocks will have the same weight as larger cap stocks. The challenges are as follows:
- Given equal weights placed to smaller cap and larger cap, equal-weighted indices (EWI) will tend to be more volatile than their market-capitalization counterparts;

- It follows that EWIs are not good reflectors of the broad market that they represent; EWIs underplay the economic importance of larger companies.
- Turnover rates will tend to be higher, as an EWI must be rebalanced back to its original target. By design, many of the transactions would be among the smaller, less-liquid stocks.

16.   a.   The ten-year Treasury bond with the higher coupon rate will sell for a higher price because its bondholder receives higher interest payments.

      b.   The call option with the lower exercise price has more value than one with a higher exercise price.

      c.   The put option written on the lower priced stock has more value than one written on a higher priced stock.

17.   a.   You bought the contract when the futures price was $7.8325 (see Figure 2.11 and remember that the number to the right of the apostrophe represents an eighth of a cent). The contract closes at a price of $7.8725, which is $0.04 more than the original futures price. The contract multiplier is 5000. Therefore, the gain will be: $0.04 \times 5000 = 200.00

      b.   Open interest is 135,778 contracts.

18.   a.   Owning the call option gives you the right, but not the obligation, to buy at $180, while the stock is trading in the secondary market at $193. Since the stock price exceeds the exercise price, you exercise the call.

         The payoff on the option will be: $193 – $180 = $13

         The cost was originally $12.58, so the profit is: $13 – $12.58 = $0.42

      b.   Since the stock price is greater than the exercise price, you will exercise the call. The payoff on the option will be: $193 – $185 = $8

         The option originally cost $9.75, so the profit is $8 – $9.75 = –$1.75

      c.   Owning the put option gives you the right, but not the obligation, to sell at $185, but you could sell in the secondary market for $193, so there is no value in exercising the option. Since the stock price is greater than the exercise price, you will not exercise the put. The loss on the put will be the initial cost of $12.01.

19.   There is always a possibility that the option will be in-the-money at some time prior to expiration. Investors will pay something for this possibility of a positive payoff.

20.

	Value of Call at Expiration	Initial Cost	Profit
a.	0	4	–4
b.	0	4	–4
c.	0	4	–4
d.	5	4	1
e.	10	4	6

	Value of Put at Expiration	Initial Cost	Profit
a.	10	6	4
b.	5	6	–1
c.	0	6	–6
d.	0	6	–6
e.	0	6	–6

21.   A put option conveys the *right* to sell the underlying asset at the exercise price. A short position in a futures contract carries an *obligation* to sell the underlying asset at the futures price. Both positions, however, benefit if the price of the underlying asset falls.

22.   A call option conveys the *right* to buy the underlying asset at the exercise price. A long position in a futures contract carries an *obligation* to buy the underlying asset at the futures price. Both positions, however, benefit if the price of the underlying asset rises.

CFA PROBLEMS

1.   (d) There are tax advantages for corporations that own preferred shares.

2.   The equivalent taxable yield is: $6.75\%/(1 - 0.34) = 10.23\%$

3.   (a) Writing a call entails unlimited potential losses as the stock price rises.

4.   a. The taxable bond. With a zero tax bracket, the after-tax yield for the taxable bond is the same as the before-tax yield (5%), which is greater than the yield on the municipal bond.

        b. The taxable bond. The after-tax yield for the taxable bond is:

        $0.05 \times (1 - 0.10) = 4.5\%$

    c. You are indifferent. The after-tax yield for the taxable bond is:

$$0.05 \times (1 - 0.20) = 4.0\%$$

The after-tax yield is the same as that of the municipal bond.

    d. The municipal bond offers the higher after-tax yield for investors in tax brackets above 20%.

5.   If the after-tax yields are equal, then: $0.056 = 0.08 \times (1 - t)$

This implies that $t = 0.30 = 30\%$.

CHAPTER 3: HOW SECURITIES ARE TRADED

PROBLEM SETS

1. Stop-loss order: allows a stock to be sold if the price falls below a predetermined level. Stop-loss orders often accompany short sales. Limit sell order: sells stock when the price rises above a predetermined level. Market order: either a buy or sell order that is executed immediately at the current market price

2. In response to the potential negative reaction to large [block] trades, trades will be split up into many small trades, effectively hiding the total number of shares bought or sold.

3. The use of leverage necessarily magnifies returns to investors. Leveraging borrowed money allows for greater return on investment if the stock price increases. However, if the stock price declines, the investor must repay the loan, regardless of how far the stock price drops, and incur a negative rate of return. For example, if an investor buys an asset at $100 and the price rises to $110, the investor earns 10%. If an investor takes out a $40 loan at 5% and buys the same stock, the return will be 13.3%, computed as follows: $10 capital gain minus $2 interest expense divided by the $60 original investment. Of course, if the stock price falls below $100, the negative return will be greater for the leveraged account.

4. (a) A market order is an order to execute the trade immediately at the best possible price. The emphasis in a market order is the speed of execution (the reduction of execution uncertainty). The disadvantage of a market order is that the price at which it will be executed is not known ahead of time; it thus has price uncertainty.

5. (a) A broker market consists of intermediaries who have the discretion to trade for their clients. A large block trade in an illiquid security would most likely trade in this market as the brokers would have the best access to clients interested in this type of security.

   The advantage of an electronic communication network (ECN) is that it can execute large block orders without affecting the public quote. Since this security is illiquid, large block orders are less likely to occur and thus it would not likely trade through an ECN.

   Electronic limit-order markets (ELOM) transact securities with high trading volume. This illiquid security is unlikely to be traded on an ELOM.

3-1

6.   a.   The stock is purchased for: $300 \times \$40 = \$12,000$

The amount borrowed is $4,000. Therefore, the investor put up equity, or margin, of $8,000.

   b.   If the share price falls to $30, then the value of the stock falls to $9,000. By the end of the year, the amount of the loan owed to the broker grows to:

$$\$4,000 \times 1.08 = \$4,320$$

Therefore, the remaining margin in the investor's account is:

$$\$9,000 - \$4,320 = \$4,680$$

The percentage margin is now: $\$4,680/\$9,000 = 0.52$, or 52%

Therefore, the investor will not receive a margin call.

   c.   The rate of return on the investment over the year is:

(Ending equity in the account − Initial equity)/Initial equity

$$= (\$4,680 - \$8,000)/\$8,000 = -0.415, \text{ or } -41.5\%$$

Alternatively, divide the initial equity investments into the change in value plus the interest payment:

$$(\$3,000 \text{ loss} + \$320 \text{ interest})/\$8,000 = -0.415.$$

7.   a.   The initial margin was: $0.50 \times 1,000 \times \$40 = \$20,000$

As a result of the increase in the stock price Old Economy Traders loses:

$$\$10 \times 1,000 = \$10,000$$

Therefore, margin decreases by $10,000. Moreover, Old Economy Traders must pay the dividend of $2 per share to the lender of the shares, so that the margin in the account decreases by an additional $2,000. Therefore, the remaining margin is:

$$\$20,000 - \$10,000 - \$2,000 = \$8,000$$

   b.   The percentage margin is: $\$8,000/\$50,000 = 0.16$, or 16%

So there will be a margin call.

   c.   The equity in the account decreased from $20,000 to $8,000 in one year, for a rate of return of: $(-\$12,000/\$20,000) = -0.60$, or −60%

8. a.   The buy order will be filled at the best limit-sell order price: $50.25

    b.   The next market buy order will be filled at the next-best limit-sell order price: $51.50

    c.   You would want to increase your inventory. There is considerable buying demand at prices just below $50, indicating that downside risk is limited. In contrast, limit sell orders are sparse, indicating that a moderate buy order could result in a substantial price increase.

9. a.   You buy 200 shares of Telecom for $10,000. These shares increase in value by 10%, or $1,000. You pay interest of: $0.08 \times \$5,000 = \$400$

         The rate of return will be: $\dfrac{\$1,000 - \$400}{\$5,000} = 0.12 = 12\%$

    b.   The value of the 200 shares is $200P$. Equity is ($200P - \$5,000$). You will receive a margin call when:

         $$\frac{200P - \$5,000}{200P} = 0.30 \Rightarrow \text{when } P = \$35.71 \text{ or lower}$$

10. a.   Initial margin is 50% of $5,000, or $2,500.

    b.   Total assets are $7,500 ($5,000 from the sale of the stock and $2,500 put up for margin). Liabilities are $100P$. Therefore, equity is ($7,500 - 100P$). A margin call will be issued when:

         $$\frac{\$7,500 - 100P}{100P} = 0.30 \Rightarrow \text{when } P = \$57.69 \text{ or higher}$$

11. The total cost of the purchase is: $\$20 \times 1,000 = \$20,000$

    You borrow $5,000 from your broker and invest $15,000 of your own funds. Your margin account starts out with equity of $15,000.

    a.   (i)   Equity increases to: ($22 \times 1,000$) $- \$5,000 = \$17,000$

                Percentage gain = $2,000/$15,000 = 0.1333, or 13.33%

         (ii)   With price unchanged, equity is unchanged.

                Percentage gain = zero

         (iii) Equity falls to ($18 \times 1,000$) $- \$5,000 = \$13,000$

                Percentage gain = ($-\$2,000/\$15,000$) = -0.1333, or -13.33%

The relationship between the percentage return and the percentage change in the price of the stock is given by:

$$\% \text{ return} = \% \text{ change in price} \times \frac{\text{Total investment}}{\text{Investor's initial equity}} = \% \text{ change in price} \times 1.333$$

For example, when the stock price rises from $20 to $22, the percentage change in price is 10%, while the percentage gain for the investor is:

$$\% \text{ return} = 10\% \times \frac{\$20,000}{\$15,000} = 13.33\%$$

b. The value of the 1,000 shares is 1,000P. Equity is (1,000P – $5,000). You will receive a margin call when:

$$\frac{1,000P - \$5,000}{1,000P} = 0.25 \Rightarrow \text{ when } P = \$6.67 \text{ or lower}$$

c. The value of the 1,000 shares is 1,000P. But now you have borrowed $10,000 instead of $5,000. Therefore, equity is (1,000P – $10,000). You will receive a margin call when:

$$\frac{1,000P - \$10,000}{1,000P} = 0.25 \Rightarrow \text{ when } P = \$13.33 \text{ or lower}$$

With less equity in the account, you are far more vulnerable to a margin call.

d. By the end of the year, the amount of the loan owed to the broker grows to:

$$\$5,000 \times 1.08 = \$5,400$$

The equity in your account is (1,000P – $5,400). Initial equity was $15,000. Therefore, your rate of return after one year is as follows:

(i) $$\frac{(1,000 \times \$22) - \$5,400 - \$15,000}{\$15,000} = 0.1067, \text{ or } 10.67\%$$

(ii) $$\frac{(1,000 \times \$20) - \$5,400 - \$15,000}{\$15,000} = -0.0267, \text{ or } -2.67\%$$

(iii) $$\frac{(1,000 \times \$18) - \$5,400 - \$15,000}{\$15,000} = -0.1600, \text{ or } -16.00\%$$

The relationship between the percentage return and the percentage change in the price of Intel is given by:

$$\% \text{ return} = \left(\% \text{ change in price} \times \frac{\text{Total investment}}{\text{Investor's initial equity}} \right) - \left(8\% \times \frac{\text{Funds borrowed}}{\text{Investor's initial equity}} \right)$$

For example, when the stock price rises from $40 to $44, the percentage change in price is 10%, while the percentage gain for the investor is:

$$\left(10\% \times \frac{\$20,000}{\$15,000}\right) - \left(8\% \times \frac{\$5,000}{\$15,000}\right) = 10.67\%$$

e. The value of the 1000 shares is $1,000P$. Equity is $(1,000P - \$5,400)$. You will receive a margin call when:

$$\frac{1,000P - \$5,400}{1,000P} = 0.25 \Rightarrow \text{when } P = \$7.20 \text{ or lower}$$

12. a. The gain or loss on the short position is: $(-1,000 \times \Delta P)$
Invested funds = $15,000

Therefore: rate of return = $(-1,000 \times \Delta P)/15,000$

The rate of return in each of the three scenarios is:

(i)   Rate of return = $(-1,000 \times \$2)/\$15,000 = -0.1333$, or -13.33%

(ii) Rate of return = $(-1,000 \times \$0)/\$15,000 = 0\%$

(iii) Rate of return = $[-1,000 \times (-\$2)]/\$15,000 = +0.1333$, or $+13.33\%$

b. Total assets in the margin account equal:

$20,000 (from the sale of the stock) + $15,000 (the initial margin) = $35,000

Liabilities are $500P$. You will receive a margin call when:

$$\frac{\$35,000 - 1,000P}{1,000P} = 0.25 \Rightarrow \text{when } P = \$28 \text{ or higher}$$

c. With a $1 dividend, the short position must now pay on the borrowed shares: ($1/share × 1000 shares) = $1000. Rate of return is now:

$$[(-1,000 \times \Delta P) - 1,000]/15,000$$

(i)   Rate of return = $[(-1,000 \times \$2) - \$1,000]/\$15,000 = -0.2000$, or -20.00%

(ii) Rate of return = $[(-1,000 \times \$0) - \$1,000]/\$15,000 = -0.0667$, or -6.67%

(iii) Rate of return = $[(-1,000) \times (-\$2) - \$1,000]/\$15,000 = +0.067$, or $+6.67\%$

Total assets are $35,000, and liabilities are $(1,000P + 1,000)$. A margin call will be issued when:

$$\frac{35,000 - 1,000P - 1,000}{1,000P} = 0.25 \Rightarrow \text{when } P = \$27.2 \text{ or higher}$$

13. The broker is instructed to attempt to sell your Marriott stock as soon as the Marriott stock trades at a bid price of $40 or less. Here, the broker will attempt to execute but may not be able to sell at $40, since the bid price is now $39.95. The price at which you sell may be more or less than $40 because the stop-loss becomes a market order to sell at current market prices.

14. a. $55.50

    b. $55.25

    c. The trade will not be executed because the bid price is lower than the price specified in the limit-sell order.

    d. The trade will not be executed because the asked price is greater than the price specified in the limit-buy order.

15. a. You will not receive a margin call. You borrowed $20,000 and with another $20,000 of your own equity you bought 1,000 shares of Disney at $40 per share. At $35 per share, the market value of the stock is $35,000, your equity is $15,000, and the percentage margin is: $15,000/$35,000 = 42.9%
    Your percentage margin exceeds the required maintenance margin.

    b. You will receive a margin call when:

    $$\frac{1,000P - \$20,000}{1,000P} = 0.35 \Rightarrow \text{when } P = \$30.77 \text{ or lower}$$

16. The proceeds from the short sale (net of commission) were: ($21 × 100) − $50 = $2,050

    A dividend payment of $200 was withdrawn from the account.

    Covering the short sale at $15 per share costs (with commission): $1,500 + $50 = $1,550

    Therefore, the value of your account is equal to the net profit on the transaction:

    $2,050 − $200 − $1,550 = $300

    Note that your profit ($300) equals (100 shares × profit per share of $3). Your net proceeds per share were:

$21	selling price of stock
−$15	repurchase price of stock
−$ 2	dividend per share
−$ 1	2 trades × $0.50 commission per share
$ 3	

CFA PROBLEMS

1. a.   In addition to the explicit fees of $70,000, FBN appears to have paid an implicit price in underpricing of the IPO. The underpricing is $3 per share, or a total of $300,000, implying total costs of $370,000.

    b.   No. The underwriters do not capture the part of the costs corresponding to the underpricing. The underpricing may be a rational marketing strategy. Without it, the underwriters would need to spend more resources in order to place the issue with the public. The underwriters would then need to charge higher explicit fees to the issuing firm. The issuing firm may be just as well off paying the implicit issuance cost represented by the underpricing.

2. (d)   The broker will sell, at current market price, after the first transaction at $55 or less.

3. (d)

CHAPTER 4: MUTUAL FUNDS AND OTHER INVESTMENT COMPANIES

PROBLEM SETS

1. The unit investment trust should have lower operating expenses. Because the investment trust portfolio is fixed once the trust is established, it does not have to pay portfolio managers to constantly monitor and rebalance the portfolio as perceived needs or opportunities change. Because the portfolio is fixed, the unit investment trust also incurs virtually no trading costs.

2. a. *Unit investment trusts*: Diversification from large-scale investing, lower transaction costs associated with large-scale trading, low management fees, predictable portfolio composition, guaranteed low portfolio turnover rate.

   b. *Open-end mutual funds*: Diversification from large-scale investing, lower transaction costs associated with large-scale trading, professional management that may be able to take advantage of buy or sell opportunities as they arise, record keeping.

   c. *Individual stocks and bonds*: No management fee; ability to coordinate realization of capital gains or losses with investors' personal tax situations; capability of designing portfolio to investor's specific risk and return profile.

3. Open-end funds are obligated to redeem investor's shares at net asset value and thus must keep cash or cash-equivalent securities on hand in order to meet potential redemptions. Closed-end funds do not need the cash reserves because there are no redemptions for closed-end funds. Investors in closed-end funds sell their shares when they wish to cash out.

4. Balanced funds keep relatively stable proportions of funds invested in each asset class. They are meant as convenient instruments to provide participation in a range of asset classes. Life-cycle funds are balanced funds whose asset mix generally depends on the age of the investor. Aggressive life-cycle funds, with larger investments in equities, are marketed to younger investors, while conservative life-cycle funds, with larger investments in fixed-income securities, are designed for older investors. Asset allocation funds, in contrast, may vary the proportions invested in each asset class by large amounts as predictions of relative performance across classes vary. Asset allocation funds therefore engage in more aggressive market timing.

5.   Unlike an open-end fund, in which underlying shares are redeemed when the fund is redeemed, a closed-end fund trades as a security in the market. Thus, their prices may differ from the NAV.

6.   Advantages of an ETF over a mutual fund:

- ETFs are continuously traded and can be sold or purchased on margin.
- There are no capital gains tax triggers when an ETF is sold (shares are just sold from one investor to another).
- Investors buy from brokers, thus eliminating the cost of direct marketing to individual small investors. This implies lower management fees.

Disadvantages of an ETF over a mutual fund:

- Prices can depart from NAV (unlike an open-end fund).
- There is a broker fee when buying and selling (unlike a no-load fund).

7.   The offering price includes a 6% front-end load, or sales commission, meaning that every dollar paid results in only $0.94 going toward purchase of shares. Therefore:

$$\text{Offering price} = \frac{\text{NAV}}{1 - \text{Load}} = \frac{\$10.70}{1 - 0.06} = \$11.38$$

8.   NAV = Offering price × (1 – Load) = $12.30 × .95 = $11.69

9.
Stock	Value Held by Fund
A	$ 7,000,000
B	12,000,000
C	8,000,000
D	15,000,000
Total	$42,000,000

$$\text{Net asset value} = \frac{\$42,000,000 - \$30,000}{4,000,000} = \$10.49$$

10. Value of stocks sold and replaced = $15,000,000

$$\text{Turnover rate} = \frac{\$15,000,000}{\$42,000,000} = 0.357, \text{ or } 35.7\%$$

11. a. $\text{NAV} = \dfrac{\$200,000,000 - \$3,000,000}{5,000,000} = \$39.40$

    b. $\text{Premium (or discount)} = \dfrac{\text{Price} - \text{NAV}}{\text{NAV}} = \dfrac{\$36 - \$39.40}{\$39.40} = -0.086, \text{ or } -8.6\%$

        The fund sells at an 8.6% discount from NAV.

12. $\dfrac{\text{NAV}_1 - \text{NAV}_0 + \text{Distributions}}{\text{NAV}_0} = \dfrac{\$12.10 - \$12.50 + \$1.50}{\$12.50} = 0.088, \text{ or } 8.8\%$

13. a. Start-of-year price: $P_0 = \$12.00 \times 1.02 = \$12.24$

        End-of-year price: $P_1 = \$12.10 \times 0.93 = \$11.25$

        Although NAV increased by $0.10, the price of the fund decreased by $0.99.

        $\text{Rate of return} = \dfrac{P_1 - P_0 + \text{Distributions}}{P_0} = \dfrac{\$11.25 - \$12.24 + \$1.50}{\$12.24} = 0.042, \text{ or } 4.2\%$

    b. An investor holding the same securities as the fund manager would have earned a rate of return based on the increase in the NAV of the portfolio:

        $\dfrac{\text{NAV}_1 - \text{NAV}_0 + \text{Distributions}}{\text{NAV}_0} = \dfrac{\$12.10 - \$12.00 + \$1.50}{\$12.00} = 0.133, \text{ or } 13.3\%$

14. a. Empirical research indicates that past performance of mutual funds is not highly predictive of future performance, especially for better-performing funds. While there *may* be some tendency for the fund to be an above average performer next year, it is unlikely to once again be a top 10% performer.

    b. On the other hand, the evidence is more suggestive of a tendency for poor performance to persist. This tendency is probably related to fund costs and turnover rates. Thus if the fund is among the poorest performers, investors should be concerned that the poor performance will persist.

15. $\text{NAV}_0 = \$200,000,000/10,000,000 = \$20$

    Dividends per share $= \$2,000,000/10,000,000 = \$0.20$

    NAV_1 is based on the 8% price gain, less the 1% 12b-1 fee:

    $\text{NAV}_1 = \$20 \times 1.08 \times (1 - 0.01) = \$21.384$

    $\text{Rate of return} = \dfrac{\$21.384 - \$20 + \$0.20}{\$20} = 0.0792, \text{ or } 7.92\%$

16.   The excess of purchases over sales must be due to new inflows into the fund. Therefore, $400 million of stock previously held by the fund was replaced by new holdings. So turnover is: $400/$2,200 = 0.182, or 18.2%.

17.   Fees paid to investment managers were: $0.007 \times \$2.2$ billion = $15.4 million
      Since the total expense ratio was 1.1% and the management fee was 0.7%, we conclude that 0.4% must be for other expenses. Therefore, other administrative expenses were: $0.004 \times \$2.2$ billion = $8.8 million.

18.   As an initial approximation, your return equals the return on the shares minus the total of the expense ratio and purchase costs: 12% − 1.2% − 4% = 6.8%.

      But the precise return is less than this because the 4% load is paid up front, not at the end of the year.

      To purchase the shares, you would have had to invest: $20,000/(1 − 0.04) = $20,833.

      The shares increase in value from $20,000 to: $20,000 \times (1.12 - 0.012) = \$22,160$.

      The rate of return is: ($22,160 − $20,833)/$20,833 = 6.37%.

19.

Assume $1,000 investment	Loaded-Up Fund	Economy Fund
Yearly growth (r is 6%)	$(1 + r - .01 - .0075)$	$(.98) \times (1 + r - .0025)$
$t = 1$ year	$1,042.50	$1,036.35
$t = 3$ years	$1,133.00	$1,158.96
$t = 10$ years	$1,516.21	$1,714.08

20.   a. $\dfrac{\$450,000,000 - \$10,000000}{44,000,000} = \$10$

      b. The redemption of 1 million shares will most likely trigger capital gains taxes which will lower the remaining portfolio by an amount greater than $10,000,000 (implying a remaining total value less than $440,000,000). The outstanding shares fall to 43 million and the NAV drops to below $10.

21.   Suppose you have $1,000 to invest. The initial investment in Class A shares is $940 net of the front-end load. After four years, your portfolio will be worth:

      $940 \times (1.10)^4 = \$1,376.25$

      Class B shares allow you to invest the full $1,000, but your investment performance net of 12b-1 fees will be only 9.5%, and you will pay a 1% back-end load fee if you sell after four years. Your portfolio value after four years will be:

      $1,000 \times (1.095)^4 = \$1,437.66$

After paying the back-end load fee, your portfolio value will be:

$1,437.66 \times .99 = \$1,423.28$

Class B shares are the better choice if your horizon is four years.

With a 15-year horizon, the Class A shares will be worth:

$\$940 \times (1.10)^{15} = \$3,926.61$

For the Class B shares, there is no back-end load in this case since the horizon is greater than five years. Therefore, the value of the Class B shares will be:

$\$1,000 \times (1.095)^{15} = \$3,901.32$

At this longer horizon, Class B shares are no longer the better choice. The effect of Class B's 0.5% 12b-1 fees accumulates over time and finally overwhelms the 6% load charged to Class A investors.

22. a. After two years, each dollar invested in a fund with a 4% load and a portfolio return equal to r will grow to: $\$0.96 \times (1 + r - 0.005)^2$.

Each dollar invested in the bank CD will grow to: $\$1 \times 1.06^2$.

If the mutual fund is to be the better investment, then the portfolio return (r) must satisfy:

$0.96 \times (1 + r - 0.005)^2 > 1.06^2$

$0.96 \times (1 + r - 0.005)^2 > 1.1236$

$(1 + r - 0.005)^2 > 1.1704$

$1 + r - 0.005 > 1.0819$

$1 + r > 1.0869$

Therefore: $r > 0.0869 = 8.69\%$

b. If you invest for six years, then the portfolio return must satisfy:

$0.96 \times (1 + r - 0.005)^6 > 1.06^6 = 1.4185$

$(1 + r - 0.005)^6 > 1.4776$

$1 + r - 0.005 > 1.0672$

$r > 7.22\%$

The cutoff rate of return is lower for the six-year investment because the "fixed cost" (the one-time front-end load) is spread over a greater number of years.

c. With a 12b-1 fee instead of a front-end load, the portfolio must earn a rate of return (r) that satisfies:

$1 + r - 0.005 - 0.0075 > 1.06$

In this case, r must exceed 7.25% regardless of the investment horizon.

23.   The turnover rate is 50%. This means that, on average, 50% of the portfolio is sold and replaced with other securities each year. Trading costs on the sell orders are 0.4% and the buy orders to replace those securities entail another 0.4% in trading costs. Total trading costs will reduce portfolio returns by: $2 \times 0.4\% \times 0.50 = 0.4\%$

24.   For the bond fund, the fraction of portfolio income given up to fees is:

$$\frac{0.6\%}{4.0\%} = 0.150, \text{ or } 15.0\%$$

For the equity fund, the fraction of investment earnings given up to fees is:

$$\frac{0.6\%}{12.0\%} = 0.050, \text{ or } 5.0\%$$

Fees are a much higher fraction of expected earnings for the bond fund and therefore may be a more important factor in selecting the bond fund.

This may help to explain why unmanaged unit investment trusts are concentrated in the fixed income market. The advantages of unit investment trusts are low turnover, low trading costs, and low management fees. This is a more important concern to bond-market investors.

25.   Suppose that finishing in the top half of all portfolio managers is purely luck, and that the probability of doing so in any year is exactly ½. Then the probability that any particular manager would finish in the top half of the sample five years in a row is $(½)^5 = 1/32$. We would then expect to find that $[350 \times (1/32)] = 11$ managers finish in the top half for each of the five consecutive years. This is precisely what we found. Thus, we should not conclude that the consistent performance after five years is proof of skill. We would expect to find 11 managers exhibiting precisely this level of "consistency" even if performance is due solely to luck.

CHAPTER 5: INTRODUCTION TO RISK, RETURN, AND THE HISTORICAL RECORD

PROBLEM SETS

1. The Fisher equation predicts that the nominal rate will equal the equilibrium real rate plus the expected inflation rate. Hence, if the inflation rate increases from 3% to 5% while there is no change in the real rate, then the nominal rate will increase by 2%. On the other hand, it is possible that an increase in the expected inflation rate would be accompanied by a change in the real rate of interest. While it is conceivable that the nominal interest rate could remain constant as the inflation rate increased, implying that the real rate decreased as inflation increased, this is not a likely scenario.

2. If we assume that the distribution of returns remains reasonably stable over the entire history, then a longer sample period (i.e., a larger sample) increases the precision of the estimate of the expected rate of return; this is a consequence of the fact that the standard error decreases as the sample size increases. However, if we assume that the mean of the distribution of returns is changing over time but we are not in a position to determine the nature of this change, then the expected return must be estimated from a more recent part of the historical period. In this scenario, we must determine how far back, historically, to go in selecting the relevant sample. Here, it is likely to be disadvantageous to use the entire data set back to 1880.

3. The true statements are (c) and (e). The explanations follow.

    Statement (c): Let σ = the annual standard deviation of the risky investments and σ_1 = the standard deviation of the first investment alternative over the two-year period. Then:

    $$\sigma_1 = \sqrt{2} \times \sigma$$

    Therefore, the annualized standard deviation for the first investment alternative is equal to:

    $$\frac{\sigma_1}{2} = \frac{\sigma}{\sqrt{2}} < \sigma$$

    Statement (e): The first investment alternative is more attractive to investors with lower degrees of risk aversion. The first alternative (entailing a sequence of two identically distributed and uncorrelated risky investments) is riskier than the second alternative (the risky investment followed by a risk-free investment). Therefore, the first alternative is more attractive to investors with lower degrees of risk aversion. Notice, however, that if you mistakenly believed that time diversification can reduce the total risk of a sequence of risky investments, you would have been tempted to conclude that the first alternative is less risky and therefore more attractive to more risk-averse investors. This is clearly not the case; the two-year standard deviation of the first alternative is greater than the two-year standard deviation of the second alternative.

4.   For the money market fund, your holding-period return for the next year depends on the level of 30-day interest rates each month when the fund rolls over maturing securities. The one-year savings deposit offers a 7.5% holding period return for the year. If you forecast that the rate on money market instruments will increase significantly above the current 6% yield, then the money market fund might result in a higher HPR than the savings deposit. The 20-year Treasury bond offers a yield to maturity of 9% per year, which is 150 basis points higher than the rate on the one-year savings deposit; however, you could earn a one-year HPR much less than 7.5% on the bond if long-term interest rates increase during the year. If Treasury bond yields rise above 9%, then the price of the bond will fall, and the resulting capital loss will wipe out some or all of the 9% return you would have earned if bond yields had remained unchanged over the course of the year.

5.   a.   If businesses reduce their capital spending, then they are likely to decrease their demand for funds. This will shift the demand curve in Figure 5.1 to the left and reduce the equilibrium real rate of interest.

     b.   Increased household saving will shift the supply of funds curve to the right and cause real interest rates to fall.

     c.   Open market purchases of U.S. Treasury securities by the Federal Reserve Board are equivalent to an increase in the supply of funds (a shift of the supply curve to the right). The FED buys treasuries with cash from its own account or it issues certificates which trade like cash. As a result, there is an increase in the money supply, and the equilibrium real rate of interest will fall.

6.   a.   The "Inflation-Plus" CD is the safer investment because it guarantees the purchasing power of the investment. Using the approximation that the real rate equals the nominal rate minus the inflation rate, the CD provides a real rate of 1.5% regardless of the inflation rate.

     b.   The expected return depends on the expected rate of inflation over the next year. If the expected rate of inflation is less than 3.5% then the conventional CD offers a higher real return than the inflation-plus CD; if the expected rate of inflation is greater than 3.5%, then the opposite is true.

     c.   If you expect the rate of inflation to be 3% over the next year, then the conventional CD offers you an expected real rate of return of 2%, which is 0.5% higher than the real rate on the inflation-protected CD. But unless you know that inflation will be 3% with certainty, the conventional CD is also riskier. The question of which is the better investment then depends on your attitude towards risk versus return. You might choose to diversify and invest part of your funds in each.

     d.   No. We cannot assume that the entire difference between the risk-free nominal rate (on conventional CDs) of 5% and the real risk-free rate (on inflation-protected CDs) of 1.5% is the expected rate of inflation. Part of the difference is probably a risk premium associated with the uncertainty surrounding the real rate of return on the conventional CDs. This implies that the expected rate of inflation is less than 3.5% per year.

7. $E(r) = [0.35 \times 44.5\%] + [0.30 \times 14.0\%] + [0.35 \times (-16.5\%)] = 14\%$

    $\sigma^2 = [0.35 \times (44.5 - 14)^2] + [0.30 \times (14 - 14)^2] + [0.35 \times (-16.5 - 14)^2] = 651.175$

    $\sigma = 25.52\%$

    The mean is unchanged, but the standard deviation has increased, as the probabilities of the high and low returns have increased.

8. Probability distribution of price and one-year holding period return for a 30-year U.S. Treasury bond (which will have 29 years to maturity at year-end):

Economy	Probability	YTM	Price	Capital Gain	Coupon Interest	HPR
Boom	0.20	11.0%	$ 74.05	−$25.95	$8.00	−17.95%
Normal growth	0.50	8.0	100.00	0.00	8.00	8.00
Recession	0.30	7.0	112.28	12.28	8.00	20.28

9. $E(q) = (0 \times 0.25) + (1 \times 0.25) + (2 \times 0.50) = 1.25$

    $\sigma_q = [0.25 \times (0 - 1.25)^2 + 0.25 \times (1 - 1.25)^2 + 0.50 \times (2 - 1.25)^2]^{1/2} = 0.8292$

10. (a) With probability 0.9544, the value of a normally distributed variable will fall within 2 standard deviations of the mean; that is, between −40% and 80%. Simply add and subtract 2 standard deviations to and from the mean.

11. From Table 5.4, the average risk premium for the period 7/1926-9/2012 was: 12.34% per year.

    Adding 12.34% to the 3% risk-free interest rate, the expected annual HPR for the Big/Value portfolio is: 3.00% + 12.34% = 15.34%.

12.

	(01/1928-06/1970)					
	Small			Big		
	Low	2	High	Low	2	High
Average	1.03%	1.21%	1.46%	0.78%	0.88%	1.18%
SD	8.55%	8.47%	10.35%	5.89%	6.91%	9.11%
Skew	1.6704	1.6673	2.3064	0.0067	1.6251	1.6348
Kurtosis	13.1505	13.5284	17.2137	6.2564	16.2305	13.6729

	(07/1970–12/2012)					
	Small			Big		
	Low	2	High	Low	2	High
Average	0.91%	1.33%	1.46%	0.93%	1.02%	1.13%
SD	7.00%	5.49%	5.66%	4.81%	4.50%	4.78%
	–	–	–			
Skew	0.3278	0.5135	0.4323	−0.3136	0.3508	−0.4954
Kurtosis	1.7962	3.1917	3.8320	1.8516	2.0756	2.8629

No. The distributions from (01/1928–06/1970) and (07/1970–12/2012) periods have distinct characteristics due to systematic shocks to the economy and subsequent government intervention. While the returns from the two periods do not differ greatly, their respective distributions tell a different story. The standard deviation for all six portfolios is larger in the first period. Skew is also positive, but negative in the second, showing a greater likelihood of higher-than-normal returns in the right tail. Kurtosis is also markedly larger in the first period.

13. a. $rr = \dfrac{1+rn}{1+i} - 1 = \dfrac{rn-i}{1+i} = \dfrac{0.80-0.70}{1.70} = 0.0588,\ or\ 5.88\%$

  b. $rr \approx rn - i = 80\% - 70\% = 10\%$
  Clearly, the approximation gives a real HPR that is too high.

14. From Table 5.2, the average real rate on T-bills has been 0.52%.

  a.   T-bills: 0.52% real rate + 3% inflation = 3.52%

  b.   Expected return on Big/Value:
  3.52% T-bill rate + 12.34% historical risk premium = 15.86%

  c.   The risk premium on stocks remains unchanged. A premium, the difference between two rates, is a real value, unaffected by inflation.

15. Real interest rates are expected to rise. The investment activity will shift the demand for funds curve (in Figure 5.1) to the right. Therefore the equilibrium real interest rate will increase.

16. a. Probability distribution of the HPR on the stock market and put:

State of the Economy	Probability	STOCK Ending Price + Dividend	HPR	PUT Ending Value	HPR
Excellent	0.25	$ 131.00	31.00%	$ 0.00	−100%
Good	0.45	114.00	14.00	$ 0.00	−100
Poor	0.25	93.25	−6.75	$ 20.25	68.75
Crash	0.05	48.00	−52.00	$ 64.00	433.33

   Remember that the cost of the index fund is $100 per share, and the cost of the put option is $12.

   b. The cost of one share of the index fund plus a put option is $112. The probability distribution of the HPR on the portfolio is:

State of the Economy	Probability	Ending Price + Put + Dividend	HPR	
Excellent	0.25	$ 131.00	17.0%	= (131 − 112)/112
Good	0.45	114.00	1.8	= (114 − 112)/112
Poor	0.25	113.50	1.3	= (113.50 − 112)/112
Crash	0.05	112.00	0.0	= (112 − 112)/112

   c. Buying the put option guarantees the investor a minimum HPR of 0.0% regardless of what happens to the stock's price. Thus, it offers insurance against a price decline.

17. The probability distribution of the dollar return on CD plus call option is:

State of the Economy	Probability	Ending Value of CD	Ending Value of Call	Combined Value
Excellent	0.25	$ 114.00	$16.50	$130.50
Good	0.45	114.00	0.00	114.00
Poor	0.25	114.00	0.00	114.00
Crash	0.05	114.00	0.00	114.00

18. a. Total return of the bond is $(100/84.49) - 1 = 0.1836$. With $t = 10$, the annual rate on the real bond is $(1 + EAR) = 1.1836^{1/10} = 1.69\%$.

   b. With a per quarter yield of 2%, the annual yield is $(1 + .02)^4 = 1.0824$, or 8.24%. The equivalent continuously compounding (cc) rate is $\ln(1+.0824) = .0792$, or 7.92%. The risk-free rate is 3.55% with a cc rate of $\ln(1+.0355) = .0349$, or 3.49%. The cc risk premium will equal $.0792 - .0349 = .0443$, or 4.433%.

c. The appropriate formula is σ^2 (effective) $= e^{2 \times m(cc)} \times [e^{\sigma^{2}(cc)} - 1]$, where

$m(cc) = g + \frac{1}{2} \times \sigma^2 (cc)$. Using solver or goal seek, setting the target cell to the known effective cc rate by changing the unknown variance (cc) rate, the equivalent standard deviation (cc) is $\approx 18.03\%$ (excel may yield slightly different solutions).

d. The expected value of the excess return will grow by 120 months (12 months over a 10-year horizon). Therefore the excess return will be $120 \times 4.433\% = 531.9\%$. The expected SD grows by the square root of time resulting in $18.03\% \times \sqrt{120} = 197.5\%$. The resulting Sharpe ratio is $531.9/197.5 = 2.6929$. Normsdist $(-2.6929) = .0035$, or a .35% probability of shortfall over a 10-year horizon.

CFA PROBLEMS

1. The expected dollar return on the investment in equities is $18,000 (0.6 × $50,000 + 0.4 × −$30,000) compared to the $5,000 expected return for T-bills. Therefore, the expected risk premium is $13,000.

2. $E(r) = [0.2 \times (-25\%)] + [0.3 \times 10\%] + [0.5 \times 24\%] = 10\%$

3. $E(r_X) = [0.2 \times (-20\%)] + [0.5 \times 18\%] + [0.3 \times 50\%] = 20\%$

    $E(r_Y) = [0.2 \times (-15\%)] + [0.5 \times 20\%] + [0.3 \times 10\%] = 10\%$

4. $\sigma_X^2 = [0.2 \times (-20 - 20)^2] + [0.5 \times (18 - 20)^2] + [0.3 \times (50 - 20)^2] = 592$

    $\sigma_X = 24.33\%$

    $\sigma_Y^2 = [0.2 \times (-15 - 10)^2] + [0.5 \times (20 - 10)^2] + [0.3 \times (10 - 10)^2] = 175$

    $\sigma_Y = 13.23\%$

5. $E(r) = (0.9 \times 20\%) + (0.1 \times 10\%) = 19\%$ ➔ $1,900 in returns

6. The probability that the economy will be neutral is 0.50, or 50%. Given a neutral economy, the stock will experience poor performance 30% of the time. The probability of both poor stock performance and a neutral economy is therefore:

    $0.30 \times 0.50 = 0.15 = 15\%$

7. $E(r) = (0.1 \times 15\%) + (0.6 \times 13\%) + (0.3 \times 7\%) = 11.4\%$

CHAPTER 6: RISK AVERSION AND CAPITAL ALLOCATION TO RISKY ASSETS

PROBLEM SETS

1. (e) The first two answer choices are incorrect because a highly risk averse investor would avoid portfolios with higher risk premiums and higher standard deviations. In addition, higher or lower Sharpe ratios are not an indication of an investor's tolerance for risk. The Sharpe ratio is simply a tool to absolutely measure the return premium earned per unit of risk.

2. (b) A higher borrowing rate is a consequence of the risk of the borrowers' default. In perfect markets with no additional cost of default, this increment would equal the value of the borrower's option to default, and the Sharpe measure, with appropriate treatment of the default option, would be the same. However, in reality there are costs to default so that this part of the increment lowers the Sharpe ratio. Also, notice that answer (c) is not correct because doubling the expected return with a fixed risk-free rate will more than double the risk premium and the Sharpe ratio.

3. Assuming no change in risk tolerance, that is, an unchanged risk-aversion coefficient (A), higher perceived volatility increases the denominator of the equation for the optimal investment in the risky portfolio (Equation 6.7). The proportion invested in the risky portfolio will therefore decrease.

4. a. The expected cash flow is: $(0.5 \times \$70,000) + (0.5 \times 200,000) = \$135,000$.

    With a risk premium of 8% over the risk-free rate of 6%, the required rate of return is 14%. Therefore, the present value of the portfolio is:

    $\$135,000/1.14 = \$118,421$

    b. If the portfolio is purchased for \$118,421 and provides an expected cash inflow of \$135,000, then the expected rate of return $[E(r)]$ is as follows:

    $\$118,421 \times [1 + E(r)] = \$135,000$

    Therefore, $E(r) = 14\%$. The portfolio price is set to equate the expected rate of return with the required rate of return.

    c. If the risk premium over T-bills is now 12%, then the required return is:

    $6\% + 12\% = 18\%$

    The present value of the portfolio is now:

    $\$135,000/1.18 = \$114,407$

d. For a given expected cash flow, portfolios that command greater risk premiums must sell at lower prices. The extra discount from expected value is a penalty for risk.

5. When we specify utility by $U = E(r) - 0.5A\sigma^2$, the utility level for T-bills is: 0.07

The utility level for the risky portfolio is:

$$U = 0.12 - 0.5 \times A \times (0.18)^2 = 0.12 - 0.0162 \times A$$

In order for the risky portfolio to be preferred to bills, the following must hold:

$$0.12 - 0.0162A > 0.07 \Rightarrow A < 0.05/0.0162 = 3.09$$

A must be less than 3.09 for the risky portfolio to be preferred to bills.

6. Points on the curve are derived by solving for $E(r)$ in the following equation:

$$U = 0.05 = E(r) - 0.5A\sigma^2 = E(r) - 1.5\sigma^2$$

The values of $E(r)$, given the values of σ^2, are therefore:

σ	σ^2	$E(r)$
0.00	0.0000	0.05000
0.05	0.0025	0.05375
0.10	0.0100	0.06500
0.15	0.0225	0.08375
0.20	0.0400	0.11000
0.25	0.0625	0.14375

The bold line in the graph on the next page (labeled Q6, for Question 6) depicts the indifference curve.

7. Repeating the analysis in Problem 6, utility is now:

$$U = E(r) - 0.5A\sigma^2 = E(r) - 2.0\sigma^2 = 0.05$$

The equal-utility combinations of expected return and standard deviation are presented in the table below. The indifference curve is the upward sloping line in the graph on the next page, labeled Q7 (for Question 7).

σ	σ^2	$E(r)$
0.00	0.0000	0.0500
0.05	0.0025	0.0550
0.10	0.0100	0.0700
0.15	0.0225	0.0950
0.20	0.0400	0.1300
0.25	0.0625	0.1750

The indifference curve in Problem 7 differs from that in Problem 6 in slope. When *A* increases from 3 to 4, the increased risk aversion results in a greater slope for the indifference curve since more expected return is needed in order to compensate for additional σ.

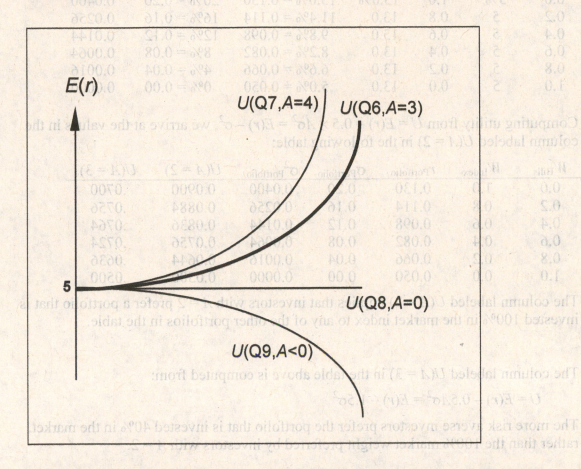

8. The coefficient of risk aversion for a risk neutral investor is zero. Therefore, the corresponding utility is equal to the portfolio's expected return. The corresponding indifference curve in the expected return-standard deviation plane is a horizontal line, labeled Q8 in the graph above (see Problem 6).

9. A risk lover, rather than penalizing portfolio utility to account for risk, derives greater utility as variance increases. This amounts to a negative coefficient of risk aversion. The corresponding indifference curve is downward sloping in the graph above (see Problem 6), and is labeled Q9.

10. The portfolio expected return and variance are computed as follows:

(1) W_{Bills}	(2) r_{Bills}	(3) W_{Index}	(4) r_{Index}	$r_{Portfolio}$ $(1)\times(2)+(3)\times(4)$	$\sigma_{Portfolio}$ $(3)\times 20\%$	$\sigma^2_{Portfolio}$
0.0	5%	1.0	13.0%	13.0% = 0.130	20% = 0.20	0.0400
0.2	5	0.8	13.0	11.4% = 0.114	16% = 0.16	0.0256
0.4	5	0.6	13.0	9.8% = 0.098	12% = 0.12	0.0144
0.6	5	0.4	13.0	8.2% = 0.082	8% = 0.08	0.0064
0.8	5	0.2	13.0	6.6% = 0.066	4% = 0.04	0.0016
1.0	5	0.0	13.0	5.0% = 0.050	0% = 0.00	0.0000

11. Computing utility from $U = E(r) - 0.5 \times A\sigma^2 = E(r) - \sigma^2$, we arrive at the values in the column labeled $U(A = 2)$ in the following table:

W_{Bills}	W_{Index}	$r_{Portfolio}$	$\sigma_{Portfolio}$	$\sigma^2_{Portfolio}$	$U(A = 2)$	$U(A = 3)$
0.0	1.0	0.130	0.20	0.0400	0.0900	.0700
0.2	0.8	0.114	0.16	0.0256	0.0884	.0756
0.4	0.6	0.098	0.12	0.0144	0.0836	.0764
0.6	0.4	0.082	0.08	0.0064	0.0756	.0724
0.8	0.2	0.066	0.04	0.0016	0.0644	.0636
1.0	0.0	0.050	0.00	0.0000	0.0500	.0500

The column labeled $U(A = 2)$ implies that investors with $A = 2$ prefer a portfolio that is invested 100% in the market index to any of the other portfolios in the table.

12. The column labeled $U(A = 3)$ in the table above is computed from:

$$U = E(r) - 0.5A\sigma^2 = E(r) - 1.5\sigma^2$$

The more risk averse investors prefer the portfolio that is invested 40% in the market, rather than the 100% market weight preferred by investors with $A = 2$.

13. Expected return = $(0.7 \times 18\%) + (0.3 \times 8\%) = 15\%$
Standard deviation = $0.7 \times 28\% = 19.6\%$

14. Investment proportions: 30.0% in T-bills
$0.7 \times 25\% = $ 17.5% in Stock A
$0.7 \times 32\% = $ 22.4% in Stock B
$0.7 \times 43\% = $ 30.1% in Stock C

15. Your reward-to-volatility ratio: $S = \dfrac{.18 - .08}{.28} = 0.3571$

Client's reward-to-volatility ratio: $S = \dfrac{.15 - .08}{.196} = 0.3571$

16.

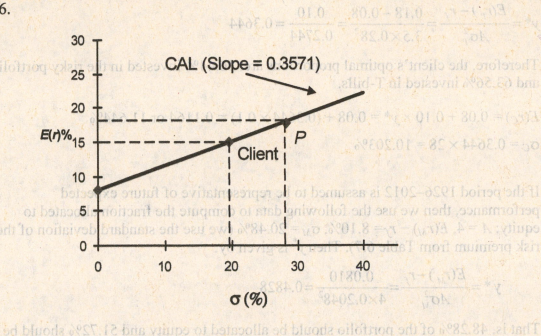

17. a. $E(r_C) = r_f + y \times [E(r_P) - r_f] = 8 + y \times (18 - 8)$

If the expected return for the portfolio is 16%, then:

$$16\% = 8\% + 10\% \times y \Rightarrow y = \frac{.16 - .08}{.10} = 0.8$$

Therefore, in order to have a portfolio with expected rate of return equal to 16%, the client must invest 80% of total funds in the risky portfolio and 20% in T-bills.

b.

Client's investment proportions:		20.0% in T-bills
	$0.8 \times 25\% =$	20.0% in Stock A
	$0.8 \times 32\% =$	25.6% in Stock B
	$0.8 \times 43\% =$	34.4% in Stock C

c. $\sigma_C = 0.8 \times \sigma_P = 0.8 \times 28\% = 22.4\%$

18. a. $\sigma_C = y \times 28\%$

If your client prefers a standard deviation of at most 18%, then:
$y = 18/28 = 0.6429 = 64.29\%$ invested in the risky portfolio.

b. $E(r_C) = .08 + .1 \times y = .08 + (0.6429 \times .1) = 14.429\%$

19. a. $y^* = \dfrac{E(r_P) - r_f}{A\sigma_P^2} = \dfrac{0.18 - 0.08}{3.5 \times 0.28^2} = \dfrac{0.10}{0.2744} = 0.3644$

    Therefore, the client's optimal proportions are: 36.44% invested in the risky portfolio and 63.56% invested in T-bills.

    b. $E(r_C) = 0.08 + 0.10 \times y^* = 0.08 + (0.3644 \times 0.1) = 0.1164$ or 11.644%

    $\sigma_C = 0.3644 \times 28 = 10.203\%$

20. a. If the period 1926–2012 is assumed to be representative of future expected performance, then we use the following data to compute the fraction allocated to equity: $A = 4$, $E(r_M) - r_f = 8.10\%$, $\sigma_M = 20.48\%$ (we use the standard deviation of the risk premium from Table 6.7). Then y^* is given by:

    $$y^* = \dfrac{E(r_M) - r_f}{A\sigma_M^2} = \dfrac{0.0810}{4 \times 0.2048^2} = 0.4828$$

    That is, 48.28% of the portfolio should be allocated to equity and 51.72% should be allocated to T-bills.

    b. If the period 1968–1988 is assumed to be representative of future expected performance, then we use the following data to compute the fraction allocated to equity: $A = 4$, $E(r_M) - r_f = 3.44\%$, $\sigma_M = 16.71\%$ and y^* is given by:

    $$y^* = \dfrac{E(r_M) - r_f}{A\sigma_M^2} = \dfrac{0.0344}{4 \times 0.1671^2} = 0.3080$$

    Therefore, 30.80% of the complete portfolio should be allocated to equity and 69.20% should be allocated to T-bills.

    c. In part (b), the market risk premium is expected to be lower than in part (a) and market risk is higher. Therefore, the reward-to-volatility *ratio* is expected to be lower in part (b), which explains the greater proportion invested in T-bills.

21. a. $E(r_C) = 8\% = 5\% + y \times (11\% - 5\%) \Rightarrow y = \dfrac{.08 - .05}{.11 - .05} = 0.5$

    b. $\sigma_C = y \times \sigma_p = 0.50 \times 15\% = 7.5\%$

    c. The first client is more risk averse, preferring investments that have less risk as evidenced by the lower standard deviation.

22. Johnson requests the portfolio standard deviation to equal one half the market portfolio standard deviation. The market portfolio $\sigma_M = 20\%$, which implies $\sigma_P = 10\%$. The intercept of the CML equals $r_f = 0.05$ and the slope of the CML equals the Sharpe ratio for the market portfolio (35%). Therefore using the CML:

$$E(r_P) = r_f + \frac{E(r_M) - r_f}{\sigma_M} \sigma_P = 0.05 + 0.35 \times 0.10 = 0.085 = 8.5\%$$

23. Data: r_f = 5%, $E(r_M)$ = 13%, σ_M = 25%, and r_f^B = 9%

The CML and indifference curves are as follows:

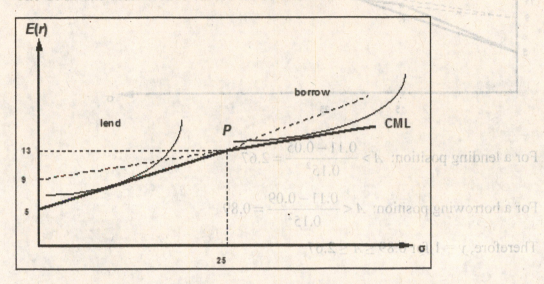

24. For y to be less than 1.0 (that the investor is a lender), risk aversion (A) must be large enough such that:

$$y = \frac{E(r_M) - r_f}{A\sigma_M^2} < 1 \Rightarrow A > \frac{0.13 - 0.05}{0.25^2} = 1.28$$

For y to be greater than 1 (the investor is a borrower), A must be small enough:

$$y = \frac{E(r_M) - r_f}{A\sigma_M^2} > 1 \Rightarrow A < \frac{0.13 - 0.09}{0.25^2} = 0.64$$

For values of risk aversion within this range, the client will neither borrow nor lend but will hold a portfolio composed only of the optimal risky portfolio:

$$y = 1 \text{ for } 0.64 \leq A \leq 1.28$$

25. a.   The graph for Problem 23 has to be redrawn here, with:
$$E(r_P) = 11\% \text{ and } \sigma_P = 15\%$$

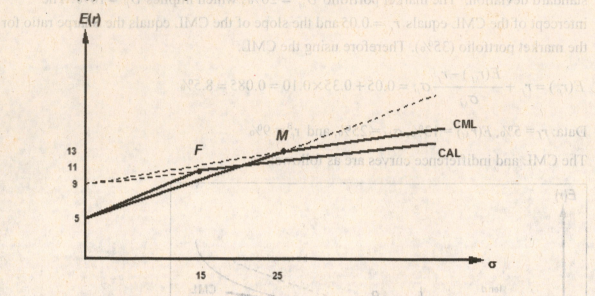

b.   For a lending position: $A > \dfrac{0.11 - 0.05}{0.15^2} = 2.67$

For a borrowing position: $A < \dfrac{0.11 - 0.09}{0.15^2} = 0.89$

Therefore, $y = 1$ for $0.89 \leq A \leq 2.67$

26.   The maximum feasible fee, denoted f, depends on the reward-to-variability ratio.
For $y < 1$, the lending rate, 5%, is viewed as the relevant risk-free rate, and we solve for f as follows:

$$\frac{.11 - .05 - f}{.15} = \frac{.13 - .05}{.25} \Rightarrow f = .06 - \frac{.15 \times .08}{.25} = .012, \text{ or } 1.2\%$$

For $y > 1$, the borrowing rate, 9%, is the relevant risk-free rate. Then we notice that, even without a fee, the active fund is inferior to the passive fund because:

$$\frac{.11 - .09 - f}{.15} = 0.13 < \frac{.13 - .09}{.25} = 0.16 \rightarrow f = -.004$$

More risk tolerant investors (who are more inclined to borrow) will not be clients of the fund. We find that f is negative: that is, you would need to *pay* investors to choose your active fund. These investors desire higher risk–higher return complete portfolios and thus are in the borrowing range of the relevant CAL. In this range, the reward-to-variability ratio of the index (the passive fund) is better than that of the managed fund.

27. a. Slope of the CML = $\dfrac{.13 - .08}{.25} = 0.20$

The diagram follows.

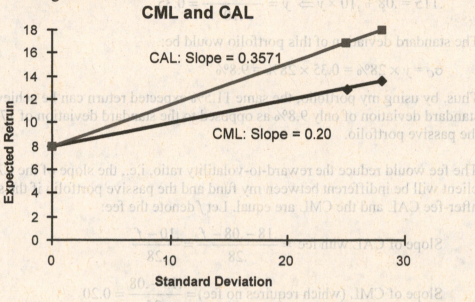

CML and CAL

CAL: Slope = 0.3571

CML: Slope = 0.20

b. My fund allows an investor to achieve a higher mean for any given standard deviation than would a passive strategy, i.e., a higher expected return for any given level of risk.

28. a. With 70% of his money invested in my fund's portfolio, the client's expected return is 15% per year with a standard deviation of 19.6% per year. If he shifts that money to the passive portfolio (which has an expected return of 13% and standard deviation of 25%), his overall expected return becomes:

$$E(r_C) = r_f + 0.7 \times [E(r_M) - r_f] = .08 + [0.7 \times (.13 - .08)] = .115, \text{ or } 11.5\%$$

The standard deviation of the complete portfolio using the passive portfolio would be:

$$\sigma_C = 0.7 \times \sigma_M = 0.7 \times 25\% = 17.5\%$$

Therefore, the shift entails a decrease in mean from 15% to 11.5% and a decrease in standard deviation from 19.6% to 17.5%. Since both mean return *and* standard deviation decrease, it is not yet clear whether the move is beneficial. The disadvantage of the shift is that, if the client is willing to accept a mean return on his total portfolio of 11.5%, he can achieve it with a lower standard deviation using my fund rather than the passive portfolio.

To achieve a target mean of 11.5%, we first write the mean of the complete portfolio as a function of the proportion invested in my fund (y):

$$E(r_C) = .08 + y \times (.18 - .08) = .08 + .10 \times y$$

Our target is: $E(r_C) = 11.5\%$. Therefore, the proportion that must be invested in my fund is determined as follows:

$$.115 = .08 + .10 \times y \Rightarrow y = \frac{.115 - .08}{.10} = 0.35$$

The standard deviation of this portfolio would be:

$$\sigma_C = y \times 28\% = 0.35 \times 28\% = 9.8\%$$

Thus, by using my portfolio, the same 11.5% expected return can be achieved with a standard deviation of only 9.8% as opposed to the standard deviation of 17.5% using the passive portfolio.

b. The fee would reduce the reward-to-volatility ratio, i.e., the slope of the CAL. The client will be indifferent between my fund and the passive portfolio if the slope of the after-fee CAL and the CML are equal. Let f denote the fee:

$$\text{Slope of CAL with fee} = \frac{.18 - .08 - f}{.28} = \frac{.10 - f}{.28}$$

$$\text{Slope of CML (which requires no fee)} = \frac{.13 - .08}{.25} = 0.20$$

Setting these slopes equal we have:

$$\frac{.10 - f}{.28} = 0.20 \Rightarrow f = 0.044 = 4.4\% \text{ per year}$$

29. a. The formula for the optimal proportion to invest in the passive portfolio is:

$$y^* = \frac{E(r_M) - r_f}{A\sigma_M^2}$$

Substitute the following: $E(r_M) = 13\%$; $r_f = 8\%$; $\sigma_M = 25\%$; $A = 3.5$:

$$y^* = \frac{0.13 - 0.08}{3.5 \times 0.25^2} = 0.2286, \text{ or } 22.86\% \text{ in the passive portfolio}$$

b. The answer here is the same as the answer to Problem 28(b). The fee that you can charge a client is the same regardless of the asset allocation mix of the client's portfolio. You can charge a fee that will equate the reward-to-volatility *ratio* of your portfolio to that of your competition.

CFA PROBLEMS

1. Utility for each investment $= E(r) - 0.5 \times 4 \times \sigma^2$

   We choose the investment with the highest utility value, Investment 3.

Investment	Expected return $E(r)$	Standard deviation σ	Utility U
1	0.12	0.30	-0.0600
2	0.15	0.50	-0.3500
3	0.21	0.16	0.1588
4	0.24	0.21	0.1518

2. When investors are risk neutral, then $A = 0$; the investment with the highest utility is Investment 4 because it has the highest expected return.

3. (b)

4. Indifference curve 2 because it is tangent to the CAL.

5. Point E

6. $(0.6 \times \$50,000) + [0.4 \times (-\$30,000)] - \$5,000 = \$13,000$

7. (b) Higher borrowing rates will reduce the total return to the portfolio and this results in a part of the line that has a lower slope.

8. Expected return for equity fund = T-bill rate + Risk premium = 6% + 10% = 16%

   Expected rate of return of the client's portfolio = $(0.6 \times 16\%) + (0.4 \times 6\%) = 12\%$

   Expected return of the client's portfolio = $0.12 \times \$100,000 = \$12,000$

   (which implies expected total wealth at the end of the period = $112,000)

   Standard deviation of client's overall portfolio = $0.6 \times 14\% = 8.4\%$

9. Reward-to-volatility ratio $= \dfrac{.10}{.14} = 0.71$

CHAPTER 6: APPENDIX

1. By year-end, the $50,000 investment will grow to: $50,000 × 1.06 = $53,000
   Without insurance, the probability distribution of end-of-year wealth is:

	Probability	Wealth
No fire	0.999	$253,000
Fire	0.001	53,000

   For this distribution, expected utility is computed as follows:

   $$E[U(W)] = [0.999 \times ln(253,000)] + [0.001 \times ln(53,000)] = 12.439582$$

   The certainty equivalent is:

   $$W_{CE} = e^{12.439582} = \$252,604.85$$

   With fire insurance, at a cost of $P, the investment in the risk-free asset is:

   $$\$(50,000 - P)$$

   Year-end wealth will be certain (since you are fully insured) and equal to:

   $$[\$(50,000 - P) \times 1.06] + \$200,000$$

   Solve for P in the following equation:

   $$[\$(50,000 - P) \times 1.06] + \$200,000 = \$252,604.85 \Rightarrow P = \$372.78$$

   This is the most you are willing to pay for insurance. Note that the expected loss is "only" $200, so you are willing to pay a substantial risk premium over the expected value of losses. The primary reason is that the value of the house is a large proportion of your wealth.

2. a. With insurance coverage for one-half the value of the house, the premium is $100, and the investment in the safe asset is $49,900. By year-end, the investment of $49,900 will grow to: $49,900 × 1.06 = $52,894

   If there is a fire, your insurance proceeds will be $100,000, and the probability distribution of end-of-year wealth is:

	Probability	Wealth
No fire	0.999	$252,894
Fire	0.001	152,894

   For this distribution, expected utility is computed as follows:

   $$E[U(W)] = [0.999 \times ln(252,894)] + [0.001 \times ln(152,894)] = 12.4402225$$

   The certainty equivalent is:

   $$W_{CE} = e^{12.4402225} = \$252,766.77$$

b. With insurance coverage for the full value of the house, costing $200, end-of-year wealth is certain, and equal to:

$$[(\$50,000 - \$200) \times 1.06] + \$200,000 = \$252,788$$

Since wealth is certain, this is also the certainty equivalent wealth of the fully insured position.

c. With insurance coverage for 1½ times the value of the house, the premium is $300, and the insurance pays off $300,000 in the event of a fire. The investment in the safe asset is $49,700. By year-end, the investment of $49,700 will grow to: $49,700 × 1.06 = $52,682

The probability distribution of end-of-year wealth is:

	Probability	Wealth
No fire	0.999	$252,682
Fire	0.001	352,682

For this distribution, expected utility is computed as follows:

$$E[U(W)] = [0.999 \times ln(252,682)] + [0.001 \times ln(352,682)] = 12.4402205$$

The certainty equivalent is:

$$W_{CE} = e^{12.440222} = \$252,766.27$$

Therefore, full insurance dominates both over- and underinsurance. Overinsuring creates a gamble (you actually gain when the house burns down). Risk is minimized when you insure exactly the value of the house.

CHAPTER 7: OPTIMAL RISKY PORTFOLIOS

PROBLEM SETS

1. (a) and (e). Short-term rates and labor issues are factors that are common to all firms and therefore must be considered as market risk factors. The remaining three factors are unique to this corporation and are not a part of market risk.

2. (a) and (c). After real estate is added to the portfolio, there are four asset classes in the portfolio: stocks, bonds, cash, and real estate. Portfolio variance now includes a variance term for real estate returns and a covariance term for real estate returns with returns for each of the other three asset classes. Therefore, portfolio risk is affected by the variance (or standard deviation) of real estate returns and the correlation between real estate returns and returns for each of the other asset classes. (Note that the correlation between real estate returns and returns for cash is most likely zero.)

3. (a) Answer (a) is valid because it provides the definition of the minimum variance portfolio.

4. The parameters of the opportunity set are:

$E(r_S) = 20\%$, $E(r_B) = 12\%$, $\sigma_S = 30\%$, $\sigma_B = 15\%$, $\rho = 0.10$

From the standard deviations and the correlation coefficient we generate the covariance matrix [note that $Cov(r_S, r_B) = \rho \times \sigma_S \times \sigma_B$]:

	Bonds	Stocks
Bonds	225	45
Stocks	45	900

The minimum-variance portfolio is computed as follows:

$$w_{Min}(S) = \frac{\sigma_B^2 - Cov(r_S, r_B)}{\sigma_S^2 + \sigma_B^2 - 2Cov(r_S, r_B)} = \frac{225 - 45}{900 + 225 - (2 \times 45)} = 0.1739$$

$$w_{Min}(B) = 1 - 0.1739 = 0.8261$$

The minimum variance portfolio mean and standard deviation are:

$$E(r_{Min}) = (0.1739 \times .20) + (0.8261 \times .12) = .1339 = 13.39\%$$

$$\sigma_{Min} = [w_S^2 \sigma_S^2 + w_B^2 \sigma_B^2 + 2w_S w_B Cov(r_S, r_B)]^{1/2}$$

$$= [(0.1739^2 \times 900) + (0.8261^2 \times 225) + (2 \times 0.1739 \times 0.8261 \times 45)]^{1/2}$$

$$= 13.92\%$$

5.

Proportion in Stock Fund	Proportion in Bond Fund	Expected Return	Standard Deviation	
0.00%	100.00%	12.00%	15.00%	
17.39	82.61	13.39	13.92	minimum variance
20.00	80.00	13.60	13.94	
40.00	60.00	15.20	15.70	
45.16	54.84	15.61	16.54	tangency portfolio
60.00	40.00	16.80	19.53	
80.00	20.00	18.40	24.48	
100.00	0.00	20.00	30.00	

Graph shown below.

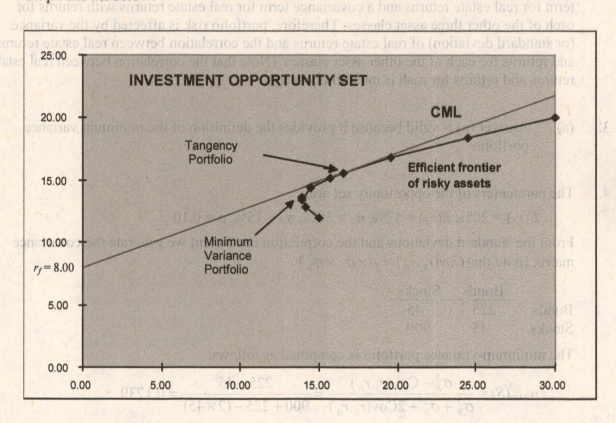

6. The above graph indicates that the optimal portfolio is the tangency portfolio with expected return approximately 15.6% and standard deviation approximately 16.5%.

7. The proportion of the optimal risky portfolio invested in the stock fund is given by:

$$w_S = \frac{[E(r_S)-r_f]\times\sigma_B^2 - [E(r_B)-r_f]\times Cov(r_S,r_B)}{[E(r_S)-r_f]\times\sigma_B^2 + [E(r_B)-r_f]\times\sigma_S^2 - [E(r_S)-r_f + E(r_B)-r_f]\times Cov(r_S,r_B)}$$

$$= \frac{[(.20-.08)\times 225] - [(.12-.08)\times 45]}{[(.20-.08)\times 225] + [(.12-.08)\times 900] - [(.20-.08+.12-.08)\times 45]} = 0.4516$$

$$w_B = 1 - 0.4516 = 0.5484$$

The mean and standard deviation of the optimal risky portfolio are:

$$E(r_P) = (0.4516 \times .20) + (0.5484 \times .12) = .1561$$

$$= 15.61\%$$

$$\sigma_P = [(0.4516^2 \times 900) + (0.5484^2 \times 225) + (2 \times 0.4516 \times 0.5484 \times 45)]^{1/2}$$

$$= 16.54\%$$

8. The reward-to-volatility ratio of the optimal CAL is:

$$\frac{E(r_p)-r_f}{\sigma_p} = \frac{.1561-.08}{.1654} = 0.4601$$

9. a. If you require that your portfolio yield an expected return of 14%, then you can find the corresponding standard deviation from the optimal CAL. The equation for this CAL is:

$$E(r_C) = r_f + \frac{E(r_p)-r_f}{\sigma_P}\sigma_C = .08 + 0.4601\sigma_C$$

If $E(r_C)$ is equal to 14%, then the standard deviation of the portfolio is 13.04%.

b. To find the proportion invested in the T-bill fund, remember that the mean of the complete portfolio (i.e., 14%) is an average of the T-bill rate and the optimal combination of stocks and bonds (P). Let y be the proportion invested in the portfolio P. The mean of any portfolio along the optimal CAL is:

$$E(r_C) = (1-y)\times r_f + y\times E(r_P) = r_f + y\times[E(r_P)-r_f] = .08 + y\times(.1561-.08)$$

Setting $E(r_C) = 14\%$ we find: $y = 0.7884$ and $(1-y) = 0.2119$ (the proportion invested in the T-bill fund).

To find the proportions invested in each of the funds, multiply 0.7884 times the respective proportions of stocks and bonds in the optimal risky portfolio:

Proportion of stocks in complete portfolio = $0.7884 \times 0.4516 = 0.3560$

Proportion of bonds in complete portfolio = $0.7884 \times 0.5484 = 0.4323$

10. Using only the stock and bond funds to achieve a portfolio expected return of 14%, we must find the appropriate proportion in the stock fund (w_S) and the appropriate proportion in the bond fund ($w_B = 1 - w_S$) as follows:

$$0.14 = 0.20 \times w_S + 0.12 \times (1 - w_S) = 0.12 + 0.08 \times w_S \Rightarrow w_S = 0.25$$

So the proportions are 25% invested in the stock fund and 75% in the bond fund. The standard deviation of this portfolio will be:

$$\sigma_P = [(0.25^2 \times 900) + (0.75^2 \times 225) + (2 \times 0.25 \times 0.75 \times 45)]^{1/2} = 14.13\%$$

This is considerably greater than the standard deviation of 13.04% achieved using T-bills and the optimal portfolio.

11. a.

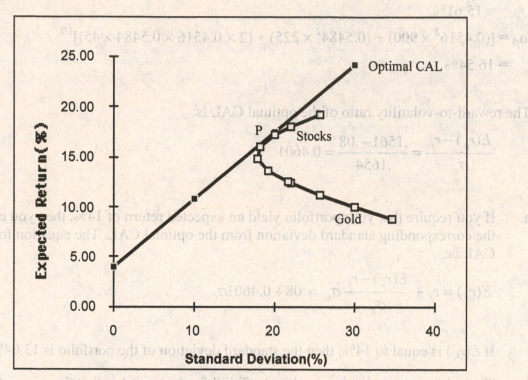

Even though it seems that gold is dominated by stocks, gold might still be an attractive asset to hold as a *part* of a portfolio. If the correlation between gold and stocks is sufficiently low, gold will be held as a component in a portfolio, specifically, the optimal tangency portfolio.

b. If the correlation between gold and stocks equals +1, then no one would hold gold. The optimal CAL would be composed of bills and stocks only. Since the set of risk/return combinations of stocks and gold would plot as a straight line with a negative slope (see the following graph), these combinations would be dominated by the stock portfolio. Of course, this situation could not persist. If no one desired gold, its price would fall and its expected rate of return would increase until it became sufficiently attractive to include in a portfolio.

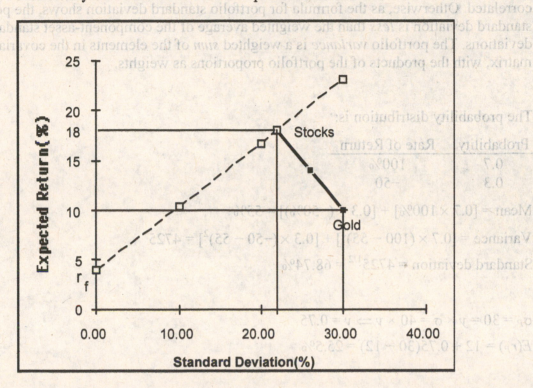

12. Since Stock A and Stock B are perfectly negatively correlated, a risk-free portfolio can be created and the rate of return for this portfolio, in equilibrium, will be the risk-free rate. To find the proportions of this portfolio [with the proportion w_A invested in Stock A and $w_B = (1 - w_A)$ invested in Stock B], set the standard deviation equal to zero. With perfect negative correlation, the portfolio standard deviation is:

σ_P = Absolute value $[w_A\sigma_A - w_B\sigma_B]$

$0 = 5 \times w_A - [10 \times (1 - w_A)] \Rightarrow w_A = 0.6667$

The expected rate of return for this risk-free portfolio is:

$E(r) = (0.6667 \times 10) + (0.3333 \times 15) = 11.667\%$

Therefore, the risk-free rate is: 11.667%

13. False. If the borrowing and lending rates are not identical, then, depending on the tastes of the individuals (that is, the shape of their indifference curves), borrowers and lenders could have different optimal risky portfolios.

14. False. The portfolio standard deviation equals the weighted average of the component-asset standard deviations *only* in the special case that all assets are perfectly positively correlated. Otherwise, as the formula for portfolio standard deviation shows, the portfolio standard deviation is *less* than the weighted average of the component-asset standard deviations. The portfolio *variance* is a weighted *sum* of the elements in the covariance matrix, with the products of the portfolio proportions as weights.

15. The probability distribution is:

Probability	Rate of Return
0.7	100%
0.3	−50

Mean = $[0.7 \times 100\%] + [0.3 \times (-50\%)] = 55\%$

Variance = $[0.7 \times (100 - 55)^2] + [0.3 \times (-50 - 55)^2] = 4725$

Standard deviation = $4725^{1/2} = 68.74\%$

16. $\sigma_P = 30 = y \times \sigma = 40 \times y \Rightarrow y = 0.75$

$E(r_P) = 12 + 0.75(30 - 12) = 25.5\%$

17. The correct choice is (c). Intuitively, we note that since all stocks have the same expected rate of return and standard deviation, we choose the stock that will result in lowest risk. This is the stock that has the lowest correlation with Stock A.

More formally, we note that when all stocks have the same expected rate of return, the optimal portfolio for any risk-averse investor is the global minimum variance portfolio (G). When the portfolio is restricted to Stock A and one additional stock, the objective is to find G for any pair that includes Stock A, and then select the combination with the lowest variance. With two stocks, I and J, the formula for the weights in G is:

$$w_{Min}(I) = \frac{\sigma_J^2 - Cov(r_I, r_J)}{\sigma_I^2 + \sigma_J^2 - 2Cov(r_I, r_J)}$$

$$w_{Min}(J) = 1 - w_{Min}(I)$$

Since all standard deviations are equal to 20%:

$$Cov(r_I, r_J) = \rho\sigma_I\sigma_J = 400\rho \text{ and } w_{Min}(I) = w_{Min}(J) = 0.5$$

This intuitive result is an implication of a property of any efficient frontier, namely, that the covariances of the global minimum variance portfolio with all other assets on the frontier are identical and equal to its own variance. (Otherwise, additional diversification would further reduce the variance.) In this case, the standard deviation of G(I, J) reduces to:

$$\sigma_{Min}(G) = [200 \times (1 + \rho_{IJ})]^{1/2}$$

This leads to the intuitive result that the desired addition would be the stock with the lowest correlation with Stock A, which is Stock D. The optimal portfolio is equally invested in Stock A and Stock D, and the standard deviation is 17.03%.

18. No, the answer to Problem 17 would not change, at least as long as investors are not risk lovers. Risk neutral investors would not care which portfolio they held since all portfolios have an expected return of 8%.

19. Yes, the answers to Problems 17 and 18 would change. The efficient frontier of risky assets is horizontal at 8%, so the optimal CAL runs from the risk-free rate through G. This implies risk-averse investors will just hold Treasury bills.

20. Rearrange the table (converting rows to columns) and compute serial correlation results in the following table:

Nominal Rates

	Small Company Stocks	Large Company Stocks	Long-Term Government Bonds	Intermed-Term Government Bonds	Treasury Bills	Inflation
1920s	−3.72	18.36	3.98	3.77	3.56	−1.00
1930s	7.28	−1.25	4.60	3.91	0.30	−2.04
1940s	20.63	9.11	3.59	1.70	0.37	5.36
1950s	19.01	19.41	0.25	1.11	1.87	2.22
1960s	13.72	7.84	1.14	3.41	3.89	2.52
1970s	8.75	5.90	6.63	6.11	6.29	7.36
1980s	12.46	17.60	11.50	12.01	9.00	5.10
1990s	13.84	18.20	8.60	7.74	5.02	2.93
Serial Correlation	0.46	−0.22	0.60	0.59	0.63	0.23

For example: to compute serial correlation in decade nominal returns for large-company stocks, we set up the following two columns in an Excel spreadsheet. Then, use the Excel function "CORREL" to calculate the correlation for the data.

	Decade	Previous
1930s	−1.25%	18.36%
1940s	9.11%	−1.25%
1950s	19.41%	9.11%
1960s	7.84%	19.41%
1970s	5.90%	7.84%
1980s	17.60%	5.90%
1990s	18.20%	17.60%

Note that each correlation is based on only seven observations, so we cannot arrive at any statistically significant conclusions. Looking at the results, however, it appears that, with the exception of large-company stocks, there is persistent serial correlation. (This conclusion changes when we turn to real rates in the next problem.)

21. The table for real rates (using the approximation of subtracting a decade's average inflation from the decade's average nominal return) is:

Real Rates

	Small Company Stocks	Large Company Stocks	Long-Term Government Bonds	Intermed-Term Government Bonds	Treasury Bills
1920s	−2.72	19.36	4.98	4.77	4.56
1930s	9.32	0.79	6.64	5.95	2.34
1940s	15.27	3.75	−1.77	−3.66	−4.99
1950s	16.79	17.19	−1.97	−1.11	−0.35
1960s	11.20	5.32	−1.38	0.89	1.37
1970s	1.39	−1.46	−0.73	−1.25	−1.07
1980s	7.36	12.50	6.40	6.91	3.90
1990s	10.91	15.27	5.67	4.81	2.09
Serial Correlation	0.29	−0.27	0.38	0.11	0.00

While the serial correlation in decade *nominal* returns seems to be positive, it appears that real rates are serially uncorrelated. The decade time series (although again too short for any definitive conclusions) suggest that real rates of return are independent from decade to decade.

22. The 3-year risk premium for the S&P portfolio is $(1+.05)^3 -1 = 0.1576 \, or \, 15.76\%$, the 3-year risk premium for the hedge fund portfolio is $(1+.1)^3 -1 = 0.3310 \, or \, 33.10\%$. S&P 3-year standard deviation is $0 \, 0.2 \times \sqrt{3} = 0.3464 \, or \, 34.64\%$. The hedge fund 3-year standard deviation is $.35 \times \sqrt{3} = 0.6062 \, or \, 60.62\%$. S&P Sharpe ratio is 15.76/34.64 = 0.4550, and the hedge fund Sharpe ratio is 33.10/60.62 = 0.5460.

23. With a $\rho = 0$, the optimal asset allocation is

$$W_{S\&P} = \frac{15.76 \times 60.62^2 - 33.10 \times (0 \times 34.64 \times 60.62)}{15.76 \times 60.62^2 + 33.10 \times 34.64^2 - [15.76 + 33.10] \times (0 \times 34.64 \times 60.62)} = 0.5932,$$

$W_{Hedge} = 1 - 0.5932 = 0.4068.$

With these weights,

$E(r_p) = 0.5932 \times 15.76 + 0.4068 \times 33.10 = 0.2281 \, or \, 22.81\%.$

$$\sigma_p = \sqrt{.5932^2 \times 34.64^2 + .4068^2 \times 60.62^2 + 2 \times .5932 \times .4068 \times (0 \times 34.64 \times 60.62)} = 0.3210 \, or \, 32.10\%$$

The resulting Sharpe ratio is $22.81/32.10 = 0.7108$. Greta has a risk aversion of A=3, Therefore, she will invest

$$y = \frac{0.2281}{3 \times .3210^2} = 0.7138 \ or \ 71.38\%$$

of her wealth in this risky portfolio. The resulting investment composition will be S&P: $0.7138 \times 59.32 = 43.78\%$ and Hedge: $0.7138 \times 40.68 = 30.02\%$. The remaining 26% will be invested in the risk-free asset.

24. With $\rho = 0.3$, the annual covariance is $.3 \times .2 \times .35 = 0.021$.

25. S&P 3-year standard deviation is $.2 \times \sqrt{3} = 0.3464 \ or \ 34.64\%$. The hedge fund 3-year standard deviation is $.35 \times \sqrt{3} = 0.6062 \ or \ 60.62\%$. Therefore, the 3-year covariance is $0.3 \times .3464 \times .6062 = 0.063$.

STOPPED

26. With a $\rho = .3$, the optimal asset allocation is

$$W_{S\&P} = \frac{15.76 \times 60.62^2 - 33.10 \times (.3 \times 34.64 \times 60.62)}{15.76 \times 60.62^2 + 33.10 \times 34.64^2 - [15.76 + 33.10] \times (.3 \times 34.64 \times 60.62)} = 0.5545,$$

$$W_{Hedge} = 1 - 0.5545 = 0.4455.$$

With these weights,

$$E(r_p) = 0.5545 \times 15.76 + 0.4455 \times 33.10 = 0.2349 \ or \ 23.49\%.$$

$$\sigma_p = \sqrt{5545^2 \times 34.64^2 + .4455^2 \times 60.62^2 + 2 \times .5545 \times .4455 \times (.3 \times 34.64 \times 60.62)} = 0.3755 \ or \ 37.55\%.$$

The resulting Sharpe ratio is $23.49/37.55 = 0.6256$. Notice that the higher covariance results in a poorer Sharpe ratio.

Greta will invest

$$y = \frac{0.2349}{3 \times .3755^2} = 0.5554 \ or \ 55.54\%$$

of her wealth in this risky portfolio. The resulting investment composition will be S&P: $0.5554 \times 55.45 = 30.79\%$ and hedge: $0.5554 \times 44.55 = 24.74\%$. The remaining 44.46% will be invested in the risk-free asset.

CFA PROBLEMS

1. a. Restricting the portfolio to 20 stocks, rather than 40 to 50 stocks, will increase the risk of the portfolio, but it is possible that the increase in risk will be minimal. Suppose that, for instance, the 50 stocks in a universe have the same standard deviation (σ) and the correlations between each pair are identical, with correlation coefficient ρ. Then, the covariance between each pair of stocks would be $\rho\sigma^2$, and the variance of an equally weighted portfolio would be:

$$\sigma_P^2 = \frac{1}{n}\sigma^2 + \frac{n-1}{n}\rho\sigma^2$$

The effect of the reduction in n on the second term on the right-hand side would be relatively small (since 49/50 is close to 19/20 and $\rho\sigma^2$ is smaller than σ^2), but the denominator of the first term would be 20 instead of 50. For example, if $\sigma = 45\%$ and $\rho = 0.2$, then the standard deviation with 50 stocks would be 20.91%, and would rise to 22.05% when only 20 stocks are held. Such an increase might be acceptable if the expected return is increased sufficiently.

    b. Hennessy could contain the increase in risk by making sure that he maintains reasonable diversification among the 20 stocks that remain in his portfolio. This entails maintaining a low correlation among the remaining stocks. For example, in part (a), with $\rho = 0.2$, the increase in portfolio risk was minimal. As a practical matter, this means that Hennessy would have to spread his portfolio among many industries; concentrating on just a few industries would result in higher correlations among the included stocks.

2. Risk reduction benefits from diversification are not a linear function of the number of issues in the portfolio. Rather, the incremental benefits from additional diversification are most important when you are least diversified. Restricting Hennessy to 10 instead of 20 issues would increase the risk of his portfolio by a greater amount than would a reduction in the size of the portfolio from 30 to 20 stocks. In our example, restricting the number of stocks to 10 will increase the standard deviation to 23.81%. The 1.76% increase in standard deviation resulting from giving up 10 of 20 stocks is greater than the 1.14% increase that results from giving up 30 of 50 stocks.

3. The point is well taken because the committee should be concerned with the volatility of the entire portfolio. Since Hennessy's portfolio is only one of six well-diversified portfolios and is smaller than the average, the concentration in fewer issues might have a minimal effect on the diversification of the total fund. Hence, unleashing Hennessy to do stock picking may be advantageous.

4. d. Portfolio Y cannot be efficient because it is dominated by another portfolio. For example, Portfolio X has both higher expected return and lower standard deviation.

5. c.

6. d.

7. b.

8. a.

9. c.

10. Since we do not have any information about expected returns, we focus exclusively on reducing variability. Stocks A and C have equal standard deviations, but the correlation of Stock B with Stock C (0.10) is less than that of Stock A with Stock B (0.90). Therefore, a portfolio composed of Stocks B and C will have lower total risk than a portfolio composed of Stocks A and B.

11. Fund D represents the single *best* addition to complement Stephenson's current portfolio, given his selection criteria. Fund D's expected return (14.0 percent) has the potential to increase the portfolio's return somewhat. Fund D's relatively low correlation with his current portfolio (+0.65) indicates that Fund D will provide greater diversification benefits than any of the other alternatives except Fund B. The result of adding Fund D should be a portfolio with approximately the same expected return and somewhat lower volatility compared to the original portfolio.

    The other three funds have shortcomings in terms of expected return enhancement or volatility reduction through diversification. Fund A offers the potential for increasing the portfolio's return but is too highly correlated to provide substantial volatility reduction benefits through diversification. Fund B provides substantial volatility reduction through diversification benefits but is expected to generate a return well below the current portfolio's return. Fund C has the greatest potential to increase the portfolio's return but is too highly correlated with the current portfolio to provide substantial volatility reduction benefits through diversification.

12. a. Subscript OP refers to the original portfolio, ABC to the new stock, and NP to the new portfolio.

    i. $E(r_{NP}) = w_{OP} E(r_{OP}) + w_{ABC} E(r_{ABC}) = (0.9 \times 0.67) + (0.1 \times 1.25) = 0.728\%$

    ii. $\text{Cov} = \rho \times \sigma_{OP} \times \sigma_{ABC} = 0.40 \times 2.37 \times 2.95 = 2.7966 \cong 2.80$

    iii. $\sigma_{NP} = [w_{OP}^2\, \sigma_{OP}^2 + w_{ABC}^2\, \sigma_{ABC}^2 + 2\, w_{OP}\, w_{ABC}\, (\text{Cov}_{OP,\,ABC})]^{1/2}$

    $= [(0.9^2 \times 2.37^2) + (0.1^2 \times 2.95^2) + (2 \times 0.9 \times 0.1 \times 2.80)]^{1/2}$

    $= 2.2673\% \cong 2.27\%$

b. Subscript *OP* refers to the original portfolio, *GS* to government securities, and *NP* to the new portfolio.

    i. $E(r_{NP}) = w_{OP} \, E(r_{OP}) + w_{GS} \, E(r_{GS}) = (0.9 \times 0.67) + (0.1 \times 0.42) = 0.645\%$

    ii. $\text{Cov} = \rho \times \sigma_{OP} \times \sigma_{GS} = 0 \times 2.37 \times 0 = 0$

    iii. $\sigma_{NP} = [w_{OP}{}^2 \, \sigma_{OP}{}^2 + w_{GS}{}^2 \, \sigma_{GS}{}^2 + 2 \, w_{OP} \, w_{GS} \, (\text{Cov}_{OP,GS})]^{1/2}$

$$= [(0.9^2 \times 2.37^2) + (0.1^2 \times 0) + (2 \times 0.9 \times 0.1 \times 0)]^{1/2}$$

$$= 2.133\% \cong 2.13\%$$

c. Adding the risk-free government securities would result in a lower beta for the new portfolio. The new portfolio beta will be a weighted average of the individual security betas in the portfolio; the presence of the risk-free securities would lower that weighted average.

d. The comment is not correct. Although the respective standard deviations and expected returns for the two securities under consideration are equal, the covariances between each security and the original portfolio are unknown, making it impossible to draw the conclusion stated. For instance, if the covariances are different, selecting one security over the other may result in a lower standard deviation for the portfolio as a whole. In such a case, that security would be the preferred investment, assuming all other factors are equal.

e.   i. Grace clearly expressed the sentiment that the risk of loss was more important to her than the opportunity for return. Using variance (or standard deviation) as a measure of risk in her case has a serious limitation because standard deviation does not distinguish between positive and negative price movements.

    ii. Two alternative risk measures that could be used instead of variance are:

Range of returns, which considers the highest and lowest expected returns in the future period, with a larger range being a sign of greater variability and therefore of greater risk.

Semivariance can be used to measure expected deviations of returns below the mean, or some other benchmark, such as zero.

Either of these measures would potentially be superior to variance for Grace. Range of returns would help to highlight the full spectrum of risk she is assuming, especially the downside portion of the range about which she is so concerned. Semivariance would also be effective, because it implicitly assumes that the investor wants to minimize the likelihood of returns falling below some target rate; in Grace's case, the target rate would be set at zero (to protect against negative returns).

13. a. Systematic risk refers to fluctuations in asset prices caused by macroeconomic factors that are common to all risky assets; hence systematic risk is often referred to as market risk. Examples of systematic risk factors include the business cycle, inflation, monetary policy, fiscal policy, and technological changes.

Firm-specific risk refers to fluctuations in asset prices caused by factors that are independent of the market, such as industry characteristics or firm characteristics. Examples of firm-specific risk factors include litigation, patents, management, operating cash flow changes, and financial leverage.

b. Trudy should explain to the client that picking only the top five best ideas would most likely result in the client holding a much more risky portfolio. The total risk of a portfolio, or portfolio variance, is the combination of systematic risk and firm-specific risk.

The systematic component depends on the sensitivity of the individual assets to market movements as measured by beta. Assuming the portfolio is well diversified, the number of assets will not affect the systematic risk component of portfolio variance. The portfolio beta depends on the individual security betas and the portfolio weights of those securities.

On the other hand, the components of firm-specific risk (sometimes called *nonsystematic risk*) are not perfectly positively correlated with each other and, as more assets are added to the portfolio, those additional assets tend to reduce portfolio risk. Hence, increasing the number of securities in a portfolio reduces firm-specific risk. For example, a patent expiration for one company would not affect the other securities in the portfolio. An increase in oil prices is likely to cause a drop in the price of an airline stock but will likely result in an increase in the price of an energy stock. As the number of randomly selected securities increases, the total risk (variance) of the portfolio approaches its systematic variance.

CHAPTER 8: INDEX MODELS

PROBLEM SETS

1. The advantage of the index model, compared to the Markowitz procedure, is the vastly reduced number of estimates required. In addition, the large number of estimates required for the Markowitz procedure can result in large aggregate estimation errors when implementing the procedure. The disadvantage of the index model arises from the model's assumption that return residuals are uncorrelated. This assumption will be incorrect if the index used omits a significant risk factor.

2. The trade-off entailed in departing from pure indexing in favor of an actively managed portfolio is between the probability (or the possibility) of superior performance against the certainty of additional management fees.

3. The answer to this question can be seen from the formulas for w^0 (equation 8.20) and w^* (equation 8.21). Other things held equal, w^0 is smaller the greater the residual variance of a candidate asset for inclusion in the portfolio. Further, we see that regardless of beta, when w^0 decreases, so does w^*. Therefore, other things equal, the greater the residual variance of an asset, the smaller its position in the optimal risky portfolio. That is, increased firm-specific risk reduces the extent to which an active investor will be willing to depart from an indexed portfolio.

4. The total risk premium equals: $\alpha + (\beta \times$ Market risk premium). We call alpha a nonmarket return premium because it is the portion of the return premium that is independent of market performance.

    The Sharpe ratio indicates that a higher alpha makes a security more desirable. Alpha, the numerator of the Sharpe ratio, is a fixed number that is not affected by the standard deviation of returns, the denominator of the Sharpe ratio. Hence, an increase in alpha increases the Sharpe ratio. Since the portfolio alpha is the portfolio-weighted average of the securities' alphas, then, holding all other parameters fixed, an increase in a security's alpha results in an increase in the portfolio Sharpe ratio.

5. a. To optimize this portfolio one would need:

    $n = 60$ estimates of means

    $n = 60$ estimates of variances

    $\dfrac{n^2 - n}{2} = 1{,}770$ estimates of covariances

Therefore, in total: $\dfrac{n^2 + 3n}{2} = 1{,}890$ estimates

b. In a single index model: $r_i - r_f = \alpha_i + \beta_i (r_M - r_f) + e_i$

Equivalently, using excess returns: $R_i = \alpha_i + \beta_i R_M + e_i$

The variance of the rate of return can be decomposed into the components:

(1) The variance due to the common market factor: $\beta_i^2 \sigma_M^2$

(2) The variance due to firm specific unanticipated events: $\sigma^2(e_i)$

In this model: $\mathrm{Cov}(r_i, r_j) = \beta_i \beta_j \sigma$

The number of parameter estimates is:

$n = 60$ estimates of the mean $E(r_i)$

$n = 60$ estimates of the sensitivity coefficient β_i

$n = 60$ estimates of the firm-specific variance $\sigma^2(e_i)$

1 estimate of the market mean $E(r_M)$

1 estimate of the market variance σ_M^2

Therefore, in total, 182 estimates.

The single index model reduces the total number of required estimates from 1,890 to 182. In general, the number of parameter estimates is reduced from:

$$\left(\frac{n^2 + 3n}{2}\right) \text{ to } (3n + 2)$$

6. a. The standard deviation of each individual stock is given by: $\sigma_i = [\beta_i^2 \sigma_M^2 + \sigma^2(e_i)]^{1/2}$

Since $\beta_A = 0.8$, $\beta_B = 1.2$, $\sigma(e_A) = 30\%$, $\sigma(e_B) = 40\%$, and $\sigma_M = 22\%$, we get:

$\sigma_A = (0.8^2 \times 22^2 + 30^2)^{1/2} = 34.78\%$

$\sigma_B = (1.2^2 \times 22^2 + 40^2)^{1/2} = 47.93\%$

b. The expected rate of return on a portfolio is the weighted average of the expected returns of the individual securities:

$E(r_P) = w_A \times E(r_A) + w_B \times E(r_B) + w_f \times r_f$

$E(r_P) = (0.30 \times 13\%) + (0.45 \times 18\%) + (0.25 \times 8\%) = 14\%$

The beta of a portfolio is similarly a weighted average of the betas of the individual securities:

$$\beta_P = w_A \times \beta_A + w_B \times \beta_B + w_f \times \beta_f$$

$$\beta_P = (0.30 \times 0.8) + (0.45 \times 1.2) + (0.25 \times 0.0) = 0.78$$

The variance of this portfolio is:

$$\sigma_P^2 = \beta_P^2 \sigma_M^2 + \sigma^2(e_P)$$

where $\beta_P^2 \sigma_M^2$ is the systematic component and $\sigma^2(e_P)$ is the nonsystematic component. Since the residuals (e_i) are uncorrelated, the nonsystematic variance is:

$$\sigma^2(e_P) = w_A^2 \times \sigma^2(e_A) + w_B^2 \times \sigma^2(e_B) + w_f^2 \times \sigma^2(e_f)$$

$$= (0.30^2 \times 30^2) + (0.45^2 \times 40^2) + (0.25^2 \times 0) = 405$$

where $\sigma^2(e_A)$ and $\sigma^2(e_B)$ are the firm-specific (nonsystematic) variances of Stocks A and B, and $\sigma^2(e_f)$, the nonsystematic variance of T-bills, is zero. The residual standard deviation of the portfolio is thus:

$$\sigma(e_P) = (405)^{1/2} = 20.12\%$$

The total variance of the portfolio is then:

$$\sigma_P^2 = (0.78^2 \times 22^2) + 405 = 699.47$$

The total standard deviation is 26.45%.

7.   a.   The two figures depict the stocks' security characteristic lines (SCL). Stock A has higher firm-specific risk because the deviations of the observations from the SCL are larger for Stock A than for Stock B. Deviations are measured by the vertical distance of each observation from the SCL.

b.   Beta is the slope of the SCL, which is the measure of systematic risk. The SCL for Stock B is steeper; hence Stock B's systematic risk is greater.

c.   The R^2 (or squared correlation coefficient) of the SCL is the ratio of the explained variance of the stock's return to total variance, and the total variance is the sum of the explained variance plus the unexplained variance (the stock's residual variance):

$$R^2 = \frac{\beta_i^2 \sigma_M^2}{\beta_i^2 \sigma_M^2 + \sigma^2(e_i)}$$

Since the explained variance for Stock B is greater than for Stock A (the explained variance is $\beta_B^2 \sigma_M^2$, which is greater since its beta is higher), *and* its residual variance $\sigma^2(e_B)$ is smaller, its R^2 is higher than Stock A's.

    d.   Alpha is the intercept of the SCL with the expected return axis. Stock A has a small positive alpha whereas Stock B has a negative alpha; hence, Stock A's alpha is larger.

    e.   The correlation coefficient is simply the square root of R^2, so Stock B's correlation with the market is higher.

8.   a.   Firm-specific risk is measured by the residual standard deviation. Thus, stock A has more firm-specific risk: 10.3% > 9.1%

    b.   Market risk is measured by beta, the slope coefficient of the regression. A has a larger beta coefficient: 1.2 > 0.8

    c. R^2 measures the fraction of total variance of return explained by the market return. A's R^2 is larger than B's: 0.576 > 0.436

    d.   Rewriting the SCL equation in terms of total return (r) rather than excess return (R):

$$r_A - r_f = \alpha + \beta \times (r_M - r_f) \Rightarrow$$

$$r_A = \alpha + r_f \times (1 - \beta) + \beta \times r_M$$

The intercept is now equal to:

$$\alpha + r_f \times (1 - \beta) = 1\% + r_f \times (1 - 1.2)$$

Since $r_f = 6\%$, the intercept would be: $1\% + 6\%(1 - 1.2) = 1\% - 1.2\% = -0.2\%$

9.   The standard deviation of each stock can be derived from the following equation for R^2:

$$R_i^2 = \frac{\beta_i^2 \sigma_M^2}{\sigma_i^2} = \frac{\text{Explained variance}}{\text{Total variance}}$$

Therefore:

$$\sigma_A^2 = \frac{\beta_A^2 \sigma_M^2}{R_A^2} = \frac{0.7^2 \times 20^2}{0.20} = 980$$

$$\sigma_A = 31.30\%$$

For stock B:

$$\sigma_B^2 = \frac{1.2^2 \times 20^2}{0.12} = 4,800$$

$$\sigma_B = 69.28\%$$

10. The systematic risk for A is:

$$\beta_A^2 \times \sigma_M^2 = 0.70^2 \times 20^2 = 196$$

The firm-specific risk of A (the residual variance) is the difference between A's total risk and its systematic risk:

$$980 - 196 = 784$$

The systematic risk for B is:

$$\beta_B^2 \times \sigma_M^2 = 1.20^2 \times 20^2 = 576$$

B's firm-specific risk (residual variance) is:

$$4,800 - 576 = 4,224$$

11. The covariance between the returns of A and B is (since the residuals are assumed to be uncorrelated):

$$Cov(r_A, r_B) = \beta_A \beta_B \sigma_M^2 = 0.70 \times 1.20 \times 400 = 336$$

The correlation coefficient between the returns of A and B is:

$$\rho_{AB} = \frac{Cov(r_A, r_B)}{\sigma_A \sigma_B} = \frac{336}{31.30 \times 69.28} = 0.155$$

12. Note that the correlation is the square root of R^2: $\rho = \sqrt{R^2}$

$$Cov(r_A, r_M) = \rho\sigma_A\sigma_M = 0.20^{1/2} \times 31.30 \times 20 = 280$$

$$Cov(r_B, r_M) = \rho\sigma_B\sigma_M = 0.12^{1/2} \times 69.28 \times 20 = 480$$

13. For portfolio P we can compute:

$$\sigma_P = [(0.6^2 \times 980) + (0.4^2 \times 4800) + (2 \times 0.4 \times 0.6 \times 336)]^{1/2} = [1282.08]^{1/2} = 35.81\%$$

$$\beta_P = (0.6 \times 0.7) + (0.4 \times 1.2) = 0.90$$

$$\sigma^2(e_P) = \sigma_P^2 - \beta_P^2\sigma_M^2 = 1282.08 - (0.90^2 \times 400) = 958.08$$

$$Cov(r_P, r_M) = \beta_P\sigma_M^2 = 0.90 \times 400 = 360$$

This same result can also be attained using the covariances of the individual stocks with the market:

$$Cov(r_P, r_M) = Cov(0.6r_A + 0.4r_B, r_M) = 0.6 \times Cov(r_A, r_M) + 0.4 \times Cov(r_B, r_M)$$

$$= (0.6 \times 280) + (0.4 \times 480) = 360$$

14. Note that the variance of T-bills is zero, and the covariance of T-bills with any asset is zero. Therefore, for portfolio Q:

$$\sigma_Q = \left[w_P^2 \sigma_P^2 + w_M^2 \sigma_M^2 + 2 \times w_P \times w_M \times Cov(r_P, r_M) \right]^{1/2}$$

$$= \left[(0.5^2 \times 1,282.08) + (0.3^2 \times 400) + (2 \times 0.5 \times 0.3 \times 360) \right]^{1/2} = 21.55\%$$

$$\beta_Q = w_P \beta_P + w_M \beta_M = (0.5 \times 0.90) + (0.3 \times 1) + (0.20 \times 0) = 0.75$$

$$\sigma^2(e_Q) = \sigma_Q^2 - \beta_Q^2 \sigma_M^2 = 464.52 - (0.75^2 \times 400) = 239.52$$

$$Cov(r_Q, r_M) = \beta_Q \sigma_M^2 = 0.75 \times 400 = 300$$

15. a. Beta Books adjusts beta by taking the sample estimate of beta and averaging it with 1.0, using the weights of 2/3 and 1/3, as follows:

adjusted beta = [(2/3) × 1.24] + [(1/3) × 1.0] = 1.16

b. If you use your current estimate of beta to be $\beta_{t-1} = 1.24$, then

$$\beta_t = 0.3 + (0.7 \times 1.24) = 1.168$$

16. For Stock A:

$$\alpha_A = r_A - [r_f + \beta_A \times (r_M - r_f)] = .11 - [.06 + 0.8 \times (.12 - .06)] = 0.2\%$$

For stock B:

$$\alpha_B = r_B - [r_f + \beta_B \times (r_M - r_f)] = .14 - [.06 + 1.5 \times (.12 - .06)] = -1\%$$

Stock A would be a good addition to a well-diversified portfolio. A short position in Stock B may be desirable.

17. a.

	Alpha (α) $\alpha_i = r_i - [r_f + \beta_i \times (r_M - r_f)]$	Expected excess return $E(r_i) - r_f$
α_A = 20% − [8% + 1.3 × (16% − 8%)] = 1.6%		20% − 8% = 12%
α_B = 18% − [8% + 1.8 × (16% − 8%)] = − 4.4%		18% − 8% = 10%
α_C = 17% − [8% + 0.7 × (16% − 8%)] = 3.4%		17% − 8% = 9%
α_D = 12% − [8% + 1.0 × (16% − 8%)] = − 4.0%		12% − 8% = 4%

Stocks A and C have positive alphas, whereas stocks B and D have negative alphas. The residual variances are:

$$\sigma^2(e_A) = 58^2 = 3,364$$
$$\sigma^2(e_B) = 71^2 = 5,041$$
$$\sigma^2(e_C) = 60^2 = 3,600$$
$$\sigma^2(e_D) = 55^2 = 3,025$$

b. To construct the optimal risky portfolio, we first determine the optimal active portfolio. Using the Treynor-Black technique, we construct the active portfolio:

	$\dfrac{a}{\sigma^2(e)}$	$\dfrac{a/\sigma^2(e)}{Sa/\sigma^2(e)}$
A	0.000476	−0.6142
B	−0.000873	1.1265
C	0.000944	−1.2181
D	−0.001322	1.7058
Total	−0.000775	1.0000

Be unconcerned with the negative weights of the positive α stocks—the entire active position will be negative, returning everything to good order.

With these weights, the forecast for the active portfolio is:

$$\alpha = [-0.6142 \times 1.6] + [1.1265 \times (-4.4)] - [1.2181 \times 3.4] + [1.7058 \times (-4.0)]$$
$$= -16.90\%$$

$$\beta = [-0.6142 \times 1.3] + [1.1265 \times 1.8] - [1.2181 \times 0.70] + [1.7058 \times 1] = 2.08$$

The high beta (higher than any individual beta) results from the short positions in the relatively low beta stocks and the long positions in the relatively high beta stocks.

$$\sigma^2(e) = [(-0.6142)^2 \times 3364] + [1.1265^2 \times 5041] + [(-1.2181)^2 \times 3600] + [1.7058^2 \times 3025]$$
$$= 21,809.6$$

$$\sigma(e) = 147.68\%$$

The levered position in B [with high $\sigma^2(e)$] overcomes the diversification effect and results in a high residual standard deviation. The optimal risky portfolio has a proportion w^* in the active portfolio, computed as follows:

$$w_0 = \frac{\alpha/\sigma^2(e)}{[E(r_M) - r_f]/\sigma_M^2} = \frac{-.1690/21,809.6}{.08/23^2} = -0.05124$$

The negative position is justified for the reason stated earlier.

The adjustment for beta is:

$$w^* = \frac{w_0}{1 + (1 - \beta)w_0} = \frac{-0.05124}{1 + (1 - 2.08)(-0.05124)} = -0.0486$$

Since w^* is negative, the result is a positive position in stocks with positive alphas and a negative position in stocks with negative alphas. The position in the index portfolio is:

$$1 - (-0.0486) = 1.0486$$

c. To calculate the Sharpe ratio for the optimal risky portfolio, we compute the information ratio for the active portfolio and Sharpe's measure for the market portfolio. The information ratio for the active portfolio is computed as follows:

$$A = \frac{\alpha}{\sigma(e)} = -16.90/147.68 = -0.1144$$

$$A^2 = 0.0131$$

Hence, the square of the Sharpe ratio (S) of the optimized risky portfolio is:

$$S^2 = S_M^2 + A^2 = \left(\frac{8}{23}\right)^2 + 0.0131 = 0.1341$$

$$S = 0.3662$$

Compare this to the market's Sharpe ratio:

$$S_M = 8/23 = 0.3478 \rightarrow \text{ A difference of: } 0.0184$$

The only moderate improvement in performance results from only a small position taken in the active portfolio A because of its large residual variance.

d. To calculate the makeup of the complete portfolio, first compute the beta, the mean excess return, and the variance of the optimal risky portfolio:

$$\beta_P = w_M + (w_A \times \beta_A) = 1.0486 + [(-0.0486) \times 2.08] = 0.95$$

$$E(R_P) = \alpha_P + \beta_P E(R_M) = [(-0.0486) \times (-16.90\%)] + (0.95 \times 8\%) = 8.42\%$$

$$\sigma_P^2 = \beta_P^2 \sigma_M^2 + \sigma^2(e_P) = (0.95 \times 23)^2 + \left((-0.0486^2) \times 21,809.6\right) = 528.94$$

$$\sigma_P = 23.00\%$$

Since $A = 2.8$, the optimal position in this portfolio is:

$$y = \frac{8.42}{0.01 \times 2.8 \times 528.94} = 0.5685$$

In contrast, with a passive strategy:

$$y = \frac{8}{0.01 \times 2.8 \times 23^2} = 0.5401 \rightarrow \text{A difference of: } 0.0284$$

The final positions are (M may include some of stocks A through D):

Bills	$1 - 0.5685 =$	43.15%
M	$0.5685 \times 1.0486 =$	59.61
A	$0.5685 \times (-0.0486) \times (-0.6142) =$	1.70
B	$0.5685 \times (-0.0486) \times 1.1265 =$	-3.11
C	$0.5685 \times (-0.0486) \times (-1.2181) =$	3.37
D	$0.5685 \times (-0.0486) \times 1.7058 =$	-4.71
	(subject to rounding error)	100.00%

18. a. If a manager is not allowed to sell short, he will not include stocks with negative alphas in his portfolio, so he will consider only A and C:

	A	$\sigma^2(e)$	$\dfrac{a}{\sigma^2(e)}$	$\dfrac{a/\sigma^2(e)}{Sa/\sigma^2(e)}$
A	1.6	3,364	0.000476	0.3352
C	3.4	3,600	0.000944	0.6648
			0.001420	1.0000

The forecast for the active portfolio is:

$$\alpha = (0.3352 \times 1.6) + (0.6648 \times 3.4) = 2.80\%$$

$$\beta = (0.3352 \times 1.3) + (0.6648 \times 0.7) = 0.90$$

$$\sigma^2(e) = (0.3352^2 \times 3,364) + (0.6648^2 \times 3,600) = 1,969.03$$

$$\sigma(e) = 44.37\%$$

The weight in the active portfolio is:

$$w_0 = \frac{\alpha/\sigma^2(e)}{E(R_M)/\sigma_M^2} = \frac{2.80/1,969.03}{8/23^2} = 0.0940$$

Adjusting for beta:

$$w^* = \frac{w_0}{1+(1-\beta)w_0} = \frac{0.094}{1+[(1-0.90)\times 0.094]} = 0.0931$$

The information ratio of the active portfolio is:

$$A = \frac{\alpha}{\sigma(e)} = \frac{2.80}{44.37} = 0.0631$$

Hence, the square of the Sharpe ratio is:

$$S^2 = \left(\frac{8}{23}\right)^2 + 0.0631^2 = 0.1250$$

Therefore: $S = 0.3535$

The market's Sharpe ratio is: $S_M = 0.3478$

When short sales are allowed (Problem 17), the manager's Sharpe ratio is higher (0.3662). The reduction in the Sharpe ratio is the cost of the short sale restriction.

The characteristics of the optimal risky portfolio are:

$$\beta_P = w_M + w_A \times \beta_A = (1 - 0.0931) + (0.0931 \times 0.9) = 0.99$$
$$E(R_P) = \alpha_P + \beta_P \times E(R_M) = (0.0931 \times 2.8\%) + (0.99 \times 8\%) = 8.18\%$$
$$\sigma_P^2 = \beta_P^2 \times \sigma_M^2 + \sigma^2(e_P) = (0.99 \times 23)^2 + (0.0931^2 \times 1969.03) = 535.54$$
$$\sigma_P = 23.14\%$$

With $A = 2.8$, the optimal position in this portfolio is:

$$y = \frac{8.18}{0.01 \times 2.8 \times 535.54} = 0.5455$$

The final positions in each asset are:

Bills	$1 - 0.5455 =$	45.45%
M	$0.5455 \times (1 - 0.0931) =$	49.47
A	$0.5455 \times 0.0931 \times 0.3352 =$	1.70
C	$0.5455 \times 0.0931 \times 0.6648 =$	3.38
		100.00

b. The mean and variance of the optimized complete portfolios in the unconstrained and short-sales constrained cases, and for the passive strategy are:

	$E(R_C)$	σ_C^2
Unconstrained	$0.5685 \times 8.42\% = 4.79$	$0.5685^2 \times 528.94 = 170.95$
Constrained	$0.5455 \times 8.18\% = 4.46$	$0.5455^2 \times 535.54 = 159.36$
Passive	$0.5401 \times 8.00\% = 4.32$	$0.5401^2 \times 529.00 = 154.31$

The utility levels below are computed using the formula: $E(r_C) - 0.005A\sigma_C^2$

Unconstrained	$8\% + 4.79\% - (0.005 \times 2.8 \times 170.95) = 10.40\%$
Constrained	$8\% + 4.46\% - (0.005 \times 2.8 \times 159.36) = 10.23\%$
Passive	$8\% + 4.32\% - (0.005 \times 2.8 \times 154.31) = 10.16\%$

19. All alphas are reduced to 0.3 times their values in the original case. Therefore, the relative weights of each security in the active portfolio are unchanged, but the alpha of the active portfolio is only 0.3 times its previous value: $0.3 \times -16.90\% = -5.07\%$

The investor will take a smaller position in the active portfolio. The optimal risky portfolio has a proportion w^* in the active portfolio as follows:

$$w_0 = \frac{\alpha / \sigma^2(e)}{E(r_M - r_f)/\sigma_M^2} = \frac{-0.0507 / 21,809.6}{0.08 / 23^2} = -0.01537$$

The negative position is justified for the reason given earlier.

The adjustment for beta is:

$$w^* = \frac{w_0}{1+(1-\beta)w_0} = \frac{-0.01537}{1+[(1-2.08)\times(-0.01537)]} = -0.0151$$

Since w^* is negative, the result is a positive position in stocks with positive alphas and a negative position in stocks with negative alphas. The position in the index portfolio is:
$1 - (-0.0151) = 1.0151$

To calculate the Sharpe ratio for the optimal risky portfolio we compute the information ratio for the active portfolio and the Sharpe ratio for the market portfolio. The information ratio of the *active portfolio* is 0.3 times its previous value:

$$A = \frac{\alpha}{\sigma(e)} = \frac{-5.07}{147.68} = -0.0343 \text{ and } A^2 = 0.00118$$

Hence, the square of the Sharpe ratio of the *optimized risky portfolio* is:

$$S^2 = S_M^2 + A^2 = (8\%/23\%)^2 + 0.00118 = 0.1222$$
$$S = 0.3495$$

Compare this to the market's Sharpe ratio: $S_M = \frac{8\%}{23\%} = 0.3478$

The difference is: 0.0017

Note that the reduction of the forecast alphas by a factor of 0.3 reduced the squared information ratio and the improvement in the squared Sharpe ratio by a factor of:

$$0.3^2 = 0.09$$

20. If each of the alpha forecasts is doubled, then the alpha of the active portfolio will also double. Other things equal, the information ratio (IR) of the active portfolio also doubles. The square of the Sharpe ratio for the optimized portfolio (*S*-square) equals the square of the Sharpe ratio for the market index (*SM*-square) plus the square of the information ratio. Since the information ratio has doubled, its square quadruples. Therefore: *S*-square = *SM*-square + (4 × *IR*)

Compared to the previous *S*-square, the difference is: 3*IR*

Now you can embark on the calculations to verify this result.

CFA PROBLEMS

1. The regression results provide quantitative measures of return and risk based on monthly returns over the five-year period.

    β for ABC was 0.60, considerably less than the average stock's β of 1.0. This indicates that, when the S&P 500 rose or fell by 1 percentage point, ABC's return on average rose or fell by only 0.60 percentage point. Therefore, ABC's systematic risk (or market risk) was low relative to the typical value for stocks. ABC's alpha (the intercept of the regression) was –3.2%, indicating that when the market return was 0%, the average return on ABC was –3.2%. ABC's unsystematic risk (or residual risk), as measured by $\sigma(e)$, was 13.02%. For ABC, R^2 was 0.35, indicating closeness of fit to the linear regression greater than the value for a typical stock.

    β for XYZ was somewhat higher, at 0.97, indicating XYZ's return pattern was very similar to the β for the market index. Therefore, XYZ stock had average systematic risk for the period examined. Alpha for XYZ was positive and quite large, indicating a return of 7.3%, on average, for XYZ independent of market return. Residual risk was 21.45%, half again as much as ABC's, indicating a wider scatter of observations around the regression line for XYZ. Correspondingly, the fit of the regression model was considerably less than that of ABC, consistent with an R^2 of only 0.17.

    The effects of including one or the other of these stocks in a diversified portfolio may be quite different. If it can be assumed that both stocks' betas will remain stable over time, then there is a large difference in systematic risk level. The betas obtained from the two brokerage houses may help the analyst draw inferences for the future. The three estimates of ABC's β are similar, regardless of the sample period of the underlying data. The range of these estimates is 0.60 to 0.71, well below the market average β of 1.0. The three estimates of XYZ's β vary significantly among the three sources, ranging as high as 1.45 for the weekly data over the most recent two years. One could infer that XYZ's β for the future might be well above 1.0, meaning it might have somewhat greater systematic risk than was implied by the monthly regression for the five-year period.

    These stocks appear to have significantly different systematic risk characteristics. If these stocks are added to a diversified portfolio, XYZ will add more to total volatility.

2. The R^2 of the regression is: $0.70^2 = 0.49$

    Therefore, 51% of total variance is unexplained by the market; this is nonsystematic risk.

3. $9 = 3 + \beta (11 - 3) \Rightarrow \beta = 0.75$

4. d.

5. b.

CHAPTER 9: THE CAPITAL ASSET PRICING MODEL

PROBLEM SETS

1. $E(r_P) = r_f + \beta_P \times [E(r_M) - r_f]$

    $.18 = .06 + \beta_P \times [.14 - .06] \rightarrow \beta_P = \dfrac{.12}{.08} = 1.5$

2. If the security's correlation coefficient with the market portfolio doubles (with all other variables such as variances unchanged), then beta, and therefore the risk premium, will also double. The current risk premium is: 14% – 6% = 8%
    The new risk premium would be 16%, and the new discount rate for the security would be: 16% + 6% = 22%

    If the stock pays a constant perpetual dividend, then we know from the original data that the dividend (D) must satisfy the equation for the present value of a perpetuity:

    Price = Dividend/Discount rate

    $50 = D/0.14 \Rightarrow D = 50 \times 0.14 = \$7.00$

    At the new discount rate of 22%, the stock would be worth: $7/0.22 = $31.82
    The increase in stock risk has lowered its value by 36.36%.

3. a. False. $\beta = 0$ implies $E(r) = r_f$, not zero.

    b. False. Investors require a risk premium only for bearing systematic (undiversifiable or market) risk. Total volatility, as measured by the standard deviation, includes diversifiable risk.

    c. False. Your portfolio should be invested 75% in the market portfolio and 25% in T-bills. Then: $\beta_P = (0.75 \times 1) + (0.25 \times 0) = 0.75$

4. The expected return is the return predicted by the CAPM for a given level of systematic risk.

    $$E(r_i) = r_f + \beta_i \times [E(r_M) - r_f]$$

    $$E(r_{\$1\,Discount}) = .04 + 1.5 \times (.10 - .04) = .13, \text{or } 13\%$$

    $$E(r_{Everything\,\$5}) = .04 + 1.0 \times (.10 - .04) = .10, \text{or } 10\%$$

5. According to the CAPM, $1 Discount Stores requires a return of 13% based on its systematic risk level of $\beta = 1.5$. However, the forecasted return is only 12%. Therefore, the security is currently overvalued.

Everything $5 requires a return of 10% based on its systematic risk level of $\beta = 1.0$. However, the forecasted return is 11%. Therefore, the security is currently undervalued.

6. Correct answer is choice a. The expected return of a stock with a $\beta = 1.0$ must, on average, be the same as the expected return of the market which also has a $\beta = 1.0$.

7. Correct answer is choice a. Beta is a measure of systematic risk. Since only systematic risk is rewarded, it is safe to conclude that the expected return will be higher for Kaskin's stock than for Quinn's stock.

8. The appropriate discount rate for the project is:

$$r_f + \beta \times [E(r_M) - r_f] = .08 + [1.8 \times (.16 - .08)] = .224, \text{ or } 22.4\%$$

Using this discount rate:

$$NPV = -\$40 + \sum_{t=1}^{10} \frac{\$15}{1.224^t} = -\$40 + [\$15 \times \text{Annuity factor } (22.4\%, 10 \text{ years})] = \$18.09$$

The internal rate of return (IRR) for the project is 35.73%. Recall from your introductory finance class that NPV is positive if IRR > discount rate (or, equivalently, hurdle rate). The highest value that beta can take before the hurdle rate exceeds the IRR is determined by:

$$.3573 = .08 + \beta \times (.16 - .08) \Rightarrow \beta = .2773/.08 = 3.47$$

9. a. Call the aggressive stock A and the defensive stock D. Beta is the sensitivity of the stock's return to the market return, i.e., the change in the stock return per unit change in the market return. Therefore, we compute each stock's beta by calculating the difference in its return across the two scenarios divided by the difference in the market return:

$$\beta_{A} = \frac{-.02 - .38}{.05 - .25} = 2.00 \qquad \beta_{D} = \frac{.06 - .12}{.05 - .25} = 0.30$$

b. With the two scenarios equally likely, the expected return is an average of the two possible outcomes:

$$E(r_A) = 0.5 \times (-.02 + .38) = .18 = 18\%$$
$$E(r_D) = 0.5 \times (.06 + .12) = .09 = 9\%$$

c. The SML is determined by the market expected return of $[0.5 \times (.25 + .05)] = 15\%$, with $\beta_M = 1$, and $r_f = 6\%$ (which has $\beta_f = 0$). See the following graph:

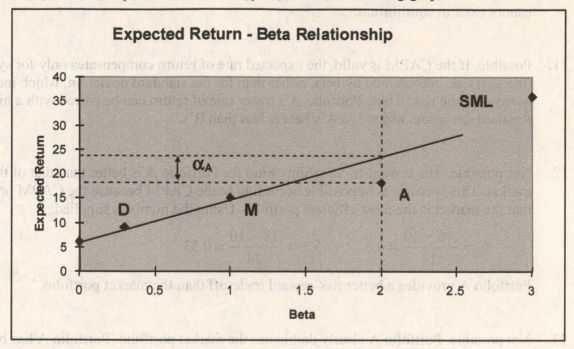

The equation for the security market line is:

$$E(r) = .06 + \beta \times (.15 - .06)$$

d. Based on its risk, the aggressive stock has a required expected return of:

$$E(r_A) = .06 + 2.0 \times (.15 - .06) = .24 = 24\%$$

The analyst's forecast of expected return is only 18%. Thus the stock's alpha is:

α_A = actually expected return − required return (given risk)

$= 18\% - 24\% = -6\%$

Similarly, the required return for the defensive stock is:

$$E(r_D) = .06 + 0.3 \times (.15 - .06) = 8.7\%$$

The analyst's forecast of expected return for D is 9%, and hence, the stock has a positive alpha:

α_D = Actually expected return − Required return (given risk)

$= .09 - .087 = +0.003 = +0.3\%$

The points for each stock plot on the graph as indicated above.

e. The hurdle rate is determined by the project beta (0.3), not the firm's beta. The correct discount rate is 8.7%, the fair rate of return for stock D.

10. Not possible. Portfolio A has a higher beta than Portfolio B, but the expected return for Portfolio A is lower than the expected return for Portfolio B. Thus, these two portfolios cannot exist in equilibrium.

11. Possible. If the CAPM is valid, the expected rate of return compensates only for systematic (market) risk, represented by beta, rather than for the standard deviation, which includes nonsystematic risk. Thus, Portfolio A's lower rate of return can be paired with a higher standard deviation, as long as A's beta is less than B's.

12. Not possible. The reward-to-variability ratio for Portfolio A is better than that of the market. This scenario is impossible according to the CAPM because the CAPM predicts that the market is the most efficient portfolio. Using the numbers supplied:

$$S_A = \frac{.16-.10}{.12} = 0.5 \qquad S_M = \frac{.18-.10}{.24} = 0.33$$

Portfolio A provides a better risk-reward trade-off than the market portfolio.

13. Not possible. Portfolio A clearly dominates the market portfolio. Portfolio A has both a lower standard deviation and a higher expected return.

14. Not possible. The SML for this scenario is: $E(r) = 10 + \beta \times (18 - 10)$

Portfolios with beta equal to 1.5 have an expected return equal to:

$$E(r) = 10 + [1.5 \times (18 - 10)] = 22\%$$

The expected return for Portfolio A is 16%; that is, Portfolio A plots below the SML ($\alpha_A = -6\%$) and, hence, is an overpriced portfolio. This is inconsistent with the CAPM.

15. Not possible. The SML is the same as in Problem 14. Here, Portfolio A's required return is: $.10 + (.9 \times .08) = 17.2\%$

This is greater than 16%. Portfolio A is overpriced with a negative alpha:
$\alpha_A = -1.2\%$

16. Possible. The CML is the same as in Problem 12. Portfolio A plots below the CML, as any asset is expected to. This scenario is not inconsistent with the CAPM.

17. Since the stock's beta is equal to 1.2, its expected rate of return is:

.06 + [1.2 × (.16 – .06)] = 18%

$$E(r) = \frac{D_1 + P_1 - P_0}{P_0} \rightarrow 0.18 = \frac{P_1 - \$50 + \$6}{\$50} \rightarrow P_1 = \$53$$

18. The series of $1,000 payments is a perpetuity. If beta is 0.5, the cash flow should be discounted at the rate:

.06 + [0.5 × (.16 – .06)] = .11 = 11%

PV = $1,000/0.11 = $9,090.91

If, however, beta is equal to 1, then the investment should yield 16%, and the price paid for the firm should be:

PV = $1,000/0.16 = $6,250

The difference, $2,840.91, is the amount you will overpay if you erroneously assume that beta is 0.5 rather than 1.

19. Using the SML: .04 = .06 + β × (.16 – .06) ⇒ β = –.02/.10 = –0.2

20. r_1 = 19%; r_2 = 16%; β_1 = 1.5; β_2 = 1

a.   To determine which investor was a better selector of individual stocks we look at abnormal return, which is the ex-post alpha; that is, the abnormal return is the difference between the actual return and that predicted by the SML. Without information about the parameters of this equation (risk-free rate and market rate of return) we cannot determine which investor was more accurate.

b.   If r_f = 6% and r_M = 14%, then (using the notation alpha for the abnormal return):

α_1 = .19 – [.06 + 1.5 × (.14 – .06)] = .19 – .18 = 1%

α_2 = .16 – [.06 + 1 × (.14 – .06)] = .16 – .14 = 2%

Here, the second investor has the larger abnormal return and thus appears to be the superior stock selector. By making better predictions, the second investor appears to have tilted his portfolio toward underpriced stocks.

c.   If r_f = 3% and r_M = 15%, then:

α_1 = .19 – [.03 + 1.5 × (.15 – .03)] = .19 – .21 = –2%

α_2 = .16 – [.03 + 1 × (.15 – .03)] = .16 – .15 = 1%

Here, not only does the second investor appear to be the superior stock selector, but the first investor's predictions appear valueless (or worse).

21. a. . Since the market portfolio, by definition, has a beta of 1, its expected rate of return is 12%.

 b. $\beta = 0$ means no systematic risk. Hence, the stock's expected rate of return in market equilibrium is the risk-free rate, 5%.

 c. Using the SML, the *fair* expected rate of return for a stock with $\beta = -0.5$ is:

$$E(r) = 0.05 + [(-0.5) \times (0.12 - 0.05)] = 1.5\%$$

The *actually* expected rate of return, using the expected price and dividend for next year is:

$$E(r) = \frac{\$41 + \$3}{\$40} - 1 = 0.10 = 10\%$$

Because the actually expected return exceeds the fair return, the stock is underpriced.

22. In the zero-beta CAPM the zero-beta portfolio replaces the risk-free rate, and thus:

$$E(r) = 8 + 0.6(17 - 8) = 13.4\%$$

23. a. $E(r_P) = r_f + \beta_P \times [E(r_M) - r_f] = 5\% + 0.8 (15\% - 5\%) = 13\%$

$\alpha = 14\% - 13\% = 1\%$

You should invest in this fund because alpha is positive.

 b. The passive portfolio with the same beta as the fund should be invested 80% in the market-index portfolio and 20% in the money market account. For this portfolio:

$$E(r_P) = (0.8 \times 15\%) + (0.2 \times 5\%) = 13\%$$

$$14\% - 13\% = 1\% = \alpha$$

24. a. We would incorporate liquidity into the CCAPM in a manner analogous to the way in which liquidity is incorporated into the conventional CAPM. In the latter case, in addition to the market risk premium, expected return is also dependent on the expected cost of illiquidity and three liquidity-related betas which measure the sensitivity of: (1) the security's illiquidity to market illiquidity; (2) the security's return to market illiquidity; and, (3) the security's illiquidity to the market return. A similar approach can be used for the CCAPM, except that the liquidity betas would be measured relative to consumption growth rather than the usual market index.

 b. As in part (a), nontraded assets would be incorporated into the CCAPM in a fashion similar to part (a). Replace the market portfolio with consumption growth. The issue of liquidity is more acute with nontraded assets such as privately held businesses and labor income.

While ownership of a privately held business is analogous to ownership of an illiquid stock, expect a greater degree of illiquidity for the typical private business. If the owner of a privately held business is satisfied with the dividends paid out from the business, then the lack of liquidity is not an issue. If the owner seeks to realize income greater than the business can pay out, then selling ownership, in full or part, typically entails a substantial liquidity discount. The illiquidity correction should be treated as suggested in part (a).

The same general considerations apply to labor income, although it is probable that the lack of liquidity for labor income has an even greater impact on security market equilibrium values. Labor income has a major impact on portfolio decisions. While it is possible to borrow against labor income to some degree, and some of the risk associated with labor income can be ameliorated with insurance, it is plausible that the liquidity betas of consumption streams are quite significant, as the need to borrow against labor income is likely cyclical.

CFA PROBLEMS

1. a. Agree; Regan's conclusion is correct. By definition, the market portfolio lies on the capital market line (CML). Under the assumptions of capital market theory, all portfolios on the CML dominate, in a risk-return sense, portfolios that lie on the Markowitz efficient frontier because, given that leverage is allowed, the CML creates a portfolio possibility line that is higher than all points on the efficient frontier except for the market portfolio, which is Rainbow's portfolio. Because Eagle's portfolio lies on the Markowitz efficient frontier at a point other than the market portfolio, Rainbow's portfolio dominates Eagle's portfolio.

    b. Nonsystematic risk is the unique risk of individual stocks in a portfolio that is diversified away by holding a well-diversified portfolio. Total risk is composed of systematic (market) risk and nonsystematic (firm-specific) risk.

    Disagree; Wilson's remark is incorrect. Because both portfolios lie on the Markowitz efficient frontier, neither Eagle nor Rainbow has any nonsystematic risk. Therefore, nonsystematic risk does not explain the different expected returns. The determining factor is that Rainbow lies on the (straight) line (the CML) connecting the risk-free asset and the market portfolio (Rainbow), at the point of tangency to the Markowitz efficient frontier having the highest return per unit of risk. Wilson's remark is also countered by the fact that, since nonsystematic risk can be eliminated by diversification, the expected return for bearing nonsystematic risk is zero. This is a result of the fact that well-diversified investors bid up the price of every asset to the point where only systematic risk earns a positive return (nonsystematic risk earns no return).

2. $E(r) = r_f + \beta \times [E(r_M) - r_f]$

    Furhman Labs: $E(r) = .05 + 1.5 \times [.115 - .05] = 14.75\%$

    Garten Testing: $E(r) = .05 + 0.8 \times [.115 - .05] = 10.20\%$

If the forecast rate of return is less than (greater than) the required rate of return, then the security is overvalued (undervalued).

Furhman Labs: Forecast return – Required return = 13.25% – 14.75% = –1.50%

Garten Testing: Forecast return – Required return = 11.25% – 10.20% = 1.05%

Therefore, Furhman Labs is overvalued and Garten Testing is undervalued.

3. a.

4. d. From CAPM, the fair expected return = $8 + 1.25 \times (15 - 8) = 16.75\%$
        Actually expected return = 17%

        $\alpha = 17 - 16.75 = 0.25\%$

5. d.

6. c.

7. d.

8. d. [You need to know the risk-free rate]

9. d. [You need to know the risk-free rate]

10. Under the CAPM, the only risk that investors are compensated for bearing is the risk that cannot be diversified away (systematic risk). Because systematic risk (measured by beta) is equal to 1.0 for both portfolios, an investor would expect the same rate of return from both portfolios A and B. Moreover, since both portfolios are well diversified, it doesn't matter if the specific risk of the individual securities is high or low. The firm-specific risk has been diversified away for both portfolios.

11. a. McKay should borrow funds and invest those funds proportionately in Murray's existing portfolio (i.e., buy more risky assets on margin). In addition to increased expected return, the alternative portfolio on the capital market line will also have increased risk, which is caused by the higher proportion of risky assets in the total portfolio.

     b. McKay should substitute low-beta stocks for high-beta stocks in order to reduce the overall beta of York's portfolio. By reducing the overall portfolio beta, McKay will reduce the systematic risk of the portfolio and, therefore, reduce its volatility relative to the market. The security market line (SML) suggests such action (i.e., moving down the SML), even though reducing beta may result in a slight loss of portfolio efficiency unless full diversification is maintained. York's primary objective, however, is not to maintain efficiency but to reduce risk exposure; reducing portfolio beta meets that objective. Because York does not want to engage in borrowing or lending, McKay cannot reduce risk by selling equities and using the proceeds to buy risk-free assets (i.e., lending part of the portfolio).

12. a.

	Expected Return	Alpha
Stock X	$5\% + 0.8 \times (14\% - 5\%) = 12.2\%$	$14.0\% - 12.2\% = 1.8\%$
Stock Y	$5\% + 1.5 \times (14\% - 5\%) = 18.5\%$	$17.0\% - 18.5\% = -1.5\%$

b. i. Kay should recommend Stock X because of its positive alpha, compared to Stock Y, which has a negative alpha. In graphical terms, the expected return/risk profile for Stock X plots above the security market line (SML), while the profile for Stock Y plots below the SML. Also, depending on the individual risk preferences of Kay's clients, the lower beta for Stock X may have a beneficial effect on overall portfolio risk.

ii. Kay should recommend Stock Y because it has higher forecasted return and lower standard deviation than Stock X. The respective Sharpe ratios for Stocks X and Y and the market index are:

Stock X: $(14\% - 5\%)/36\% = 0.25$

Stock Y: $(17\% - 5\%)/25\% = 0.48$

Market index: $(14\% - 5\%)/15\% = 0.60$

The market index has an even more attractive Sharpe ratio than either of the individual stocks, but, given the choice between Stock X and Stock Y, Stock Y is the superior alternative.

When a stock is held as a single stock portfolio, standard deviation is the relevant risk measure. For such a portfolio, beta as a risk measure is irrelevant.

Although holding a single asset is not a typically recommended investment strategy, some investors may hold what is essentially a single-asset portfolio when they hold the stock of their employer company. For such investors, the relevance of standard deviation versus beta is an important issue.

CHAPTER 10: ARBITRAGE PRICING THEORY AND MULTIFACTOR MODELS OF RISK AND RETURN

PROBLEM SETS

1. The revised estimate of the expected rate of return on the stock would be the old estimate plus the sum of the products of the unexpected change in each factor times the respective sensitivity coefficient:

    Revised estimate = 12% + [(1 × 2%) + (0.5 × 3%)] = 15.5%

    Note that the IP estimate is computed as: 1 × (5% − 3%), and the IR estimate is computed as: 0.5 × (8% − 5%).

2. The APT factors must correlate with major sources of uncertainty, i.e., sources of uncertainty that are of concern to many investors. Researchers should investigate factors that correlate with uncertainty in consumption and investment opportunities. GDP, the inflation rate, and interest rates are among the factors that can be expected to determine risk premiums. In particular, industrial production (IP) is a good indicator of changes in the business cycle. Thus, IP is a candidate for a factor that is highly correlated with uncertainties that have to do with investment and consumption opportunities in the economy.

3. Any pattern of returns can be explained if we are free to choose an indefinitely large number of explanatory factors. If a theory of asset pricing is to have value, it must explain returns using a reasonably limited number of explanatory variables (i.e., systematic factors such as unemployment levels, GDP, and oil prices).

4. Equation 10.11 applies here:

    $$E(r_p) = r_f + \beta_{P1}\,[E(r_1) - r_f] + \beta_{P2}\,[E(r_2) - r_f]$$

    We need to find the risk premium (RP) for each of the two factors:

    $$RP_1 = [E(r_1) - r_f] \text{ and } RP_2 = [E(r_2) - r_f]$$

    In order to do so, we solve the following system of two equations with two unknowns:

    $$.31 = .06 + (1.5 \times RP_1) + (2.0 \times RP_2)$$
    $$.27 = .06 + (2.2 \times RP_1) + [(-0.2) \times RP_2]$$

    The solution to this set of equations is

    $$RP_1 = 10\% \text{ and } RP_2 = 5\%$$

    Thus, the expected return-beta relationship is

    $$E(r_P) = 6\% + (\beta_{P1} \times 10\%) + (\beta_{P2} \times 5\%)$$

5. The expected return for portfolio F equals the risk-free rate since its beta equals 0.
   For portfolio A, the ratio of risk premium to beta is $(12 - 6)/1.2 = 5$

   For portfolio E, the ratio is lower at $(8 - 6)/0.6 = 3.33$

   This implies that an arbitrage opportunity exists. For instance, you can create a portfolio G with beta equal to 0.6 (the same as E's) by combining portfolio A and portfolio F in equal weights. The expected return and beta for portfolio G are then:

   $$E(r_G) = (0.5 \times 12\%) + (0.5 \times 6\%) = 9\%$$

   $$\beta_G = (0.5 \times 1.2) + (0.5 \times 0\%) = 0.6$$

   Comparing portfolio G to portfolio E, G has the same beta and higher return. Therefore, an arbitrage opportunity exists by buying portfolio G and selling an equal amount of portfolio E. The profit for this arbitrage will be

   $$r_G - r_E = [9\% + (0.6 \times F)] - [8\% + (0.6 \times F)] = 1\%$$

   That is, 1% of the funds (long or short) in each portfolio.

6. Substituting the portfolio returns and betas in the expected return-beta relationship, we obtain two equations with two unknowns, the risk-free rate (r_f) and the factor risk premium (RP):

   $$12\% = r_f + (1.2 \times RP)$$

   $$9\% = r_f + (0.8 \times RP)$$

   Solving these equations, we obtain

   $$r_f = 3\% \text{ and } RP = 7.5\%$$

7. a. Shorting an equally weighted portfolio of the ten negative-alpha stocks and investing the proceeds in an equally-weighted portfolio of the 10 positive-alpha stocks eliminates the market exposure and creates a zero-investment portfolio. Denoting the systematic market factor as R_M, the expected dollar return is (noting that the expectation of nonsystematic risk, e, is zero):

   $$\$1,000,000 \times [0.02 + (1.0 \times R_M)] - \$1,000,000 \times [(-0.02) + (1.0 \times R_M)]$$

   $$= \$1,000,000 \times 0.04 = \$40,000$$

   The sensitivity of the payoff of this portfolio to the market factor is zero because the exposures of the positive alpha and negative alpha stocks cancel out. (Notice that the terms involving R_M sum to zero.) Thus, the systematic component of total risk is also zero. The variance of the analyst's profit is not zero, however, since this portfolio is not well diversified.

For $n = 20$ stocks (i.e., long 10 stocks and short 10 stocks) the investor will have a $100,000 position (either long or short) in each stock. Net market exposure is zero, but firm-specific risk has not been fully diversified. The variance of dollar returns from the positions in the 20 stocks is

$$20 \times [(100,000 \times 0.30)^2] = 18,000,000,000$$

The standard deviation of dollar returns is $134,164.

b.   If $n = 50$ stocks (25 stocks long and 25 stocks short), the investor will have a $40,000 position in each stock, and the variance of dollar returns is

$$50 \times [(40,000 \times 0.30)^2] = 7,200,000,000$$

The standard deviation of dollar returns is $84,853.

Similarly, if $n = 100$ stocks (50 stocks long and 50 stocks short), the investor will have a $20,000 position in each stock, and the variance of dollar returns is

$$100 \times [(20,000 \times 0.30)^2] = 3,600,000,000$$

The standard deviation of dollar returns is $60,000.

Notice that, when the number of stocks increases by a factor of 5 (i.e., from 20 to 100), standard deviation decreases by a factor of $\sqrt{5} = 2.23607$ (from $134,164 to $60,000).

8.   a. $\sigma^2 = \beta^2 \sigma_M^2 + \sigma^2(e)$

$\sigma_A^2 = (0.8^2 \times 20^2) + 25^2 = 881$

$\sigma_B^2 = (1.0^2 \times 20^2) + 10^2 = 500$

$\sigma_C^2 = (1.2^2 \times 20^2) + 20^2 = 976$

b.   If there are an infinite number of assets with identical characteristics, then a well-diversified portfolio of each type will have only systematic risk since the nonsystematic risk will approach zero with large n. Each variance is simply $\beta^2 \times$ market variance:

Well-diversified $\sigma_A^2 \approx 256$

Well-diversified $\sigma_B^2 \approx 400$

Well-diversified $\sigma_C^2 \approx 576$

The mean will equal that of the individual (identical) stocks.

c.   There is no arbitrage opportunity because the well-diversified portfolios all plot on the security market line (SML). Because they are fairly priced, there is no arbitrage.

9. a.   A long position in a portfolio (P) composed of portfolios A and B will offer an expected return-beta trade-off lying on a straight line between points A and B. Therefore, we can choose weights such that $\beta_P = \beta_C$ but with expected return higher than that of portfolio C. Hence, combining P with a short position in C will create an arbitrage portfolio with zero investment, zero beta, and positive rate of return.

    b.   The argument in part (a) leads to the proposition that the coefficient of β^2 must be zero in order to preclude arbitrage opportunities.

10. a. $E(r) = 6\% + (1.2 \times 6\%) + (0.5 \times 8\%) + (0.3 \times 3\%) = 18.1\%$

     b.   Surprises in the macroeconomic factors will result in surprises in the return of the stock:

          Unexpected return from macro factors =

          $$[1.2 \times (4\% - 5\%)] + [0.5 \times (6\% - 3\%)] + [0.3 \times (0\% - 2\%)] = -0.3\%$$

          $$E(r) = 18.1\% - 0.3\% = 17.8\%$$

11. The APT *required* (i.e., equilibrium) rate of return on the stock based on r_f and the factor betas is

     $$\text{Required } E(r) = 6\% + (1 \times 6\%) + (0.5 \times 2\%) + (0.75 \times 4\%) = 16\%$$

     According to the equation for the return on the stock, the actually expected return on the stock is 15% (because the *expected* surprises on all factors are zero by definition). Because the actually expected return based on risk is less than the equilibrium return, we conclude that the stock is overpriced.

12. The first two factors seem promising with respect to the likely impact on the firm's cost of capital. Both are macro factors that would elicit hedging demands across broad sectors of investors. The third factor, while important to Pork Products, is a poor choice for a multifactor SML because the price of hogs is of minor importance to most investors and is therefore highly unlikely to be a priced risk factor. Better choices would focus on variables that investors in aggregate might find more important to their welfare. Examples include: inflation uncertainty, short-term interest-rate risk, energy price risk, or exchange rate risk. The important point here is that, in specifying a multifactor SML, we not confuse risk factors that are important to a particular investor with factors that are important to investors in general; only the latter are likely to command a risk premium in the capital markets.

13. The formula is $E(r) = 0.04 + 1.25 \times 0.08 + 1.5 \times 0.02 = .17 = 17\%$

14. If $r_f = 4\%$ and based on the sensitivities to real GDP (0.75) and inflation (1.25), McCracken would calculate the expected return for the Orb Large Cap Fund to be:

$E(r) = 0.04 + 0.75 \times 0.08 + 1.25 \times 0.02 = .04 + 0.085 = 8.5\%$ above the risk free rate

Therefore, Kwon's fundamental analysis estimate is congruent with McCracken's APT estimate. If we assume that both Kwon and McCracken's estimates on the return of Orb's Large Cap Fund are accurate, then no arbitrage profit is possible.

15. In order to eliminate inflation, the following three equations must be solved simultaneously, where the GDP sensitivity will equal 1 in the first equation, inflation sensitivity will equal 0 in the second equation and the sum of the weights must equal 1 in the third equation.

    1. $1.25wx + 0.75wy + 1.0wz = 1$
    2. $1.5wz + 1.25wy + 2.0wz = 0$
    3. $wx + wy + wz = 1$

Here, x represents Orb's High Growth Fund, y represents Large Cap Fund and z represents Utility Fund. Using algebraic manipulation will yield $wx = wy = 1.6$ and $wz = -2.2$.

16. Since retirees living off a steady income would be hurt by inflation, this portfolio would not be appropriate for them. Retirees would want a portfolio with a return positively correlated with inflation to preserve value, and less correlated with the variable growth of GDP. Thus, Stiles is wrong. McCracken is correct in that supply side macroeconomic policies are generally designed to increase output at a minimum of inflationary pressure. Increased output would mean higher GDP, which in turn would increase returns of a fund positively correlated with GDP.

17. The maximum residual variance is tied to the number of securities (n) in the portfolio because, as we increase the number of securities, we are more likely to encounter securities with larger residual variances. The starting point is to determine the practical limit on the portfolio residual standard deviation, $\sigma(e_P)$, that still qualifies as a well-diversified portfolio. A reasonable approach is to compare

$\sigma^2(e_P)$ to the market variance, or equivalently, to compare $\sigma(e_P)$ to the market standard deviation. Suppose we do not allow $\sigma(e_P)$ to exceed $p\sigma_M$, where p is a small decimal fraction, for example, 0.05; then, the smaller the value we choose for p, the more stringent our criterion for defining how diversified a well-diversified portfolio must be.

Now construct a portfolio of n securities with weights $w_1, w_2, \ldots, w_n$, so that $\Sigma w_i = 1$. The portfolio residual variance is $\sigma^2(e_P) = \Sigma w_1^2 \sigma^2(e_i)$

To meet our practical definition of sufficiently diversified, we require this residual variance to be less than $(p\sigma_M)^2$. A sure and simple way to proceed is to assume the worst, that is, assume that the residual variance of each security is the highest possible value allowed under the assumptions of the problem: $\sigma^2(e_i) = n\sigma^2_M$.

In that case $\sigma^2(e_P) = \Sigma w_i^2 \, n\sigma_M^2$

Now apply the constraint: $\Sigma w_i^2 \, n \, \sigma_M^2 \leq (p\sigma_M)^2$

This requires that: $n\Sigma w_i^2 \leq p^2$

Or, equivalently, that: $\Sigma w_i^2 \leq p^2/n$

A relatively easy way to generate a set of well-diversified portfolios is to use portfolio weights that follow a geometric progression, since the computations then become relatively straightforward. Choose w_1 and a common factor q for the geometric progression such that $q < 1$. Therefore, the weight on each stock is a fraction q of the weight on the previous stock in the series. Then the sum of n terms is:

$$\Sigma w_i = w_1(1 - q^n)/(1 - q) = 1$$

or: $\quad w_1 = (1 - q)/(1 - q^n)$

The sum of the n *squared* weights is similarly obtained from w_1^2 and a common geometric progression factor of q^2. Therefore

$$\Sigma w_i^2 = w_1^2(1 - q^{2n})/(1 - q^2)$$

Substituting for w_1 from above, we obtain

$$\Sigma w_i^2 = [(1 - q)^2/(1 - q^n)^2] \times [(1 - q^{2n})/(1 - q^2)]$$

For sufficient diversification, we choose q so that $\Sigma w_i^2 \leq p^2/n$

For example, continue to assume that $p = 0.05$ and $n = 1,000$. If we choose $q = 0.9973$, then we will satisfy the required condition. At this value for q

$$w_1 = 0.0029 \text{ and } w_n = 0.0029 \times 0.9973^{1,000}$$

In this case, w_1 is about 15 times w_n. Despite this significant departure from equal weighting, this portfolio is nevertheless well diversified. Any value of q between 0.9973 and 1.0 results in a well-diversified portfolio. As q gets closer to 1, the portfolio approaches equal weighting.

18. a. Assume a single-factor economy, with a factor risk premium E_M and a (large) set of well-diversified portfolios with beta β_P. Suppose we create a portfolio Z by allocating the portion w to portfolio P and $(1 - w)$ to the market portfolio M. The rate of return on portfolio Z is:

$$R_Z = (w \times R_P) + [(1 - w) \times R_M]$$

Portfolio Z is riskless if we choose w so that $\beta_Z = 0$. This requires that:

$$\beta_Z = (w \times \beta_P) + [(1-w) \times 1] = 0 \Rightarrow w = 1/(1-\beta_P) \text{ and } (1-w) = -\beta_P/(1-\beta_P)$$

Substitute this value for w in the expression for R_Z:

$$R_Z = \{[1/(1-\beta_P)] \times R_P\} - \{[\beta_P/(1-\beta_P)] \times R_M\}$$

Since $\beta_Z = 0$, then, in order to avoid arbitrage, R_Z must be zero.

This implies that: $R_P = \beta_P \times R_M$

Taking expectations we have:

$$E_P = \beta_P \times E_M$$

This is the SML for well-diversified portfolios.

b. The same argument can be used to show that, in a three-factor model with factor risk premiums E_M, E_1 and E_2, in order to avoid arbitrage, we must have:

$$E_P = (\beta_{PM} \times E_M) + (\beta_{P1} \times E_1) + (\beta_{P2} \times E_2)$$

This is the SML for a three-factor economy.

19. a. The Fama-French (FF) three-factor model holds that one of the factors driving returns is firm size. An index with returns highly correlated with firm size (i.e., firm capitalization) that captures this factor is SMB (small minus big), the return for a portfolio of small stocks in excess of the return for a portfolio of large stocks. The returns for a small firm will be positively correlated with SMB. Moreover, the smaller the firm, the greater its residual from the other two factors, the market portfolio and the HML portfolio, which is the return for a portfolio of high book-to-market stocks in excess of the return for a portfolio of low book-to-market stocks. Hence, the ratio of the variance of this residual to the variance of the return on SMB will be larger and, together with the higher correlation, results in a high beta on the SMB factor.

b. This question appears to point to a flaw in the FF model. The model predicts that firm size affects average returns so that, if two firms merge into a larger firm, then the FF model predicts lower average returns for the merged firm. However, there seems to be no reason for the merged firm to underperform the returns of the component companies, assuming that the component firms were unrelated and that they will now be operated independently. We might therefore expect that the performance of the merged firm would be the same as the performance of a portfolio of the originally independent firms, but the FF model predicts that the increased firm size will result in lower average returns. Therefore, the question revolves around the behavior of returns for a portfolio of small firms, compared to the return for larger firms that result from merging those small firms into larger ones. Had past mergers of small firms into larger firms resulted, on average, in no change in the resultant larger firms' stock return characteristics (compared to the portfolio of stocks of the merged firms), the size factor in the FF model would have failed.

Perhaps the reason the size factor seems to help explain stock returns is that, when small firms become large, the characteristics of their fortunes (and hence their stock returns) change in a significant way. Put differently, stocks of large firms that result from a merger of smaller firms appear empirically to behave differently from portfolios of the smaller component firms. Specifically, the FF model predicts that the large firm will have a smaller risk premium. Notice that this development is not necessarily a bad thing for the stockholders of the smaller firms that merge. The lower risk premium may be due, in part, to the increase in value of the larger firm relative to the merged firms.

CFA PROBLEMS

1. a. This statement is incorrect. The CAPM requires a mean-variance efficient market portfolio, but APT does not.

    b. This statement is incorrect. The CAPM assumes normally distributed security returns, but APT does not.

    c. This statement is correct.

2. b. Since portfolio X has $\beta = 1.0$, then X is the market portfolio and $E(R_M) = 16\%$. Using $E(R_M) = 16\%$ and $r_f = 8\%$, the expected return for portfolio Y is not consistent.

3. d.

4. c.

5. d.

6. c. Investors will take on as large a position as possible only if the mispricing opportunity is an arbitrage. Otherwise, considerations of risk and diversification will limit the position they attempt to take in the mispriced security.

7. d.

8. d.

CHAPTER 11: THE EFFICIENT MARKET HYPOTHESIS

PROBLEM SETS

1. The correlation coefficient between stock returns for two nonoverlapping periods should be zero. If not, returns from one period could be used to predict returns in later periods and make abnormal profits.

2. No. Microsoft's continuing profitability does not imply that stock market investors who purchased Microsoft shares after its success was already evident would have earned an exceptionally high return on their investments. It simply means that Microsoft has made risky investments over the years that have paid off in the form of increased cash flows and profitability. Microsoft shareholders have benefited from the risk-expected return tradeoff, which is consistent with the EMH.

3. Expected rates of return differ because of differential risk premiums across all securities.

4. No. The value of dividend predictability would be already reflected in the stock price.

5. No, markets can be efficient even if some investors earn returns above the market average. Consider the Lucky Event issue: Ignoring transaction costs, about 50% of professional investors, by definition, will "beat" the market in any given year. The probability of beating it three years in a row, though small, is not insignificant. Beating the market in the past does not predict future success as three years of returns make up too small a sample on which to base correlation let alone causation.

6. Volatile stock prices could reflect volatile underlying economic conditions as large amounts of information being incorporated into the price will cause variability in stock price. The efficient market hypothesis suggests that investors cannot earn excess risk-adjusted rewards. The variability of the stock price is thus reflected in the expected returns as returns and risk are positively correlated.

7. The following effects seem to suggest predictability within equity markets and thus disprove the efficient market hypothesis. However, consider the following:

    a. Multiple studies suggest that "value" stocks (measured often by low P/E multiples) earn higher returns over time than "growth" stocks (high P/E multiples). This could suggest a strategy for earning higher returns over time. However, another rational argument may be that traditional forms of CAPM (such as Sharpe's model) do not fully account for all risk factors that affect a firm's price level. A firm viewed as riskier may have a lower price and thus P/E multiple.

b. The book-to-market effect suggests that an investor can earn excess returns by investing in companies with high book value (the value of a firm's assets minus its liabilities divided by the number of shares outstanding) to market value. A study by Fama and French[1] suggests that book-to-market value reflects a risk factor that is not accounted for by traditional one variable CAPM. For example, companies experiencing financial distress see the ratio of book to market value increase. Thus a more complex CAPM that includes book-to-market value as an explanatory variable should be used to test market anomalies.

c. Stock price momentum can be positively correlated with past performance (short to intermediate horizon) or negatively correlated (long horizon). Historical data seem to imply statistical significance to these patterns. Explanations for this include a bandwagon effect or the behaviorists' (see Chapter 12) explanation that there is a tendency for investors to underreact to new information, thus producing a positive serial correlation. However, statistical significance does not imply economic significance. Several studies that included transaction costs in the momentum models discovered that momentum traders tended to not outperform the efficient market hypothesis strategy of buy and hold.

d. The small-firm effect states that smaller firms produce better returns than larger firms. Since 1926, returns from small firms outpace large firm stock returns by about 1% per year. Do small cap investors earn excess risk-adjusted returns?

The measure of systematic risk according to Sharpe's CAPM is the stock's beta (or sensitivity of returns of the stock to market returns). If the stock's beta is the best explanation of risk, then the small-firm effect does indicate an inefficient market. Dividing the market into deciles based on their betas shows an increasing relationship between betas and returns. Fama and French[2] show that the empirical relationship between beta and stock returns is flat over a fairly long horizon (1963–1990). Breaking the market into deciles based on sizes and then examining the relationship between beta and stock returns within each size decile exhibits this flat relationship. This implies that firm size may be a better measure of risk than beta and the size-effect should not be viewed as an indicator that markets are inefficient. Heuristically this makes sense, as smaller firms are generally viewed as risky compared to larger firms and perceived risk and return are positively correlated.

In addition this effect seems to be endpoint and data sensitive. For example, smaller stocks did not outperform larger stocks from the mid-1980s through the 1990s. In addition, databases contain stock returns from companies that have survived and do not include returns of those that went bankrupt. Thus small-firm data may exhibit survivorship bias.

[1] Fama, Eugene and Kenneth French, "Common Risk Factors in the Returns on Stocks and Bonds," *Journal of Finance* 33:1, pp. 3-56.
[2] Ibid

8.   Over the long haul, there is an expected upward drift in stock prices based on their fair expected rates of return. The fair expected return over any single day is very small (e.g., 12% per year is only about 0.03% per day), so that on any day the price is virtually equally likely to rise or fall. Over longer periods, the small expected daily returns accumulate, and upward moves are more likely than downward ones. Remember that economies tend to grow over time and stock prices tend to follow economic growth, so it is only natural that there is an upward drift in equity prices.

9.   c.   This is a predictable pattern in returns that should not occur if the weak-form EMH is valid.

10. a.   Acute market inefficiencies are temporary in nature and are more easily exploited than chronic inefficiencies. A temporary drop in a stock price due to a large sale would be more easily exploited than the chronic inefficiencies mentioned in the other responses.

11. c.   This is a classic filter rule that should not produce superior returns in an efficient market.

12. b.   This is the definition of an efficient market.

13. a.   Though stock prices follow a random walk and intraday price changes do appear to be a random walk, over the long run there is compensation for bearing market risk and for the time value of money. Investing differs from a casino in that in the long-run, an investor is compensated for these risks, while a player at a casino faces less than fair-game odds.

     b.   In an efficient market, any predictable future prospects of a company have already been priced into the current value of the stock. Thus, a stock share price can still follow a random walk.

     c.   While the random nature of dart board selection seems to follow naturally from efficient markets, the role of rational portfolio management still exists. It exists to ensure a well-diversified portfolio, to assess the risk-tolerance of the investor, and to take into account tax code issues.

14. d.   In a semistrong-form efficient market, it is not possible to earn abnormally high profits by trading on publicly available information. Information about P/E ratios and recent price changes is publicly known. On the other hand, an investor who has advance knowledge of management improvements could earn abnormally high trading profits (unless the market is also strong-form efficient).

15. Market efficiency implies investors cannot earn excess risk-adjusted profits. If the stock price run-up occurs when only insiders know of the coming dividend increase, then it is a violation of strong-form efficiency. If the public also knows of the increase, then this violates semistrong-form efficiency.

16. While positive beta stocks respond well to favorable new information about the economy's progress through the business cycle, they should not show abnormal returns around already anticipated events. If a recovery, for example, is already anticipated, the actual recovery is not news. The stock price should already reflect the coming recovery.

17. a. Consistent. Based on pure luck, half of all managers should beat the market in any year.

   b. Inconsistent. This would be the basis of an "easy money" rule: simply invest with last year's best managers.

   c. Consistent. In contrast to predictable returns, predictable *volatility* does not convey a means to earn abnormal returns.

   d. Inconsistent. The abnormal performance ought to occur in January when earnings are announced.

   e. Inconsistent. Reversals offer a means to earn easy money: just buy last week's losers.

18. The return on the market is 8%. Therefore, the forecast monthly return for Ford is:

   $$0.10\% + (1.1 \times 8\%) = 8.9\%$$

   Ford's actual return was 7%, so the abnormal return was –1.9%.

19. a. Based on broad market trends, the CAPM indicates that AmbChaser stock should have increased by: $1.0\% + 2.0 \times (1.5\% - 1.0\%) = 2.0\%$
   Its firm-specific (nonsystematic) return due to the lawsuit is $1 million per $100 million initial equity, or 1%. Therefore, the total return should be 3%. (It is assumed here that the outcome of the lawsuit had a zero expected value.)

   b. If the settlement was expected to be $2 million, then the actual settlement was a "$1 million disappointment," and so the firm-specific return would be –1%, for a total return of $2\% - 1\% = 1\%$.

20. Given market performance, predicted returns on the two stocks would be:

   Apex: $0.2\% + (1.4 \times 3\%) = 4.4\%$

Bpex: $-0.1\% + (0.6 \times 3\%) = 1.7\%$

Apex underperformed this prediction; Bpex outperformed the prediction. We conclude that Bpex won the lawsuit.

21. a. $E(r_M) = 12\%$, $r_f = 4\%$ and $\beta = 0.5$

Therefore, the expected rate of return is:

$$4\% + 0.5 \times (12\% - 4\%) = 8\%$$

If the stock is fairly priced, then $E(r) = 8\%$.

b.   If r_M falls short of your expectation by 2% (that is, $10\% - 12\%$) then you would expect the return for Changing Fortunes Industries to fall short of your original expectation by: $\beta \times 2\% = 1\%$

Therefore, you would forecast a revised expectation for Changing Fortunes of: $8\% - 1\% = 7\%$

c.   Given a market return of 10%, you would forecast a return for Changing Fortunes of 7%. The actual return is 10%. Therefore, the surprise due to firm-specific factors is $10\% - 7\% = 3\%$, which we attribute to the settlement. Because the firm is initially worth $100 million, the surprise amount of the settlement is 3% of $100 million, or $3 million, implying that the prior expectation for the settlement was only $2 million.

22. Implicit in the dollar-cost averaging strategy is the notion that stock prices fluctuate around a "normal" level. Otherwise, there is no meaning to statements such as: "when the price is high." How do we know, for example, whether a price of $25 today will turn out to be viewed as high or low compared to the stock price six months from now?

23. The market responds positively to *new* news. If the eventual recovery is anticipated, then the recovery is already reflected in stock prices. Only a better-than-expected recovery should affect stock prices.

24. Buy. In your view, the firm is not as bad as everyone else believes it to be. Therefore, you view the firm as undervalued by the market. You are less pessimistic about the firm's prospects than the beliefs built into the stock price.

25. Here we need a two-factor model relating Ford's return to those of both the broad market and the auto industry. If we call r_I the industry return, then we would first estimate parameters $\alpha, \beta_M, \beta_{IND}$ in the following regression:

$$r_{FORD} = \alpha + \beta_M r_M + \beta_{IND} r_{IND} + \varepsilon$$

Given these estimates we would calculate Ford's firm-specific return as:

$$r_{\text{FORD}} - [\alpha + \beta_M r_M + \beta_{IND} r_{IND} + \varepsilon]$$

This estimate of firm-specific news would measure the market's assessment of the potential profitability of Ford's new model.

26. The market may have anticipated even greater earnings. *Compared to prior expectations,* the announcement was a disappointment.

27. Thinly traded stocks will not have a considerable amount of market research performed on the companies they represent. This neglected-firm effect implies a greater degree of uncertainty with respect to smaller companies. Thus positive CAPM alphas among thinly traded stocks do not necessarily violate the efficient market hypothesis since these higher alphas are actually risk premiums, not market inefficiencies.

28. The negative abnormal returns (downward drift in CAR) just prior to stock purchases suggest that insiders deferred their purchases until *after* bad news was released to the public. This is evidence of valuable inside information. The positive abnormal returns after purchase suggest insider purchases in anticipation of good news. The analysis is symmetric for insider sales.

29. a. The market risk premium moves countercyclical to the economy, peaking in recessions. A violation of the efficient market hypothesis would imply that investors could take advantage of this predictability and earn excess risk adjusted returns. However, several studies, including Siegel,[3] show that successfully timing the changes have eluded professional investors thus far. Moreover a changing risk premium implies changing required rates of return for stocks rather than an inefficiency with the market.

   b. As the market risk premium increases during a recession, stocks prices tend to fall. As the economy recovers, the market risk premium falls, and stock prices tend to rise. These changes could give investors the impression that markets overreact, especially if the underlying changes in the market risk premium are small but cumulative. For example, the October Crash of 1987 is commonly viewed as an example of market overreaction. However, in the weeks running up to mid-October, several underlying changes to the market risk premium occurred (in addition to changes in the yields on long-term Treasury Bonds). Congress threatened investors with a "merger tax" that would have truncated the booming merger industry and loosened the discipline that the threat of mergers provides to a firm's management. In addition, the Secretary of Treasury threatened further depreciation in the value of the dollar, frightening foreign investors. These events may have increased the market risk premium and lowered stock prices in a seeming overreaction.

---

[3] Jeremy Siegel, *Stocks for the Long Run: The Definitive Guide to Financial Market Returns and Long-Term Investment Strategies,* 2002, New York: McGraw-Hill.

CFA PROBLEMS

1. b. Semistrong form efficiency implies that market prices reflect all *publicly available* information concerning past trading history as well as fundamental aspects of the firm.

2. a. The full price adjustment should occur just as the news about the dividend becomes publicly available.

3. d. If low P/E stocks tend to have positive abnormal returns, this would represent an unexploited profit opportunity that would provide evidence that investors are not using all available information to make profitable investments.

4. c. In an efficient market, no securities are consistently overpriced or underpriced. While some securities will turn out after any investment period to have provided positive alphas (i.e., risk-adjusted abnormal returns) and some negative alphas, these past returns are not predictive of future returns.

5. c. A random walk implies that stock price changes are unpredictable, using past price changes or any other data.

6. d. A gradual adjustment to fundamental values would allow for the use of strategies based on past price movements in order to generate abnormal profits.

7. a.

8. a. Some empirical evidence that supports the EMH:

   (i) Professional money managers do not typically earn higher returns than comparable risk, passive index strategies.

   (ii) Event studies typically show that stocks respond immediately to the public release of relevant news.

   (iii) Most tests of technical analysis find that it is difficult to identify price trends that can be exploited to earn superior risk-adjusted investment returns.

   b. Some evidence that is difficult to reconcile with the EMH concerns simple portfolio strategies that apparently would have provided high risk-adjusted returns in the past. Some examples of portfolios with attractive historical returns:

   (i) Low P/E stocks.

   (ii) High book-to-market ratio stocks.

   (iii) Small firms in January.

   (iv) Firms with very poor stock price performance in the last few months.

Other evidence concerns post-earnings-announcement stock price drift and intermediate-term price momentum.

c. An investor might choose not to index even if markets are efficient because he or she may want to tailor a portfolio to specific tax considerations or to specific risk management issues, for example, the need to hedge (or at least not add to) exposure to a particular source of risk (e.g., industry exposure).

9. a. The efficient market hypothesis (EMH) states that a market is efficient if security prices immediately and fully reflect all available relevant information. If the market fully reflects information, the knowledge of that information would not allow an investor to profit from the information because stock prices already incorporate the information.

i. The *weak form* of the EMH asserts that stock prices reflect all the information that can be derived by examining market trading data such as the history of past prices and trading volume.

A strong body of evidence supports weak-form efficiency in the major U.S. securities markets. For example, test results suggest that technical trading rules do not produce superior returns after adjusting for transaction costs and taxes.

ii. The *semistrong form* states that a firm's stock price reflects all publicly available information about a firm's prospects. Examples of publicly available information are company annual reports and investment advisory data.

Evidence strongly supports the notion of semistrong efficiency, but occasional studies (e.g., identifying market anomalies such as the small-firm-in-January or book-to-market effects) and events (e.g. stock market crash of October 19, 1987) are inconsistent with this form of market efficiency. There is a question concerning the extent to which these "anomalies" result from data mining.

iii. The *strong form* of the EMH holds that current market prices reflect *all* information (whether publicly available or privately held) that can be relevant to the valuation of the firm.

Empirical evidence suggests that strong-form efficiency does not hold. If this form were correct, prices would fully reflect all information. Therefore even insiders could not earn excess returns. But the evidence is that corporate officers do have access to pertinent information long enough before public release to enable them to profit from trading on this information.

b. i. *Technical analysis* involves the search for recurrent and predictable patterns in stock prices in order to enhance returns. The EMH implies that technical analysis is without value. If past prices contain no useful information for predicting future prices, there is no point in following any technical trading rule.

ii. *Fundamental analysis* uses earnings and dividend prospects of the firm, expectations of future interest rates, and risk evaluation of the firm to determine proper stock prices. The EMH predicts that most fundamental analysis is doomed to failure. According to semistrong-form efficiency, no investor can earn excess returns from trading rules based on publicly available information. Only analysts with unique insight achieve superior returns.

In summary, the EMH holds that the market appears to adjust so quickly to information about both individual stocks and the economy as a whole that no technique of selecting a portfolio using either technical or fundamental analysis can consistently outperform a strategy of simply buying and holding a diversified portfolio of securities, such as those comprising the popular market indexes.

c. Portfolio managers have several roles and responsibilities even in perfectly efficient markets. The most important responsibility is to identify the risk/return objectives for a portfolio given the investor's constraints. In an efficient market, portfolio managers are responsible for tailoring the portfolio to meet the investor's needs, rather than to beat the market, which requires identifying the client's return requirements and risk tolerance. Rational portfolio management also requires examining the investor's constraints, including liquidity, time horizon, laws and regulations, taxes, and unique preferences and circumstances such as age and employment.

10. a. The earnings (and dividend) growth rate of growth stocks may be consistently overestimated by investors. Investors may extrapolate recent growth too far into the future and thereby downplay the inevitable slowdown. At any given time, growth stocks are likely to revert to (lower) mean returns and value stocks are likely to revert to (higher) mean returns, often over an extended future time horizon.

b. In efficient markets, the current prices of stocks already reflect all known relevant information. In this situation, growth stocks and value stocks provide the same risk-adjusted expected return.

CHAPTER 12: BEHAVIORAL FINANCE
AND TECHNICAL ANALYSIS

PROBLEM SETS

1. Technical analysis can generally be viewed as a search for trends or patterns in market prices. Technical analysts tend to view these trends as momentum, or gradual adjustments to 'correct' prices, or, alternatively, reversals of trends. A number of the behavioral biases discussed in the chapter might contribute to such trends and patterns. For example, a conservatism bias might contribute to a trend in prices as investors gradually take new information into account, resulting in gradual adjustment of prices towards their fundamental values. Another example derives from the concept of representativeness, which leads investors to inappropriately conclude, on the basis of a small sample of data, that a pattern has been established that will continue well into the future. When investors subsequently become aware of the fact that prices have overreacted, corrections reverse the initial erroneous trend.

2. Even if many investors exhibit behavioral biases, security prices might still be set efficiently if the actions of arbitrageurs move prices to their intrinsic values. Arbitrageurs who observe mispricing in the securities markets would buy underpriced securities (or possibly sell short overpriced securities) in order to profit from the anticipated subsequent changes as prices move to their intrinsic values. Consequently, securities prices would still exhibit the characteristics of an efficient market.

3. One of the major factors limiting the ability of rational investors to take advantage of any 'pricing errors' that result from the actions of behavioral investors is the fact that a mispricing can get worse over time. An example of this fundamental risk is the apparent ongoing overpricing of the NASDAQ index in the late 1990s. Related factors are the inherent costs and limits related to short selling, which restrict the extent to which arbitrage can force overpriced securities (or indexes) to move towards their fair values. Rational investors must also be aware of the risk that an apparent mispricing is, in fact, a consequence of model risk; that is, the perceived mispricing may not be real because the investor has used a faulty model to value the security.

4.   There are two reasons why behavioral biases might not affect equilibrium asset prices: first, behavioral biases might contribute to the success of technical trading rules as prices gradually adjust towards their intrinsic values, and second, the actions of arbitrageurs might move security prices towards their intrinsic values. It might be important for investors to be aware of these biases because either of these scenarios might create the potential for excess profits even if behavioral biases do not affect equilibrium prices.

In addition, an investor should be aware of his personal behavioral biases, even if those biases do not affect equilibrium prices, to help avoid some of these information processing errors (e.g. overconfidence or representativeness).

5.   Efficient market advocates believe that publicly available information (and, for advocates of strong-form efficiency, even insider information) is, at any point in time, reflected in securities prices, and that price adjustments to new information occur very quickly. Consequently, prices are at fair levels so that active management is very unlikely to improve performance above that of a broadly diversified index portfolio. In contrast, advocates of behavioral finance identify a number of investor errors in information processing and decision making that could result in mispricing of securities. However, the behavioral finance literature generally does not provide guidance as to how these investor errors can be exploited to generate excess profits. Therefore, in the absence of any profitable alternatives, even if securities markets are not efficient, the optimal strategy might still be a passive indexing strategy.

6.   a.   Davis uses loss aversion as the basis for her decision making. She holds on to stocks that are down from the purchase price in the hopes that they will recover. She is reluctant to accept a loss.

7.   a.   Shrum refuses to follow a stock after she sells it because she does not want to experience the regret of seeing it rise. The behavioral characteristic used for the basis for her decision making is the fear of regret.

8.   a.   Investors attempt to avoid regret by holding on to losers hoping the stocks will rebound. If the stock rebounds to its original purchase price, the stock can be sold with no regret. Investors also may try to avoid regret by distancing themselves from their decisions by hiring a full-service broker.

9. a.   iv

    b.   iii

    c.   v

    d.   i

    e.   ii

10. Underlying risks still exist even during a mispricing event. The market mispricing could get worse before it gets better. Other adverse effects could occur before the price corrects itself (e.g., loss of clients with no understanding or appetite for mispricing opportunities).

11. Data mining is the process by which patterns are pulled from data. Technical analysts must be careful not to engage in data mining as great is the human capacity to discern patterns where no patterns exist. Technical analysts must avoid mining data to **support** a theory rather than using data to **test** a theory.

12. Even if prices follow a random walk, the existence of irrational investors combined with the limits to arbitrage by arbitrageurs may allow persistent mispricings to be present. This implies that capital will not be allocated efficiently—capital does not immediately flow from relatively unproductive firms to relatively productive firms.

13. $$\text{Trin} = \frac{\text{Volume declining} / \text{Number declining}}{\text{Volume advancing} / \text{Number advancing}} =$$

    $$\frac{\$1,0.58,313 / 1,553}{\$852,581 / 1,455} = 1.16$$

    This trin ratio, which is above 1.0, would be taken as a bearish signal.

14. Breadth:

Advances	Declines	Net Advances
1,455	1,553	−98

Breadth is negative—bearish signal (no one would actually use a one-day measure).

15. This exercise is left to the student; answers will vary, but successful students should be able to identify time periods when upward or downward trends are obvious. This exercise also shows the benefit of hindsight, which investors do not possess when making current decisions.

16. The confidence index increases from (5%/6%) = 0.833 to (6%/7%) = 0.857.
     This indicates slightly higher confidence which would be interpreted by technicians
     as a bullish signal. But the real reason for the increase in the index is the expectation
     of higher inflation, not higher confidence about the economy.

17. At the beginning of the period, the price of Computers, Inc. divided by the industry index
     was 0.39; by the end of the period, the ratio had increased to 0.50. As the ratio increased
     over the period, it appears that Computers, Inc. outperformed other firms in its industry.
     The overall trend, therefore, indicates relative strength, although some fluctuation existed
     during the period, with the ratio falling to a low point of 0.33 on day 19.

18. Five day moving averages:
     Days 1 – 5: (19.63 + 20 + 20.5 + 22 + 21.13) / 5 = 20.65
     Days 2 – 6 = 21.13
     Days 3 – 7 = 21.50
     Days 4 – 8 = 21.90
     Days 5 – 9 = 22.13
     Days 6 – 10 = 22.68
     Days 7 – 11 = 23.18
     Days 8 – 12 = 23.45   ←Sell signal (day 12 price < moving average)
     Days 9 – 13 = 23.38
     Days 10 – 14 = 23.15
     Days 11 – 15 = 22.50
     Days 12 – 16 = 21.65
     Days 13 – 17 = 20.95
     Days 14 – 18 = 20.28
     Days 15 – 19 = 19.38
     Days 16 – 20 = 19.05
     Days 17 – 21 = 18.93   ←Buy signal (day 21 price > moving average)
     Days 18 – 22 = 19.28
     Days 19 – 23 = 19.93
     Days 20 – 24 = 21.05
     Days 21 – 25 = 22.05
     Days 22 – 26 = 23.18
     Days 23 – 27 = 24.13
     Days 24 – 28 = 25.13
     Days 25 – 29 = 26.00
     Days 26 – 30 = 26.80
     Days 27 – 31 = 27.45
     Days 28 – 32 = 27.80
     Days 29 – 33 = 27.90   ←Sell signal (day 33 price < moving average)
     Days 30 – 34 = 28.20
     Days 31 – 35 = 28.45
     Days 32 – 36 = 28.65
     Days 33 – 37 = 29.05

Days 34 – 38 = 29.25
Days 35 – 39 = 29.00
Days 36 – 40 = 28.75

19. This pattern shows a lack of breadth. Even though the index is up, more stocks declined than advanced, which indicates a "lack of broad-based support" for the rise in the index.

20.

Day	Advances	Declines	Net Advances	Cumulative Breadth
1	906	704	202	202
2	653	986	−333	−131
3	721	789	−68	−199
4	503	968	−465	−664
5	497	1,095	−598	−1,262
6	970	702	268	−994
7	1,002	609	393	−601
8	903	722	181	−420
9	850	748	102	−318
10	766	766	0	−318

The signal is bearish as cumulative breadth is negative; however, the negative number is declining in magnitude, indicative of improvement. Perhaps the worst of the bear market has passed.

21. $\text{Trin} = \dfrac{\text{Volume declining/Number declining}}{\text{Volume advancing/Number advancing}} = \dfrac{240 \text{ million}/704}{330 \text{ million}/906} = 0.936$

This is a slightly bullish indicator, with average volume in advancing issues a bit greater than average volume in declining issues.

22. $\text{Confidence Index} = \dfrac{\text{Yield on top-rated corporate bonds}}{\text{Yield on intermediate-grade corporate bonds}}$

This year: Confidence index = (8%/10.5%) = 0.762

Last year: Confidence index = (8.5%/10%) = 0.850

Thus, the confidence index is decreasing.

23.   Note: In order to create the 26-week moving average for the S&P 500, we converted the weekly returns to weekly index values, with a base of 100 for the week prior to the first week of the data set. The following graph shows the S&P 500 values and the 26-week moving average, beginning with the 26th week of the data set.

   a.   The graph summarizes the data for the 26-week moving average. The graph also shows the values of the S&P 500 index.

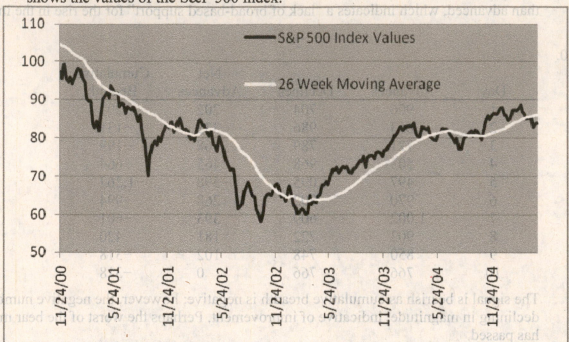

   b.   The S&P 500 crosses through its moving average from below 14 times, as indicated in the table below. The index increases seven times in weeks following a cross-through and decreases seven times.

Date of Cross-Through	Direction of S&P 500 in Subsequent Week
05/18/01	Decrease
06/08/01	Decrease
12/07/01	Decrease
12/21/01	Increase
03/01/02	Increase
11/22/02	Increase
01/03/03	Increase
03/21/03	Decrease
04/17/03	Increase
06/10/04	Decrease
09/03/04	Increase
10/01/04	Decrease
10/29/04	Increase
04/08/05	Decrease

c. The S&P 500 crosses through its moving average from above 14 times, as indicated in the table below. The index increases nine times in weeks following a cross-through and decreases five times.

Date of Cross-Through	Direction of S&P 500 in Subsequent Week	Date of Cross-Through	Direction of S&P 500 in Subsequent Week
06/01/01	Increase	03/28/03	Increase
06/15/01	Increase	04/30/04	Decrease
12/14/01	Increase	07/02/04	Decrease
02/08/02	Increase	09/24/04	Increase
04/05/02	Decrease	10/15/04	Decrease
12/13/02	Increase	03/24/05	Increase
01/24/03	Decrease	04/15/05	Increase

d. When the index crosses through its moving average from below, as in part (b), this is regarded as a bullish signal. In our sample, the index is as likely to increase as it is to decrease following such a signal. When the index crosses through its moving average from above, as in part (c), this is regarded as a bearish signal. In our sample, contrary to the bearish signal, the index is actually more likely to increase than it is to decrease following such a signal.

24. In order to create the relative strength measure, we converted the weekly returns for the Fidelity Banking Fund and for the S&P 500 to weekly index values, using a base of 100 for the week prior to the first week of the data set. The first graph shows the resulting values, along with the relative strength measure ($\times$ 100). The second graph shows the percentage change in the relative strength measure over five-week intervals.

a. The following graph summarizes the relative strength data for the fund.

b. Over five-week intervals, relative strength increased by more than 5% 29 times, as indicated in the table and graph below. The Fidelity Banking Fund underperformed the S&P 500 index 18 times and outperformed the S&P 500 index 11 times in weeks following an increase of more than 5%.

Date of Increase	Performance of Banking Fund in Subsequent Week	Date of Increase	Performance of Banking Fund in Subsequent Week
07/21/00	Outperformed	03/09/01	Outperformed
08/04/00	Outperformed	03/16/01	Underperformed
08/11/00	Underperformed	03/30/01	Underperformed
08/18/00	Outperformed	06/22/01	Underperformed
09/22/00	Outperformed	08/17/01	Underperformed
09/29/00	Underperformed	03/15/02	Outperformed
10/06/00	Underperformed	03/22/02	Underperformed
12/01/00	Underperformed	03/28/02	Outperformed
12/22/00	Underperformed	04/05/02	Outperformed
12/29/00	Outperformed	04/12/02	Underperformed
01/05/01	Underperformed	04/26/02	Outperformed
01/12/01	Underperformed	05/03/02	Underperformed
02/16/01	Underperformed	05/10/02	Underperformed
02/23/01	Outperformed	06/28/02	Underperformed
03/02/01	Underperformed		

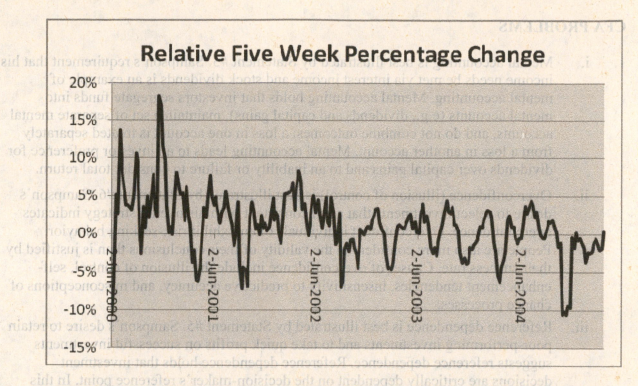

c. Over five-week intervals, relative strength decreases by more than 5% 15 times, as indicated in the graph above and table below. The Fidelity Banking Fund underperformed the S&P 500 index six times and outperformed the S&P 500 index nine times in weeks following a decrease of more than 5%.

Date of Decrease	Performance of Banking Fund in Subsequent Week	Date of Decrease	Performance of Banking Fund in Subsequent Week
07/07/00	Underperformed	04/16/04	Underperformed
07/14/00	Outperformed	04/23/04	Outperformed
05/04/01	Underperformed	12/03/04	Outperformed
05/11/01	Outperformed	12/10/04	Underperformed
10/12/01	Outperformed	12/17/04	Outperformed
11/02/01	Outperformed	12/23/04	Underperformed
10/04/02	Outperformed	12/31/04	Underperformed
10/11/02	Outperformed		

d. An increase in relative strength, as in part (b) above, is regarded as a bullish signal. However, in our sample, the Fidelity Banking Fund is more likely to underperform the S&P 500 index than it is to outperform the index following such a signal. A decrease in relative strength, as in part (c), is regarded as a bearish signal. In our sample, contrary to the bearish signal, the Fidelity Banking Fund is actually more likely to outperform the index increase than it is to underperform following such a signal.

25. It has been shown that discrepancies of price from net asset value in closed-end funds tend to be higher in funds that are more difficult to arbitrage such as less-diversified funds.

CFA PROBLEMS

1. i.   Mental accounting is best illustrated by Statement #3. Sampson's requirement that his income needs be met via interest income and stock dividends is an example of mental accounting. Mental accounting holds that investors segregate funds into mental accounts (e.g., dividends and capital gains), maintain a set of separate mental accounts, and do not combine outcomes; a loss in one account is treated separately from a loss in another account. Mental accounting leads to an investor preference for dividends over capital gains and to an inability or failure to consider total return.

    ii. Overconfidence (illusion of control) is best illustrated by Statement #6. Sampson's desire to select investments that are inconsistent with his overall strategy indicates overconfidence. Overconfident individuals often exhibit risk-seeking behavior. People are also more confident in the validity of their conclusions than is justified by their success rate. Causes of overconfidence include the illusion of control, self-enhancement tendencies, insensitivity to predictive accuracy, and misconceptions of chance processes.

    iii. Reference dependence is best illustrated by Statement #5. Sampson's desire to retain poor-performing investments and to take quick profits on successful investments suggests reference dependence. Reference dependence holds that investment decisions are critically dependent on the decision-maker's reference point. In this case, the reference point is the original purchase price. Alternatives are evaluated not in terms of final outcomes but rather in terms of gains and losses relative to this reference point. Thus, preferences are susceptible to manipulation simply by changing the reference point.

2. a.   Frost's statement is an example of reference dependence. His inclination to sell the international investments once prices return to the original cost depends not only on the terminal wealth value, but also on where he is now, that is, his reference point. This reference point, which is below the original cost, has become a critical factor in Frost's decision.

    In standard finance, alternatives are evaluated in terms of terminal wealth values or final outcomes, not in terms of gains and losses relative to some reference point such as original cost.

    b.   Frost's statement is an example of susceptibility to cognitive error, in at least two ways. First, he is displaying the behavioral flaw of overconfidence. He likely is more confident about the validity of his conclusion than is justified by his rate of success. He is very confident that the past performance of Country XYZ indicates future performance. Behavioral investors could, and often do, conclude that a five-year record is ample evidence to suggest future performance. Second, by choosing to invest in the securities of only Country XYZ, Frost is also exemplifying the behavioral finance phenomenon of asset segregation. That is, he is evaluating Country XYZ investment in terms of its anticipated gains or losses viewed in isolation.

    Individuals are typically more confident about the validity of their conclusions than is justified by their success rate or by the principles of standard finance, especially with regard to relevant time horizons. In standard finance, investors know that five years of returns on Country XYZ securities relative to all other markets provide little information about future performance. A standard finance investor would not be fooled by this "law of small numbers." In standard finance, investors evaluate performance in portfolio terms, in this case defined by combining the Country XYZ holding with all other securities held. Investments in Country XYZ, like all other potential investments, should be evaluated in terms of the anticipated contribution to the risk–reward profile of the entire portfolio.

c. Frost's statement is an example of mental accounting. Mental accounting holds that investors segregate money into mental accounts (e.g., safe versus speculative), maintain a set of separate mental accounts, and do not combine outcomes; a loss in one account is treated separately from a loss in another account. One manifestation of mental accounting, in which Frost is engaging, is building a portfolio as a pyramid of assets, layer by layer, with the retirement account representing a layer separate from the speculative fund. Each layer is associated with different goals and attitudes toward risk. He is more risk averse with respect to the retirement account than he is with respect to the speculative fund account. The money in the retirement account is a downside protection layer, designed to avoid future poverty. The money in the speculative fund account is the upside potential layer, designed for a chance at being rich.

In standard finance, decisions consider the risk and return profile of the entire portfolio rather than anticipated gains or losses on any particular account, investment, or class of investments. Alternatives should be considered in terms of final outcomes in a total portfolio context rather than in terms of contributions to a safe or a speculative account. Standard finance investors seek to maximize the mean-variance structure of the portfolio as a whole and consider covariances between assets as they construct their portfolios. Standard finance investors have consistent attitudes toward risk across their entire portfolio.

3. a. *Illusion of knowledge*: Maclin believes he is an expert on, and can make accurate forecasts about, the real estate market solely because he has studied housing market data on the Internet. He may have access to a large amount of real estate-related information, but he may not understand how to analyze the information nor have the ability to apply it to a proposed investment.

Overconfidence: Overconfidence causes us to misinterpret the accuracy of our information and our skill in analyzing it. Maclin has assumed that the information he collected on the Internet is accurate without attempting to verify it or consult other sources. He also assumes he has skill in evaluating and analyzing the real estate-related information he has collected, although there is no information in the question that suggests he possesses such ability.

b. *Reference point*: Maclin's reference point for his bond position is the purchase price, as evidenced by the fact that he will not sell a position for less than he paid for it. This fixation on a reference point, and the subsequent waiting for the price of the security to move above that reference point before selling the security, prevents Maclin from undertaking a risk/return-based analysis of his portfolio position.

c. *Familiarity*: Maclin is evaluating his holding of company stock based on his familiarity with the company rather than on sound investment and portfolio principles. Company employees, because of this familiarity, may have a distorted perception of their own company, assuming a "good company" will also be a good investment. Irrational investors believe an investment in a company with which they are familiar will produce higher returns and have less risk than nonfamiliar investments.

Representativeness: Maclin is confusing his company (which may well be a good company) with the company's stock (which may or may not be an appropriate holding for his portfolio and/or a good investment) and its future performance. This can result in employees' overweighting their company stock, thereby holding an underdiversified portfolio.

4. a. The behavioral finance principle of biased expectations/overconfidence is most consistent with the investor's first statement. Petrie stock provides a level of confidence and comfort for the investor because of the circumstances in which she acquired the stock and her recent history with the returns and income from the stock. However, the investor exhibits overconfidence in the stock given the needs of her portfolio (she is retired) and the brevity of the recent performance history.

b. The behavioral finance principle of mental accounting is most consistent with the investor's second statement. The investor has segregated the monies distributed from her portfolio into two "accounts": the returns her portfolio receives on the Petrie stock and the returns on the rest of her portfolio. She is maintaining a separate set of mental accounts with regard to the total funds distributed. The investor's specific uses should be viewed in the overall context of her spending needs and she should consider the risk and return profile of the entire portfolio.

5. i. *Overconfidence (Biased Expectations and Illusion of Control)*: Pierce is basing her investment strategy for supporting her parents on her confidence in the economic forecasts. This is a cognitive error reflecting overconfidence in the form of both biased expectations and an illusion of control. Pierce is likely more confident in the validity of those forecasts than is justified by the accuracy of prior forecasts. Analysts' consensus forecasts have proven routinely and widely inaccurate. Pierce also appears to be overly confident that the recent performance of the Pogo Island economy is a good indicator of future performance. Behavioral investors often conclude that a short track record is ample evidence to suggest future performance.

Standard finance investors understand that individuals typically have greater confidence in the validity of their conclusions than is justified by their success rate. The calibration paradigm, which compares confidence to predictive ability, suggests that there is significantly lower probability of success than the confidence levels reported by individuals. In addition, standard finance investors know that recent performance provides little information about future performance and are not deceived by this "law of small numbers."

ii.   *Loss Aversion (Risk Seeking)*: Pierce is exhibiting *risk aversion* in deciding to sell the Core Bond Fund despite its gains and favorable prospects. She prefers a certain gain over a possibly larger gain coupled with a smaller chance of a loss. Pierce is exhibiting *loss aversion* (risk seeking) by holding the High Yield Bond Fund despite its uncertain prospects. She prefers the modest possibility of recovery coupled with the chance of a larger loss over a certain loss. People tend to exhibit risk seeking, rather than risk aversion, behavior when the probability of loss is large. There is considerable evidence indicating that risk aversion holds for gains and risk seeking behavior holds for losses, and that attitudes toward risk vary depending on particular goals and circumstances.

Standard finance investors are consistently risk averse and systematically prefer a certain outcome over a gamble with the same expected value. Such investors also take a symmetrical view of gains and losses of the same magnitude, and their sensitivity (aversion) to changes in value is not a function of a specified value reference point.

iii.   *Reference Dependence:* Pierce's inclination to sell her Small Company Fund once it returns to her original cost is an example of *reference dependence*. This is predicated on the current value as related to original cost, her reference point. Her decision ignores any analysis of expected terminal value or the impact of this sale on her total portfolio. This reference point of original cost has become a critical but inappropriate factor in Pierce's decision.

In standard finance, alternatives are evaluated in terms of terminal wealth values or final outcomes, not in terms of gains and losses relative to a reference point such as original cost. Standard finance investors also consider the risk and return profile of the entire portfolio rather than anticipated gains or losses on any particular investment or asset class.

CHAPTER 13: EMPIRICAL EVIDENCE ON SECURITY RETURNS

PROBLEM SETS

1. Even if the single-factor CCAPM (with a consumption-tracking portfolio used as the index) performs better than the CAPM, it is still quite possible that the consumption portfolio does not capture the size and growth characteristics captured by the SMB (i.e., small minus big capitalization) and HML (i.e., high minus low book-to-market ratio) factors of the Fama-French three-factor model. Therefore, it is expected that the Fama-French model with consumption provides a better explanation of returns than does the model with consumption alone.

2. Wealth and consumption should be positively correlated and, therefore, market volatility and consumption volatility should also be positively correlated. Periods of high market volatility might coincide with periods of high consumption volatility. The conventional CAPM focuses on the covariance of security returns with returns for the market portfolio (which in turn tracks aggregate wealth), while the consumption-based CAPM focuses on the covariance of security returns with returns for a portfolio that tracks consumption growth. However, to the extent that wealth and consumption are correlated, both versions of the CAPM might represent patterns in actual returns reasonably well.

    To see this formally, suppose that the CAPM and the consumption-based model are approximately true. According to the conventional CAPM, the market price of risk equals expected excess market return divided by the variance of that excess return. According to the consumption-beta model, the price of risk equals expected excess market return divided by the covariance of R_M with g, where g is the rate of consumption growth. This covariance equals the correlation of R_M with g times the product of the standard deviations of the variables. Combining the two models, the correlation between R_M and g equals the standard deviation of R_M divided by the standard deviation of g. Accordingly, if the correlation between R_M and g is relatively stable, then an increase in market volatility will be accompanied by an increase in the volatility of consumption growth.

    <u>Note:</u> For the following problems, the focus is on the estimation *procedure*. To keep the exercise feasible, the sample was limited to returns on nine stocks plus a market index and a second factor over a period of 12 years. The data were generated to conform to a two-factor CAPM so that actual rates of return equal CAPM expectations plus random noise, and the true intercept of the SCL is zero for all stocks. The exercise will provide a feel for the pitfalls of verifying social-science models. However, due to the small size of the sample, results are not always consistent with the findings of other studies as reported in the chapter.

3. Using the regression feature of Excel with the data presented in the text, the first-pass (SCL) estimation results are:

Stock:	A	B	C	D	E	F	G	H	I
R-square	0.06	0.06	0.06	0.37	0.17	0.59	0.06	0.67	0.70
Observations	12	12	12	12	12	12	12	12	12
Alpha	9.00	−0.63	−0.64	−5.05	0.73	−4.53	5.94	−2.41	5.92
Beta	−0.47	0.59	0.42	1.38	0.90	1.78	0.66	1.91	2.08
t-Alpha	0.73	−0.04	−0.06	−0.41	0.05	−0.45	0.33	−0.27	0.64
t-Beta	−0.81	0.78	0.78	2.42	1.42	3.83	0.78	4.51	4.81

4. The hypotheses for the second-pass regression for the SML are:
   - The intercept is zero.
   - The slope is equal to the average return on the index portfolio.

5. The second-pass data from first-pass (SCL) estimates are:

	Average Excess Return	Beta
A	5.18	−0.47
B	4.19	0.59
C	2.75	0.42
D	6.15	1.38
E	8.05	0.90
F	9.90	1.78
G	11.32	0.66
H	13.11	1.91
I	22.83	2.08
M	8.12	

The second-pass regression yields:

Regression Statistics	
Multiple R	0.7074
R-square	0.5004
Adjusted R-square	0.4291
Standard error	4.6234
Observations	9

	Coefficients	Standard Error	t Statistic for β=0	t Statistic for β=8.12
Intercept	3.92	2.54	1.54	
Slope	5.21	1.97	2.65	−1.48

6. As we saw in the chapter, the intercept is too high (3.92% per year instead of 0) and the slope is too flat (5.21% instead of a predicted value equal to the sample-average risk premium: $r_M - r_f = 8.12\%$). The intercept is not significantly greater than zero (the t-statistic is less than 2) and the slope is not significantly different from its theoretical value (the t-statistic for this hypothesis is -1.48). This lack of statistical significance is probably due to the small size of the sample.

7. Arranging the securities in three portfolios based on betas from the SCL estimates, the first pass input data are:

Year	ABC	DEG	FHI
1	15.05	25.86	56.69
2	−16.76	−29.74	−50.85
3	19.67	−5.68	8.98
4	−15.83	−2.58	35.41
5	47.18	37.70	−3.25
6	−2.26	53.86	75.44
7	−18.67	15.32	12.50
8	−6.35	36.33	32.12
9	7.85	14.08	50.42
10	21.41	12.66	52.14
11	−2.53	−50.71	−66.12
12	−0.30	−4.99	−20.10
Average	4.04	8.51	15.28
Std. Dev.	19.30	29.47	43.96

The first-pass (SCL) estimates are:

	ABC	DEG	FHI
R-square	0.04	0.48	0.82
Observations	12	12	12
Alpha	2.58	0.54	−0.34
Beta	0.18	0.98	1.92
t-Alpha	0.42	0.08	−0.06
t-Beta	0.62	3.02	6.83

Grouping into portfolios has improved the SCL estimates as is evident from the higher R-square for Portfolio DEG and Portfolio FHI. This means that the beta (slope) is measured with greater precision, reducing the error-in-measurement problem at the expense of leaving fewer observations for the second pass.

The inputs for the second pass regression are:

	Average Excess Return	Beta
ABC	4.04	0.18
DEH	8.51	0.98
FGI	15.28	1.92
M	8.12	

The second-pass estimates are:

Regression Statistics	
Multiple R	0.9975
R-square	0.9949
Adjusted R-square	0.9899
Standard error	0.5693
Observations	3

	Coefficients	Standard Error	t Statistic for $\beta = 0$	t Statistic for $\beta = 8.12$
Intercept	2.62	0.58	4.55	
Slope	6.47	0.46	14.03	−3.58

Despite the decrease in the intercept and the increase in slope, the intercept is now significantly positive, and the slope is significantly less than the hypothesized value by more than three times the standard error.

8. Roll's critique suggests that the problem begins with the market index, which is not the theoretical portfolio against which the second pass regression should hold. Remember that Roll suggests the true market portfolio contains every asset available to investors, including real estate, commodities, artifacts, and collectible items such as Hollywood memorabilia, which this index obviously does not have. Hence, even if the relationship is valid with respect to the true (unknown) index, we may not find it. As a result, the second pass relationship may be meaningless.

9.

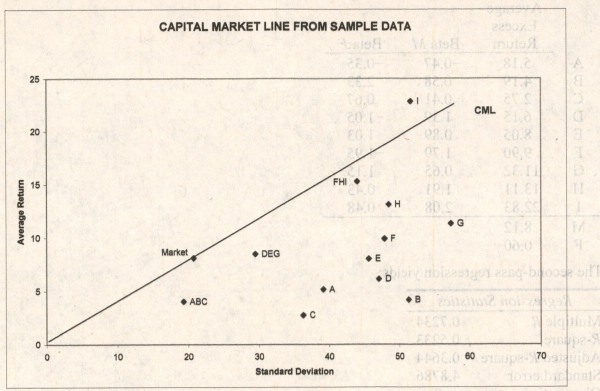

CAPITAL MARKET LINE FROM SAMPLE DATA

Except for Stock I, which realized an extremely positive surprise, the CML shows that the index dominates all other securities, and the three portfolios dominate all individual stocks. The power of diversification is evident despite the very small sample size.

10. The first-pass (SCL) regression results are summarized below:

	A	B	C	D	E	F	G	H	I
R-square	0.07	0.36	0.11	0.44	0.24	0.84	0.12	0.68	0.71
Observations	12	12	12	12	12	12	12	12	12
Intercept	9.19	−1.89	−1.00	−4.48	0.17	−3.47	5.32	−2.64	5.66
Beta M	−0.47	0.58	0.41	1.39	0.89	1.79	0.65	1.91	2.08
Beta F	−0.35	2.33	0.67	−1.05	1.03	−1.95	1.15	0.43	0.48
t-intercept	0.71	−0.13	−0.08	−0.37	0.01	−0.52	0.29	−0.28	0.59
t-Beta M	−0.77	0.87	0.75	2.46	1.40	5.80	0.75	4.35	4.65
t-Beta F	−0.34	2.06	0.71	−1.08	0.94	−3.69	0.77	0.57	0.63

11. The hypotheses for the second-pass regression for the two-factor SML are:
   • The intercept is zero.
   • The market-index slope coefficient equals the market-index average return.
   • The factor slope coefficient equals the average return on the factor.
   (Note that the first two hypotheses are the same as those for the single factor model.)

12.   The inputs for the second pass regression are:

	Average Excess Return	Beta M	Beta F
A	5.18	−0.47	−0.35
B	4.19	0.58	2.33
C	2.75	0.41	0.67
D	6.15	1.39	−1.05
E	8.05	0.89	1.03
F	9.90	1.79	−1.95
G	11.32	0.65	1.15
H	13.11	1.91	0.43
I	22.83	2.08	0.48
M	8.12		
F	0.60		

The second-pass regression yields:

Regression Statistics	
Multiple R	0.7234
R-square	0.5233
Adjusted R-square	0.3644
Standard error	4.8786
Observations	9

	Coefficients	Standard Error	t Statistic for $\beta = 0$	t Statistic for $\beta = 8.12$	t Statistic for $\beta = 0.6$
Intercept	3.35	2.88	1.16		
Beta M	5.53	2.16	2.56	−1.20	
Beta F	0.80	1.42	0.56		0.14

These results are slightly better than those for the single factor test; that is, the intercept is smaller and the slope of M is slightly greater. We cannot expect a great improvement since the factor we added does not appear to carry a large risk premium (average excess return is less than 1%), and its effect on mean returns is therefore small. The data do not reject the second factor because the slope is close to the average excess return and the difference is less than one standard error. However, with this sample size, the power of this test is extremely low.

13. When we use the actual factor, we implicitly assume that investors can perfectly replicate it, that is, they can invest in a portfolio that is perfectly correlated with the factor. When this is not possible, one cannot expect the CAPM equation (the second pass regression) to hold. Investors can use a replicating portfolio (a proxy for the factor) that maximizes the correlation with the factor. The CAPM equation is then expected to hold with respect to the proxy portfolio.

Using the bordered covariance matrix of the nine stocks and the Excel Solver, we produce a proxy portfolio for factor F, denoted PF. To preserve the scale, we include constraints that require the nine weights to be in the range of $[-1,1]$ and that the mean equals the factor mean of 0.60%. The resultant weights for the proxy and period returns are:

Proxy Portfolio for Factor F (PF)

	Weights on Universe Stocks	Year	PF Holding Period Returns
A	−0.14	1	−33.51
B	1.00	2	62.78
C	0.95	3	9.87
D	−0.35	4	−153.56
E	0.16	5	200.76
F	−1.00	6	−36.62
G	0.13	7	−74.34
H	0.19	8	−10.84
I	0.06	9	28.11
		10	59.51
		11	−59.15
		12	14.22
		Average	0.60

This proxy (PF) has an R-square with the actual factor of 0.80.

We next perform the first pass regressions for the two factor model using PF instead of P:

	A	B	C	D	E	F	G	H	I
R-square	0.08	0.55	0.20	0.43	0.33	0.88	0.16	0.71	0.72
Observations	12	12	12	12	12	12	12	12	12
Intercept	9.28	−2.53	−1.35	−4.45	−0.23	−3.20	4.99	−2.92	5.54
Beta M	−0.50	0.80	0.49	1.32	1.00	1.64	0.76	1.97	2.12
Beta PF	−0.06	0.42	0.16	−0.13	0.21	−0.29	0.21	0.11	0.08
t-intercept	0.72	−0.21	−0.12	−0.36	−0.02	−0.55	0.27	−0.33	0.58
t-Beta M	−0.83	1.43	0.94	2.29	1.66	6.00	0.90	4.67	4.77
t-Beta PF	−0.44	3.16	1.25	−0.97	1.47	−4.52	1.03	1.13	0.78

Note that the betas of the nine stocks on M and the proxy (PF) are different from those in the first pass when we use the actual proxy.

The first-pass regression for the two-factor model with the proxy yields:

	Average Excess Return	Beta M	Beta PF
A	5.18	−0.50	−0.06
B	4.19	0.80	0.42
C	2.75	0.49	0.16
D	6.15	1.32	−0.13
E	8.05	1.00	0.21
F	9.90	1.64	−0.29
G	11.32	0.76	0.21
H	13.11	1.97	0.11
I	22.83	2.12	0.08
M	8.12		
PF	0.6		

The second-pass regression yields:

Regression Statistics	
Multiple R	0.71
R-square	0.51
Adjusted R-square	0.35
Standard error	4.95
Observations	9

	Coefficients	Standard Error	t Statistic for $\beta = 0$	t Statistic for $\beta = 8.12$	t Statistic for $\beta = 0.6$
Intercept	3.50	2.99	1.17		
Beta M	5.39	2.18	2.48	−1.25	
Beta PF	0.26	8.36	0.03		−0.04

We can see that the results are similar to, but slightly inferior to, those with the actual factor, since the intercept is larger and the slope coefficient smaller. Note also that we use here an in-sample test rather than tests with future returns, which is more forgiving than an out-of-sample test.

14. We assume that the value of your labor is incorporated in the calculation of the rate of return for your business. It would likely make sense to commission a valuation of your business at least once each year. The resultant sequence of figures for percentage change in the value of the business (including net cash withdrawals from the business in the calculations) will allow you to derive a reasonable estimate of the correlation between the rate of return for your business and returns for other assets. You would then search for industries having the lowest correlations with your portfolio and identify exchange traded funds (ETFs) for these industries. Your asset allocation would then comprise your business, a market portfolio ETF, and the low-correlation (hedge) industry ETFs. Assess the standard deviation of such a portfolio with reasonable proportions of the portfolio invested in the market and in the hedge industries. Now determine where you want to be on the resultant CAL. If you wish to hold a less risky overall portfolio and to mix it with the risk-free asset, reduce the portfolio weights for the market and for the hedge industries in an efficient way.

CFA PROBLEMS

1. (i)   Betas are estimated with respect to market indexes that are proxies for the true market portfolio, which is inherently unobservable.

    (ii) Empirical tests of the CAPM show that average returns are not related to beta in the manner predicted by the theory. The empirical SML is flatter than the theoretical one.

    (iii) Multi-factor models of security returns show that beta, which is a one-dimensional measure of risk, may not capture the true risk of the stock of portfolio.

2. a.   The basic procedure in portfolio evaluation is to compare the returns on a managed portfolio to the return expected on an unmanaged portfolio having the same risk, using the SML. That is, expected return is calculated from:

    $$E(r_P) = r_f + \beta_P [E(r_M) - r_f]$$

    where r_f is the risk-free rate, $E(r_M)$ is the expected return for the *unmanaged* portfolio (or the market portfolio), and β_P is the beta coefficient (or systematic risk) of the managed portfolio. The performance benchmark then is the unmanaged portfolio. The typical proxy for this unmanaged portfolio is an aggregate stock market index such as the S&P 500.

    b.   The benchmark error might occur when the unmanaged portfolio used in the evaluation process is not optimized. That is, market indices, such as the S&P 500, chosen as benchmarks are not on the manager's *ex ante* mean/variance efficient frontier.

    c.   Your graph should show an efficient frontier obtained from actual returns, and a different one that represents (unobserved) ex-ante expectations. The CML and SML generated from actual returns do not conform to the CAPM predictions, while the hypothesized lines do conform to the CAPM.

    d.   The answer to this question depends on one's prior beliefs. Given a consistent track record, an agnostic observer might conclude that the data support the claim of superiority. Other observers might start with a strong prior that, since so many managers are attempting to beat a passive portfolio, a small number are bound to produce seemingly convincing track records.

    e.   The question is really whether the CAPM is at all testable. The problem is that even a slight inefficiency in the benchmark portfolio may completely invalidate any test of the expected return-beta relationship. It appears from Roll's argument that the best guide to the question of the validity of the CAPM is the difficulty of beating a passive strategy.

3.   The effect of an incorrectly specified market proxy is that the beta of Black's portfolio is likely to be underestimated (i.e., too low) relative to the beta calculated based on the true market portfolio. This is because the Dow Jones Industrial Average (DJIA) and other market proxies are likely to have less diversification and therefore a higher variance of returns than the true market portfolio as specified by the capital asset pricing model. Consequently, beta computed using an overstated variance will be underestimated. This result is clear from the following formula:

$$\beta_{Portfolio} = \frac{Cov(r_{Portfolio}, r_{Market\ Proxy})}{\sigma^2_{Market\ Proxy}}$$

An incorrectly specified market proxy is likely to produce a slope for the security market line (i.e., the market risk premium) that is underestimated relative to the true market portfolio. This results from the fact that the true market portfolio is likely to be more efficient (plotting on a higher return point for the same risk) than the DJIA and similarly misspecified market proxies. Consequently, the proxy-based SML would offer less expected return per unit of risk.

CHAPTER 14: BOND PRICES AND YIELDS

PROBLEM SETS

1.   a.   *Catastrophe bond*—A bond that allows the issuer to transfer "catastrophe risk" from the firm to the capital markets. Investors in these bonds receive a compensation for taking on the risk in the form of higher coupon rates. In the event of a catastrophe, the bondholders will receive only part or perhaps none of the principal payment due to them at maturity. *Disaster* can be defined by total insured losses or by criteria such as wind speed in a hurricane or Richter level in an earthquake.

        b.   *Eurobond*—A bond that is denominated in one currency, usually that of the issuer, but sold in other national markets.

        c.   *Zero-coupon bond*—A bond that makes no coupon payments. Investors receive par value at the maturity date but receive no interest payments until then. These bonds are issued at prices below par value, and the investor's return comes from the difference between issue price and the payment of par value at maturity (capital gain).

        d.   *Samurai bond*—Yen-dominated bonds sold in Japan by non-Japanese issuers.

        e.   *Junk bond*—A bond with a low credit rating due to its high default risk; also known as high-yield bonds.

        f.   *Convertible bond*—A bond that gives the bondholders an option to exchange the bond for a specified number of shares of common stock of the firm.

        g.   *Serial bonds*—Bonds issued with staggered maturity dates. As bonds mature sequentially, the principal repayment burden for the firm is spread over time.

        h.   *Equipment obligation bond*—A collateralized bond for which the collateral is equipment owned by the firm. If the firm defaults on the bond, the bondholders would receive the equipment.

        i.   *Original issue discount bond*—A bond issued at a discount to the face value.

        j.   *Indexed bond*— A bond that makes payments that are tied to a general price index or the price of a particular commodity.

        k.   *Callable bond*—A bond that gives the issuer the option to repurchase the bond at a specified call price before the maturity date.

        l.   *Puttable bond*—A bond that gives the bondholder the option to sell back the bond at a specified put price before the maturity date.

2.   The bond callable at 105 should sell at a lower price because the call provision is more valuable to the firm. Therefore, its yield to maturity should be higher.

3.   Zero coupon bonds provide no coupons to be reinvested. Therefore, the investor's proceeds from the bond are independent of the rate at which coupons could be reinvested (if they were paid). There is no reinvestment rate uncertainty with zeros.

4.   A bond's coupon interest payments and principal repayment are not affected by changes in market rates. Consequently, if market rates increase, bond investors in the secondary markets are not willing to pay as much for a claim on a given bond's fixed interest and principal payments as they would if market rates were lower. This relationship is apparent from the inverse relationship between interest rates and present value. An increase in the discount rate (i.e., the market rate) decreases the present value of the future cash flows).

5.   Annual coupon rate: 4.80% → $48 Coupon payments
      Current yield:
      $$\left(\frac{\$48}{\$970}\right) = 4.95\%$$

6.   a.   Effective annual rate for 3-month T-bill:
            $$\left(\frac{100,000}{97,645}\right)^{4} -1 = 1.02412^{4} -1 = 0.100 = 10.0\%$$

      b.   Effective annual interest rate for coupon bond paying 5% semiannually:
            $$(1.05.^{2} - 1) = 0.1025 \text{ or } 10.25\%$$
            Therefore the coupon bond has the higher effective annual interest rate.

7.   The effective annual yield on the semiannual coupon bonds is 8.16%. If the annual coupon bonds are to sell at par they must offer the same yield, which requires an annual coupon rate of 8.16%.

8.   The bond price will be lower. As time passes, the bond price, which is now above par value, will approach par.

9.   *Yield to maturity:* Using a financial calculator, enter the following:

$n = 3$; PV = –953.10; FV = 1000; PMT = 80; COMP i

This results in: YTM = 9.88%

Realized compound yield: First, find the future value (FV) of reinvested coupons and principal:

FV = ($80 * 1.10 *1.12) + ($80 * 1.12) + $1,080 = $1,268.16

Then find the rate ($y_{realized}$) that makes the FV of the purchase price equal to $1,268.16:

$953.10 \times (1 + y_{realized})^3 = \$1,268.16 \Rightarrow y_{realized} = 9.99\%$ or approximately 10%

Using a financial calculator, enter the following: N = 3; PV = –953.10; FV = 1,268.16; PMT = 0; COMP I. Answer is 9.99%.

10.

a.

	Zero coupon	8% coupon	10% coupon
Current prices	$463.19	$1,000.00	$1,134.20
b. Price 1 year from now	$500.25	$1,000.00	$1,124.94
Price increase	$ 37.06	$ 0.00	– $ 9.26
Coupon income	$ 0.00	$ 80.00	$ 100.00
Pretax income	$ 37.06	$ 80.00	$ 90.74
Pretax rate of return	8.00%	8.00%	8.00%
Taxes*	$ 11.12	$ 24.00	$ 28.15
After-tax income	$ 25.94	$ 56.00	$ 62.59
After-tax rate of return	5.60%	5.60%	5.52%
c. Price 1 year from now	$543.93	$1,065.15	$1,195.46
Price increase	$ 80.74	$ 65.15	$ 61.26
Coupon income	$ 0.00	$ 80.00	$ 100.00
Pretax income	$ 80.74	$ 145.15	$ 161.26
Pretax rate of return	17.43%	14.52%	14.22%
Taxes†	$ 19.86	$ 37.03	$ 42.25
After-tax income	$ 60.88	$ 108.12	$ 119.01
After-tax rate of return	13.14%	10.81%	10.49%

* In computing taxes, we assume that the 10% coupon bond was issued at par and that the decrease in price when the bond is sold at year-end is treated as a capital loss and therefore is not treated as an offset to ordinary income.

† In computing taxes for the zero coupon bond, $37.06 is taxed as ordinary income (see part b); the remainder of the price increase is taxed as a capital gain.

11. a. On a financial calculator, enter the following:
$n = 40$; $FV = 1000$; $PV = -950$; $PMT = 40$

You will find that the yield to maturity on a semiannual basis is 4.26%. This implies a bond equivalent yield to maturity equal to: $4.26\% * 2 = 8.52\%$
Effective annual yield to maturity = $(1.0426)^2 - 1 = 0.0870 = 8.70\%$

   b. Since the bond is selling at par, the yield to maturity on a semiannual basis is the same as the semiannual coupon rate, i.e., 4%. The bond equivalent yield to maturity is 8%.

Effective annual yield to maturity = $(1.04)^2 - 1 = 0.0816 = 8.16\%$

   c. Keeping other inputs unchanged but setting $PV = -1050$, we find a bond equivalent yield to maturity of 7.52%, or 3.76% on a semiannual basis.

Effective annual yield to maturity = $(1.0376)^2 - 1 = 0.0766 = 7.66\%$

12. Since the bond payments are now made annually instead of semiannually, the bond equivalent yield to maturity is the same as the effective annual yield to maturity.
[On a financial calculator, $n = 20$; $FV = 1000$; $PV = -price$; $PMT = 80$]
The resulting yields for the three bonds are:

Bond Price	Bond Equivalent Yield = Effective Annual Yield
$950	8.53%
1,000	8.00
1,050	7.51

The yields computed in this case are lower than the yields calculated with semiannual payments. All else equal, bonds with annual payments are less attractive to investors because more time elapses before payments are received. If the bond price is the same with annual payments, then the bond's yield to maturity is lower.

13.

Price	Maturity (years)	Bond Equivalent YTM
$400.00	20.00	4.688%
500.00	20.00	3.526
500.00	10.00	7.177
385.54	10.00	10.000
463.19	10.00	8.000
400.00	11.91	8.000

14.   a.   The bond pays $50 every 6 months. The current price is:

[$50 × Annuity factor (4%, 6)] + [$1,000 × PV factor (4%, 6)] = $1,052.42

Alternatively, PMT = $50; FV = $1,000; I = 4; N = 6. Solve for PV = $1,052.42.

If the market interest rate remains 4% per half year, price six months from now is:

[$50 × Annuity factor (4%, 5)] + [$1,000 × PV factor (4%, 5)] = $1,044.52

Alternatively, PMT = $50; FV = $1,000; I = 4; N = 5. Solve for PV = $1,044.52.

   b. $\text{Rate of return} = \dfrac{\$50 + (\$1,044.52 - \$1,052.42)}{\$1,052.42} = \dfrac{\$50 - \$7.90}{\$1,052.42} = 4.0\%$

15. The *reported* bond price is: $1,001.250

However, 15 days have passed since the last semiannual coupon was paid, so:

Accrued interest = $35 * (15/182) = $2.885

The invoice price is the reported price plus accrued interest: $1,004.14

16. If the yield to maturity is greater than the current yield, then the bond offers the prospect of price appreciation as it approaches its maturity date. Therefore, the bond must be selling below par value.

17. The coupon rate is less than 9%. If coupon divided by price equals 9%, and price is less than par, then price divided by par is less than 9%.

18.

Time	Inflation in Year Just Ended	Par Value	Coupon Payment	Principal Repayment
0		$1,000.00		
1	2%	1,020.00	$40.80	$ 0.00
2	3%	$1,050.60	$42.02	$ 0.00
3	1%	$1,061.11	$42.44	$1,061.11

The *nominal* rate of return and *real* rate of return on the bond in each year are computed as follows:

$$\text{Nominal rate of return} = \frac{\text{interest} + \text{price appreciation}}{\text{initial price}}$$

$$\text{Real rate of return} = \frac{1 + \text{nominal return}}{1 + \text{inflation}} - 1$$

	Second Year	Third Year
Nominal return	$\dfrac{\$42.02 + \$30.60}{\$1,020} = 0.071196$	$\dfrac{\$42.44 + \$10.51}{\$1,050.60} = 0.050400$
Real return	$\dfrac{1.071196}{1.03} - 1 = 0.040 = 4.0\%$	$\dfrac{1.050400}{1.01} - 1 = 0.040 = 4.0\%$

The real rate of return in each year is precisely the 4% real yield on the bond.

19. The price schedule is as follows:

Year	Remaining Maturity (T).	Constant Yield Value $\$1,000/(1.08)^T$	Imputed Interest (increase in constant yield value)
0 (now)	20 years	$214.55	
1	19	231.71	$17.16
2	18	250.25	18.54
19	1	925.93	
20	0	1,000.00	74.07

20. The bond is issued at a price of $800. Therefore, its yield to maturity is: 6.8245% Therefore, using the constant yield method, we find that the price in one year (when maturity falls to 9 years) will be (at an unchanged yield) $814.60, representing an increase of $14.60. Total taxable income is: $40.00 + $14.60 = $54.60

21. a. The bond sells for $1,124.72 based on the 3.5% yield to *maturity*.
    [$n = 60$; $i = 3.5$; FV = 1000; PMT = 40]

    Therefore, yield to *call* is 3.368% semiannually, 6.736% annually.
    [$n = 10$ semiannual periods; PV = –1124.72; FV = 1100; PMT = 40]

    b. If the call price were $1,050, we would set FV = 1,050 and redo part (a) to find that yield to call is 2.976% semiannually, 5.952% annually. With a lower call price, the yield to call is lower.

    c. Yield to call is 3.031% semiannually, 6.062% annually.
    [$n = 4$; PV = –1124.72; FV = 1100; PMT = 40]

22. The stated yield to maturity, based on promised payments, equals 16.075%.
    [$n = 10$; PV = –900; FV = 1000; PMT = 140]

    Based on *expected* reduced coupon payments of $70 annually, the expected yield to maturity is 8.526%.

23.   The bond is selling at par value. Its yield to maturity equals the coupon rate, 10%. If the first-year coupon is reinvested at an interest rate of *r* percent, then total proceeds at the end of the second year will be: $[\$100 * (1 + r)] + \$1,100$

Therefore, realized compound yield to maturity is a function of *r*, as shown in the following table:

r	Total proceeds	Realized YTM = $\sqrt{\text{Proceeds}/1000}$ -1
8%	$1,208	$\sqrt{1208/1000}$ $-1 = 0.0991 = 9.91\%$
10%	$1,210	$\sqrt{1210/1000}$ $-1 = 0.1000 = 10.00\%$
12%	$1,212	$\sqrt{1212/1000}$ $-1 = 0.1009 = 10.09\%$

24.   April 15 is midway through the semiannual coupon period. Therefore, the invoice price will be higher than the stated ask price by an amount equal to one-half of the semiannual coupon. The ask price is 101.25 percent of par, so the invoice price is:

$$\$1,012.50 + (\tfrac{1}{2} *\$50) = \$1,037.50$$

25.   Factors that might make the ABC debt more attractive to investors, therefore justifying a lower coupon rate and yield to maturity, are:

   i.   The ABC debt is a larger issue and therefore may sell with greater liquidity.
   ii. An option to extend the term from 10 years to 20 years is favorable if interest rates 10 years from now are lower than today's interest rates. In contrast, if interest rates increase, the investor can present the bond for payment and reinvest the money for a higher return.
   iii. In the event of trouble, the ABC debt is a more senior claim. It has more underlying security in the form of a first claim against real property.
   iv. The call feature on the XYZ bonds makes the ABC bonds relatively more attractive since ABC bonds cannot be called from the investor.
   v.   The XYZ bond has a sinking fund requiring XYZ to retire part of the issue each year. Since most sinking funds give the firm the option to retire this amount at the lower of par or market value, the sinking fund can be detrimental for bondholders.

26.   A. If an investor believes the firm's credit prospects are poor in the near term and wishes to capitalize on this, the investor should buy a credit default swap. Although a short sale of a bond could accomplish the same objective, liquidity is often greater in the swap market than it is in the underlying cash market. The investor could pick a swap with a maturity similar to the expected time horizon of the credit risk. By buying the swap, the investor would receive compensation if the bond experiences an increase in credit risk.

27. a. When credit risk increases, credit default swaps increase in value because the protection they provide is more valuable. Credit default swaps do not provide protection against interest rate risk however.

28. a. An increase in the firm's times interest-earned ratio decreases the default risk of the firm→increases the bond's price → decreases the YTM.

   b. An increase in the issuing firm's debt-equity ratio increases the default risk of the firm → decreases the bond's price → increases YTM.

   c. An increase in the issuing firm's quick ratio increases short-run liquidity, → implying a decrease in default risk of the firm → increases the bond's price → decreases YTM.

29. a. The floating rate note pays a coupon that adjusts to market levels. Therefore, it will not experience dramatic price changes as market yields fluctuate. The fixed rate note will therefore have a greater price range.

   b. Floating rate notes may not sell at par for any of several reasons:
       (i)   The yield spread between one-year Treasury bills and other money market instruments of comparable maturity could be wider (or narrower) than when the bond was issued.
       (ii) The credit standing of the firm may have eroded (or improved) relative to Treasury securities, which have no credit risk. Therefore, the 2% premium would become insufficient to sustain the issue at par.
       (iii) The coupon increases are implemented with a lag, i.e., once every year. During a period of changing interest rates, even this brief lag will be reflected in the price of the security.

   c. The risk of call is low. Because the bond will almost surely not sell for much above par value (given its adjustable coupon rate), it is unlikely that the bond will ever be called.

   d. The fixed-rate note currently sells at only 88% of the call price, so that yield to maturity is greater than the coupon rate. Call risk is currently low, since yields would need to fall substantially for the firm to use its option to call the bond.

   e. The 9% coupon notes currently have a remaining maturity of 15 years and sell at a yield to maturity of 9.9%. This is the coupon rate that would be needed for a newly issued 15-year maturity bond to sell at par.

   f. Because the floating rate note pays a variable stream of interest payments to maturity, the effective maturity for comparative purposes with other debt securities is closer to the next coupon reset date than the final maturity date. Therefore, yield-to-maturity is an indeterminable calculation for a floating rate note, with "yield-to-recoupon date" a more meaningful measure of return.

30. a. The yield to maturity on the par bond equals its coupon rate, 8.75%. All else equal, the 4% coupon bond would be more attractive because its coupon rate is far below current market yields, and its price is far below the call price. Therefore, if yields fall, capital gains on the bond will not be limited by the call price. In contrast, the 8¾% coupon bond can increase in value to at most $1,050, offering a maximum possible gain of only 0.5%. The disadvantage of the 8¾% coupon bond, in terms of vulnerability to being called, shows up in its higher *promised* yield to maturity.

   b. If an investor expects yields to fall substantially, the 4% bond offers a greater expected return.

   c. Implicit call protection is offered in the sense that any likely fall in yields would not be nearly enough to make the firm consider calling the bond. In this sense, the call feature is almost irrelevant.

31. a. Initial price $P_0 = \$705.46$ [$n = 20$; PMT = 50; FV = 1000; $i = 8$]
       Next year's price $P_1 = \$793.29$ [$n = 19$; PMT = 50; FV = 1000; $i = 7$]

$$HPR = \frac{\$50 + (\$793.29 - \$705.46)}{\$705.46} = 0.1954 = 19.54\%$$

   b. Using OID tax rules, the cost basis and imputed interest under the constant yield method are obtained by discounting bond payments at the *original* 8% yield and simply reducing maturity by one year at a time:

Constant yield prices (compare these to actual prices to compute capital gains):
   $P_0 = \$705.46$
   $P_1 = \$711.89 \Rightarrow$ implicit interest over first year = $6.43
   $P_2 = \$718.84 \Rightarrow$ implicit interest over second year = $6.95

Tax on explicit interest plus implicit interest in first year =

$$0.40*(\$50 + \$6.43) = \$22.57$$

Capital gain in first year = Actual price at 7% YTM—constant yield price =

$$\$793.29 - \$711.89 = \$81.40$$

Tax on capital gain = 0.30*$81.40 = $24.42

Total taxes = $22.57 + $24.42 = $46.99

   c. After tax HPR = $\dfrac{\$50 + (\$793.29 - \$705.46) - \$46.99}{\$705.46} = 0.1288 = 12.88\%$

d. Value of bond after two years = $798.82 [using $n = 18$; $i = 7\%$; PMT = $50; FV = $1,000]

Reinvested income from the coupon interest payments = $50*1.03 + $50 = $101.50

Total funds after two years = $798.82 + $101.50 = $900.32

Therefore, the investment of $705.46 grows to $900.32 in two years:

$705.46 $(1 + r)^2$ = $900.32 $\Rightarrow r = 0.1297 = 12.97\%$

e. Coupon interest received in first year: $50.00
Less: tax on coupon interest @ 40%: – 20.00
Less: tax on imputed interest (0.40*$6.43): – 2.57
Net cash flow in first year: $27.43

The year-1 cash flow can be invested at an after-tax rate of:

$3\% \times (1 - 0.40) = 1.8\%$

By year 2, this investment will grow to: $27.43 × 1.018 = $27.92

In two years, sell the bond for: $798.82 [$n = 18$; $i = 7\%\%$; PMT = $50; FV = $1,000]

Less: tax on *imputed* interest in second year: – 2.78 [0.40 × $6.95]
Add: after-tax coupon interest received
in second year: + 30.00 [$50 × (1 – 0.40)]
Less: Capital gains tax on
(sales price – constant yield value): – 23.99 [0.30 × (798.82 – 718.84)]
Add: CF from first year's coupon (reinvested): + 27.92 [from above]
Total $829.97

$705.46 $(1 + r)^2$ = $829.97 $\Rightarrow r = 0.0847 = 8.47\%$

CFA PROBLEMS

1. a. A sinking fund provision requires the early redemption of a bond issue. The provision may be for a specific number of bonds or a percentage of the bond issue over a specified time period. The sinking fund can retire all or a portion of an issue over the life of the issue.

b. (i) Compared to a bond without a sinking fund, the sinking fund reduces the average life of the overall issue because some of the bonds are retired prior to the stated maturity.

(ii) The company will make the same total principal payments over the life of the issue, although the timing of these payments will be affected. The total interest payments associated with the issue will be reduced given the early redemption of principal.

c. From the investor's point of view, the key reason for demanding a sinking fund is to reduce credit risk. Default risk is reduced by the orderly retirement of the issue.

2.   a.   (i)   Current yield = Coupon/Price = $70/$960 = 0.0729 = 7.29%

       (ii)   YTM = 3.993% semiannually, or 7.986% annual bond equivalent yield.
On a financial calculator, enter: $n = 10$; PV = -960; FV = 1000; PMT = 35
Compute the interest rate.

     (iii)   Realized compound yield is 4.166% (semiannually), or 8.332% annual bond
equivalent yield. To obtain this value, first find the future value (FV) of
reinvested coupons and principal. There will be six payments of $35 each,
reinvested semiannually at 3% per period. On a financial calculator, enter:
PV = 0; PMT = 35; $n = 6$; $i = 3\%$. Compute: FV = 226.39

Three years from now, the bond will be selling at the par value of $1,000
because the yield to maturity is forecast to equal the coupon rate. Therefore, total
proceeds in three years will be: $226.39 + $1,000 = $1,226.39

Then find the rate ($y_{realized}$) that makes the FV of the purchase price equal
to $1,226.39:

$$\$960 \times (1 + y_{realized})^6 = \$1,226.39 \Rightarrow y_{realized} = 4.166\% \text{ (semiannual)}$$

Alternatively, PV = $-\$960$; FV = $\$1,226.39$; N = 6; PMT = $0. Solve for I = 4.16%.

   b.   Shortcomings of each measure:

      (i)   Current yield does not account for capital gains or losses on bonds bought at
prices other than par value. It also does not account for reinvestment income on
coupon payments.

     (ii)   Yield to maturity assumes the bond is held until maturity and that all coupon
income can be reinvested at a rate equal to the yield to maturity.

    (iii)   Realized compound yield is affected by the forecast of reinvestment rates,
holding period, and yield of the bond at the end of the investor's holding period.

3.   a.   The maturity of each bond is 10 years, and we assume that coupons are paid
semiannually. Since both bonds are selling at par value, the current yield for each
bond is equal to its coupon rate.

If the yield declines by 1% to 5% (2.5% semiannual yield), the Sentinal bond will
increase in value to $107.79 [$n=20$; $i = 2.5\%$; FV = 100; PMT = 3].

The price of the Colina bond will increase, but only to the call price of 102. The
present value of *scheduled* payments is greater than 102, but the call price puts a
ceiling on the actual bond price.

b. If rates are expected to fall, the Sentinal bond is more attractive: since it is not subject to call, its potential capital gains are greater.

If rates are expected to rise, Colina is a relatively better investment. Its higher coupon (which presumably is compensation to investors for the call feature of the bond) will provide a higher rate of return than the Sentinal bond.

c. An increase in the volatility of rates will increase the value of the firm's option to call back the Colina bond. If rates go down, the firm can call the bond, which puts a cap on possible capital gains. So, greater volatility makes the option to call back the bond more valuable to the issuer. This makes the bond less attractive to the investor.

4.   Market conversion value = Value if converted into stock = 20.83 × $28 = $583.24

Conversion premium = Bond price – Market conversion value

= $775.00 – $583.24 = $191.76

5. a. The call feature requires the firm to offer a higher coupon (or higher promised yield to maturity) on the bond in order to compensate the investor for the firm's option to call back the bond at a specified price if interest rate falls sufficiently. Investors are willing to grant this valuable option to the issuer, but only for a price that reflects the possibility that the bond will be called. That price is the higher promised yield at which they are willing to buy the bond.

b. The call feature reduces the expected life of the bond. If interest rates fall substantially so that the likelihood of a call increases, investors will treat the bond as if it will "mature" and be paid off at the call date, not at the stated maturity date. On the other hand, if rates rise, the bond must be paid off at the maturity date, not later. This asymmetry means that the expected life of the bond is less than the stated maturity.

c. The advantage of a callable bond is the higher coupon (and higher promised yield to maturity) when the bond is issued. If the bond is never called, then an investor earns a higher realized compound yield on a callable bond issued at par than a noncallable bond issued at par on the same date. The disadvantage of the callable bond is the risk of call. If rates fall and the bond is called, then the investor receives the call price and then has to reinvest the proceeds at interest rates that are lower than the yield to maturity at which the bond originally was issued. In this event, the firm's savings in interest payments is the investor's loss.

6.   a. (iii)

b. (iii) The yield to maturity on the callable bond must compensate the investor for the risk of call.

Choice (i) is wrong because, although the owner of a callable bond receives a premium plus the principal in the event of a call, the interest rate at which he can reinvest will be low. The low interest rate that makes it profitable for the issuer to call the bond also makes it a bad deal for the bond's holder.

Choice (ii) is wrong because a bond is more apt to be called when interest rates are low. Only if rates are low will there be an interest saving for the issuer.

c. (iii)

d. (ii)

CHAPTER 15: THE TERM STRUCTURE OF INTEREST RATES

PROBLEM SETS

1. In general, the forward rate can be viewed as the sum of the market's expectation of the future short rate plus a potential risk (or liquidity) premium. According to the expectations theory of the term structure of interest rates, the liquidity premium is zero so that the forward rate is equal to the market's expectation of the future short rate. Therefore, the market's expectation of future short rates (i.e., forward rates) can be derived from the yield curve, and there is no risk premium for longer maturities.

   The liquidity preference theory, on the other hand, specifies that the liquidity premium is positive so that the forward rate is greater than the market's expectation of the future short rate. This could result in an upward sloping term structure even if the market does not anticipate an increase in interest rates. The liquidity preference theory is based on the assumption that the financial markets are dominated by short-term investors who demand a premium in order to be induced to invest in long maturity securities.

2. True. Under the expectations hypothesis, there are no risk premia built into bond prices. The only reason for long-term yields to exceed short-term yields is an expectation of higher short-term rates in the future.

3. Uncertain. Expectations of lower inflation will usually lead to lower nominal interest rates. Nevertheless, if the liquidity premium is sufficiently great, long-term yields may exceed short-term yields *despite* expectations of falling short rates.

4. The liquidity theory holds that investors demand a premium to compensate them for interest rate exposure and the premium increases with maturity. Add this premium to a flat curve and the result is an upward sloping yield curve.

5. The pure expectations theory, also referred to as the *unbiased* expectations theory, purports that forward rates are solely a function of expected future spot rates. Under the pure expectations theory, a yield curve that is upward (downward) sloping, means that short-term rates are expected to rise (fall). A flat yield curve implies that the market expects short-term rates to remain constant.

6. The yield curve slopes upward because short-term rates are lower than long-term rates. Since market rates are determined by supply and demand, it follows that investors (demand side) expect rates to be higher in the future than in the near-term.

7.

Maturity	Price	YTM	Forward Rate
1	$943.40	6.00%	
2	$898.47	5.50%	$(1.055^2/1.06) - 1 = 5.0\%$
3	$847.62	5.67%	$(1.0567^3/1.055^2) - 1 = 6.0\%$
4	$792.16	6.00%	$(1.06^4/1.0567^3) - 1 = 7.0\%$

8. The expected price path of the 4-year zero coupon bond is shown below. (Note that we discount the face value by the appropriate sequence of forward rates implied by this year's yield curve.)

Beginning of Year	Expected Price	Expected Rate of Return
1	$792.16	$(\$839.69/\$792.16) - 1 = 6.00\%$
2	$\dfrac{\$1,000}{1.05 \times 1.06 \times 1.07} = \$839.69$	$(\$881.68/\$839.69) - 1 = 5.00\%$
3	$\dfrac{\$1,000}{1.06 \times 1.07} = \$881.68$	$(\$934.58/\$881.68) - 1 = 6.00\%$
4	$\dfrac{\$1,000}{1.07} = \$934.58$	$(\$1,000.00/\$934.58) - 1 = 7.00\%$

9. If expectations theory holds, then the forward rate equals the short rate, and the one-year interest rate three years from now would be

$$\frac{(1.07)^4}{(1.065)^3} - 1 = .0851 = 8.51\%$$

10. a. A 3-year zero coupon bond with face value $100 will sell today at a yield of 6% and a price of:

$100/1.06^3 = \$83.96$

Next year, the bond will have a two-year maturity, and therefore a yield of 6% (from next year's forecasted yield curve). The price will be $89, resulting in a holding period return of 6%.

b.   The forward rates based on today's yield curve are as follows:

Year	Forward Rate
2	$(1.05^2/1.04) - 1 = 6.01\%$
3	$(1.06^3/1.05^2) - 1 = 8.03\%$

Using the forward rates, the forecast for the yield curve *next* year is:

Maturity	YTM
1	6.01%
2	$(1.0601 \times 1.0803)^{1/2} - 1 = 7.02\%$

The market forecast is for a higher YTM on 2-year bonds than your forecast. Thus, the market predicts a lower price and higher rate of return.

11.   a. $$P = \frac{\$9}{1.07} + \frac{\$109}{1.08^2} = \$101.86$$

b.   The yield to maturity is the solution for y in the following equation:

$$\frac{\$9}{1+y} + \frac{\$109}{(1+y)^2} = \$101.86$$

[Using a financial calculator, enter $n = 2$; FV = 100; PMT = 9; PV = −101.86; Compute i] YTM = 7.958%

c.   The forward rate for next year, derived from the zero-coupon yield curve, is the solution for f_2 in the following equation:

$$1 + f_2 = \frac{(1.08)^2}{1.07} = 1.0901 \Rightarrow f_2 = 0.0901 = 9.01\%.$$

Therefore, using an expected rate for next year of $r_2 = 9.01\%$, we find that the forecast bond price is:

$$P = \frac{\$109}{1.0901} = \$99.99$$

d.   If the liquidity premium is 1% then the forecast interest rate is:

$$E(r_2) = f_2 - \text{liquidity premium} = 9.01\% - 1.00\% = 8.01\%$$

The forecast of the bond price is:

$$\frac{\$109}{1.0801} = \$100.92$$

12. a. The current bond price is:

   ($85 × 0.94340) + ($85 × 0.87352) + ($1,085 × 0.81637) = $1,040.20

   This price implies a yield to maturity of 6.97%, as shown by the following:

   [$85 × Annuity factor (6.97%, 3)] + [$1,000 × PV factor (6.97%, 3)] = $1,040.17

   b. If one year from now y = 8%, then the bond price will be:

   [$85 × Annuity factor (8%, 2)] + [$1,000 × PV factor (8%, 2)] = $1,008.92

   The holding period rate of return is:

   [$85 + ($1,008.92 − $1,040.20)]/$1,040.20 = 0.0516 = 5.16%

13.

Year	Forward Rate	PV of $1 received at period end
1	5%	$1/1.05 = $0.9524
2	7	1/(1.05×1.07) = $0.8901
3	8	1/(1.05×1.07×1.08) = $0.8241

   a. Price = ($60 × 0.9524) + ($60 × 0.8901) + ($1,060 × 0.8241) = $984.14

   b. To find the yield to maturity, solve for y in the following equation:

   $984.10 = [$60 × Annuity factor $(y, 3)$] + [$1,000 × PV factor $(y, 3)$]

   This can be solved using a financial calculator to show that y = 6.60%:

   PV = −$984.10; N = 3; FV = $1,000; PMT = $60. Solve for I = 6.60%.

   c.

Period	Payment Received at End of Period:	Will Grow by a Factor of:	To a Future Value of:
1	$60.00	1.07 × 1.08	$ 69.34
2	60.00	1.08	64.80
3	1,060.00	1.00	1,060.00
			$1,194.14

   $984.10 × (1 + y_{realized})^3 = $1,194.14

   $$1 + y_{\text{realized}} = \left(\frac{\$1,194.14}{\$984.10}\right)^{1/3} = 1.0666 \Rightarrow y_{\text{realized}} = 6.66\%$$

   Alternatively, PV = −$984.10; N = 3; FV = $1,194.14; PMT = $0. Solve for I = 6.66%.

   d. Next year, the price of the bond will be:

   [$60 × Annuity factor (7%, 2)] + [$1,000 × PV factor (7%, 2)] = $981.92

Therefore, there will be a capital loss equal to: $984.10 − $981.92 = $2.18

The holding period return is: $\dfrac{\$60 + (-\$2.18)}{\$984.10} = 0.0588 = 5.88\%$

14. a. The return on the one-year zero-coupon bond will be 6.1%.

    The price of the 4-year zero today is:

    $\$1,000/1.064^4 = \$780.25$

    Next year, if the yield curve is unchanged, today's 4-year zero coupon bond will have a 3-year maturity, a YTM of 6.3%, and therefore the price will be:

    $\$1,000/1.063^3 = \$832.53$

    The resulting one-year rate of return will be: 6.70%

    Therefore, in this case, the longer-term bond is expected to provide the higher return because its YTM is expected to decline during the holding period.

   b. If you believe in the expectations hypothesis, you would not expect that the yield curve next year will be the same as today's curve. The upward slope in today's curve would be evidence that expected short rates are rising and that the yield curve will shift upward, reducing the holding period return on the four-year bond. Under the expectations hypothesis, all bonds have equal expected holding period returns. Therefore, you would predict that the HPR for the 4-year bond would be 6.1%, the same as for the 1-year bond.

15. The price of the coupon bond, based on its yield to maturity, is:

    [$120 × Annuity factor (5.8%, 2)] + [$1,000 × PV factor (5.8%, 2)] = $1,113.99

    If the coupons were stripped and sold separately as zeros, then, based on the yield to maturity of zeros with maturities of one and two years, respectively, the coupon payments could be sold separately for:

    $\dfrac{\$120}{1.05} + \dfrac{\$1,120}{1.06^2} = \$1,111.08$

    The arbitrage strategy is to buy zeros with face values of $120 and $1,120, and respective maturities of one year and two years, and simultaneously sell the coupon bond. The profit equals $2.91 on each bond.

16. a. The one-year zero-coupon bond has a yield to maturity of 6%, as shown below:

    $\$94.34 = \dfrac{\$100}{1 + y_1} \Rightarrow y_1 = 0.06000 = 6.000\%$

    The yield on the two-year zero is 8.472%, as shown below:

$$\$84.99 = \frac{\$100}{(1+y_2)^2} \Rightarrow y_2 = 0.08472 = 8.472\%$$

The price of the coupon bond is: $\dfrac{\$12}{1.06} + \dfrac{\$112}{(1.08472)^2} = \$106.51$

Therefore: yield to maturity for the coupon bond = 8.333%
[On a financial calculator, enter: $n = 2$; $PV = -106.51$; $FV = 100$; $PMT = 12$]

b. $f_2 = \dfrac{(1+y_2)^2}{1+y_1} - 1 = \dfrac{(1.08472)^2}{1.06} - 1 = 0.1100 = 11.00\%$

c. Expected price $= \dfrac{\$112}{1.11} = \$100.90$

(Note that next year, the coupon bond will have one payment left.)
Expected holding period return =

$$\frac{\$12 + (\$100.90 - \$106.51)}{\$106.51} = 0.0600 = 6.00\%$$

This holding period return is the same as the return on the one-year zero.

d. If there is a liquidity premium, then: $E(r_2) < f_2$

$$E(\text{Price}) = \frac{\$112}{1+E(r_2)} > \$100.90$$

$E(\text{HPR}) > 6\%$

17. a. We obtain forward rates from the following table:

Maturity	YTM	Forward Rate	Price (for parts c, d)
1 year	10%		$1,000/1.10 = $909.09
2 years	11%	$(1.11^2/1.10) - 1 = 12.01\%$	$1,000/1.11^2 = $811.62
3 years	12%	$(1.12^3/1.11^2) - 1 = 14.03\%$	$1,000/1.12^3 = $711.78

b. We obtain next year's prices and yields by discounting each zero's face value at the forward rates for next year that we derived in part (a):

Maturity	Price	YTM
1 year	$1,000/1.1201 = $892.78	12.01%
2 years	$1,000/(1.1201 × 1.1403) = $782.93	13.02%

Note that this year's upward sloping yield curve implies, according to the expectations hypothesis, a shift upward in next year's curve.

c. Next year, the 2-year zero will be a 1-year zero, and will therefore sell at a price of: $1,000/1.1201 = $892.78

Similarly, the current 3-year zero will be a 2-year zero and will sell for: $782.93

Expected total rate of return:

$$\text{2-year bond: } \frac{\$892.78}{\$811.62} - 1 = 1.1000 - 1 = 10.00\%$$

$$\text{3-year bond: } \frac{\$782.93}{\$711.78} - 1 = 1.1000 - 1 = 10.00\%$$

d. The current price of the bond should equal the value of each payment times the present value of $1 to be received at the "maturity" of that payment. The present value schedule can be taken directly from the prices of zero-coupon bonds calculated above.

Current price = ($120 × 0.90909) + ($120 × 0.81162) + ($1,120 × 0.71178)

= $109.0908 + $97.3944 + $797.1936 = $1,003.68

Similarly, the expected prices of zeros one year from now can be used to calculate the expected bond value at that time:

Expected price 1 year from now = ($120 × 0.89278) + ($1,120 × 0.78293)

= $107.1336 + $876.8816 = $984.02

Total expected rate of return =

$$\frac{\$120 + (\$984.02 - \$1,003.68)}{\$1,003.68} = 0.1000 = 10.00\%$$

18. a.

Maturity (years)	Price	YTM	Forward Rate
1	$925.93	8.00%	
2	853.39	8.25	8.50%
3	782.92	8.50	9.00
4	15.00	8.75	9.50
5	650.00	9.00	10.00

b.   For each 3-year zero issued today, use the proceeds to buy:

$782.92/$715.00 = 1.095 four-year zeros

Your cash flows are thus as follows:

Time	Cash Flow	
0	$ 0	
3	−$1,000	The 3-year zero issued at time 0 matures; the issuer pays out $1,000 face value
4	+$1,095	The 4-year zeros purchased at time 0 mature; receive face value

This is a synthetic one-year loan originating at time 3. The rate on the synthetic loan is 0.095 = 9.5%, precisely the forward rate for year 4.

c.   For each 4-year zero issued today, use the proceeds to buy:

$715.00/$650.00 = 1.100 five-year zeros

Your cash flows are thus as follows:

Time	Cash Flow	
0	$ 0	
4	−$1,000	The 4-year zero issued at time 0 matures; the issuer pays out $1,000 face value
5	+$1,100	The 5-year zeros purchased at time 0 mature; receive face value

This is a synthetic one-year loan originating at time 4. The rate on the synthetic loan is 0.100 = 10.0%, precisely the forward rate for year 5.

19. a.   For each three-year zero you buy today, issue:

$782.92/$650.00 = 1.2045 five-year zeros

The time-0 cash flow equals zero.

b.   Your cash flows are thus as follows:

Time	Cash Flow	
0	$ 0	
3	+$1,000.00	The 3-year zero purchased at time 0 matures; receive $1,000 face value
5	−$1,204.50	The 5-year zeros issued at time 0 mature; issuer pays face value

This is a synthetic two-year loan originating at time 3.

c.   The effective two-year interest rate on the forward loan is:

$1,204.50/$1,000 − 1 = 0.2045 = 20.45%

d.   The one-year forward rates for years 4 and 5 are 9.5% and 10%, respectively. Notice that:

$$1.095 \times 1.10 = 1.2045 =$$

$$1 + \text{(two-year forward rate on the 3-year ahead forward loan)}$$

The 5-year YTM is 9.0%. The 3-year YTM is 8.5%. Therefore, another way to derive the 2-year forward rate for a loan starting at time 3 is:

$$f_3(2) = \frac{(1+y_5)^5}{(1+y_3)^3} - 1 = \frac{1.09^5}{1.085^3} - 1 = 0.2046 = 20.46\%$$

[Note: slight discrepancies here from rounding errors in YTM calculations]

CFA PROBLEMS

1.   Expectations hypothesis: The yields on long-term bonds are geometric averages of present and expected future short rates. An upward sloping curve is explained by expected future short rates being higher than the current short rate. A downward-sloping yield curve implies expected future short rates are lower than the current short rate. Thus bonds of different maturities have different yields if expectations of future short rates are different from the current short rate.

    Liquidity preference hypothesis: Yields on long-term bonds are greater than the expected return from rolling over short-term bonds in order to compensate investors in long-term bonds for bearing interest rate risk. Thus bonds of different maturities can have different yields even if expected future short rates are all equal to the current short rate. An upward-sloping yield curve can be consistent even with expectations of falling short rates if liquidity premiums are high enough. If, however, the yield curve is downward sloping and liquidity premiums are assumed to be positive, then we can conclude that future short rates are expected to be lower than the current short rate.

2.   d. Investors bid up the price of short term securities and force yields to be relatively low, while doing just the opposite at the long end of the term structure. Therefore, they must be compensated more for giving up liquidity in the long term.

3.   a. $(1+y_4)^4 = (1+y_3)^3 (1 +f_4)$

      $(1.055)^4 = (1.05)^3 (1 +f_4)$

      $1.2388 = 1.1576 (1 +f_4) \Rightarrow f_4 = 0.0701 = 7.01\%$

    b.   The conditions would be those that underlie the expectations theory of the term structure: risk neutral market participants who are willing to substitute among maturities solely on the basis of yield differentials. This behavior would rule out liquidity or term premia relating to risk.

c. Under the expectations hypothesis, lower implied forward rates would indicate lower expected future spot rates for the corresponding period. Since the lower expected future rates embodied in the term structure are nominal rates, either lower expected future real rates or lower expected future inflation rates would be consistent with the specified change in the observed (implied) forward rate.

4. The given rates are annual rates, but each period is a half-year. Therefore, the per period spot rates are 2.5% on one-year bonds and 2% on six-month bonds. The semiannual forward rate is obtained by solving for f in the following equation:

$$1+f = \frac{1.025^2}{1.02} = 1.030$$

This means that the forward rate is 0.030 = 3.0% semiannually, or 6.0% annually.

5. The present value of each bond's payments can be derived by discounting each cash flow by the appropriate rate from the spot interest rate (i.e., the pure yield) curve:

Bond A: $PV = \dfrac{\$10}{1.05} + \dfrac{\$10}{1.08^2} + \dfrac{\$110}{1.11^3} = \$98.53$

Bond B: $PV = \dfrac{\$6}{1.05} + \dfrac{\$6}{1.08^2} + \dfrac{\$106}{1.11^3} = \$88.36$

Bond A sells for $0.13 (i.e., 0.13% of par value) less than the present value of its stripped payments. Bond B sells for $0.02 less than the present value of its stripped payments. Bond A is more attractively priced.

6. a. Based on the pure expectations theory, VanHusen's conclusion is incorrect. According to this theory, the expected return over any time horizon would be the same, regardless of the maturity strategy employed.

   b. According to the liquidity preference theory, the shape of the yield curve implies that short-term interest rates are expected to rise in the future. This theory asserts that forward rates reflect expectations about future interest rates plus a liquidity premium that increases with maturity. Given the shape of the yield curve and the liquidity premium data provided, the yield curve would still be positively sloped (at least through maturity of eight years) after subtracting the respective liquidity premiums:

   2.90% − 0.55% = 2.35%

   3.50% − 0.55% = 2.95%

   3.80% − 0.65% = 3.15%

   4.00% − 0.75% = 3.25%

   4.15% − 0.90% = 3.25%

   4.30% − 1.10% = 3.20%

$$4.45\% - 1.20\% = 3.25\%$$
$$4.60\% - 1.50\% = 3.10\%$$
$$4.70\% - 1.60\% = 3.10\%$$

7. The coupon bonds can be viewed as portfolios of stripped zeros: each coupon can stand alone as an independent zero-coupon bond. Therefore, yields on coupon bonds reflect yields on payments with dates corresponding to each coupon. When the yield curve is upward sloping, coupon bonds have lower yields than zeros with the same maturity because the yields to maturity on coupon bonds reflect the yields on the earlier interim coupon payments.

8. The following table shows the expected short-term interest rate based on the projections of Federal Reserve rate cuts, the term premium (which increases at a rate of 0.10% per 12 months), the forward rate (which is the sum of the expected rate and term premium), and the YTM, which is the geometric average of the forward rates.

Time	Expected Short Rate	Term Premium	Forward Rate (annual)	Forward Rate (semiannual)	YTM (semiannual)
0	5.00%	0.00%	5.00%	2.500%	2.500%
6 months	4.50	0.05	4.55	2.275	2.387
12 months	4.00	0.10	4.10	2.050	2.275
18 months	4.00	0.15	4.15	2.075	2.225
24 months	4.00	0.20	4.20	2.100	2.200
30 months	5.00	0.25	5.25	2.625	2.271
36 months	5.00	0.30	5.30	2.650	2.334

This analysis is predicated on the liquidity preference theory of the term structure, which asserts that the forward rate in any period is the sum of the expected short rate plus the liquidity premium.

9. a. Five-year spot rate:

$$\$1,000 = \frac{\$70}{(1+y_1)^1} + \frac{\$70}{(1+y_2)^2} + \frac{\$70}{(1+y_3)^3} + \frac{\$70}{(1+y_4)^4} + \frac{\$1,070}{(1+y_5)^5}$$

$$\$1,000 = \frac{\$70}{(1.05)} + \frac{\$70}{(1.0521)^2} + \frac{\$70}{(1.0605)^3} + \frac{\$70}{(1.0716)^4} + \frac{\$1,070}{(1+y_5)^5}$$

$$\$1,000 = \$66.67 + \$63.24 + \$58.69 + \$53.08 + \frac{\$1,070}{(1+y_5)^5}$$

$$\$758.32 = \frac{\$1,070}{(1+y_5)^5}$$

$$(1+y_5)^5 = \frac{\$1,070}{\$758.32} \Rightarrow y_5 = \sqrt[5]{1.411} - 1 = 7.13\%$$

Five-year forward rate:

$$\frac{(1.0713)^5}{(1.0716)^4} - 1 = 1.0701 - 1 = 7.01\%$$

b. The yield to maturity is the single discount rate that equates the present value of a series of cash flows to a current price. It is the internal rate of return.

The short rate for a given interval is the interest rate for that interval available at different points in time.

The spot rate for a given period is the yield to maturity on a zero-coupon bond that matures at the end of the period. A spot rate is the discount rate for each period. Spot rates are used to discount each cash flow of a coupon bond in order to calculate a current price. Spot rates are the rates appropriate for discounting future cash flows of different maturities.

A forward rate is the implicit rate that links any two spot rates. Forward rates are directly related to spot rates, and therefore to yield to maturity. Some would argue (as in the expectations hypothesis) that forward rates are the market expectations of future interest rates. A forward rate represents a break-even rate that links two spot rates. It is important to note that forward rates link spot rates, not yields to maturity.

Yield to maturity is not unique for any particular maturity. In other words, two bonds with the same maturity but different coupon rates may have different yields to maturity. In contrast, spot rates and forward rates for each date are unique.

c. The four-year spot rate is 7.16%. Therefore, 7.16% is the theoretical yield to maturity for the zero-coupon U.S. Treasury note. The price of the zero-coupon note discounted at 7.16% is the present value of $1,000 to be received in four4 years. Using annual compounding:

$$PV = \frac{\$1,000}{(1.0716)^4} = \$758.35$$

10. a. The two-year implied annually compounded forward rate for a deferred loan beginning in 3 years is calculated as follows:

$$f_3(2) = \left[\frac{(1+y_5)^5}{(1+y_3)^3} \right]^{1/2} - 1 = \left[\frac{1.09^5}{1.11^3} \right]^{1/2} - 1 = 0.0607 = 6.07\%$$

b.   Assuming a par value of $1,000, the bond price is calculated as follows:

$$P = \frac{\$90}{(1+y_1)^1} + \frac{\$90}{(1+y_2)^2} + \frac{\$90}{(1+y_3)^3} + \frac{\$90}{(1+y_4)^4} + \frac{\$1,090}{(1+y_5)^5}$$

$$= \frac{\$90}{(1.13)^1} + \frac{\$90}{(1.12)^2} + \frac{\$90}{(1.11)^3} + \frac{\$90}{(1.10)^4} + \frac{\$1,090}{(1.09)^5} = \$987.10$$

CHAPTER 16: MANAGING BOND PORTFOLIOS

PROBLEM SETS

1. While it is true that short-term rates are more volatile than long-term rates, the longer duration of the longer-term bonds makes their prices and their rates of return more volatile. The higher duration magnifies the sensitivity to interest-rate changes.

2. Duration can be thought of as a weighted average of the maturities of the cash flows paid to holders of the perpetuity, where the weight for each cash flow is equal to the present value of that cash flow divided by the total present value of all cash flows. For cash flows in the distant future, present value approaches zero (i.e., the weight becomes very small) so that these distant cash flows have little impact and, eventually, virtually no impact on the weighted average.

3. The percentage change in the bond's price is:

$$-\frac{D}{1+y}\times\Delta y = -\frac{7.194}{1.10}\times 0.005 = -0.0327 = -3.27\%, \text{ or a } 3.27\% \text{ decline}$$

4. a. **YTM = 6%**

(1) Time until Payment (Years)	(2) Cash Flow	(3) PV of CF (Discount Rate = 6%)	(4) Weight	(5) Column (1) × Column (4)
1	$ 60.00	$ 56.60	0.0566	0.0566
2	60.00	53.40	0.0534	0.1068
3	1,060.00	890.00	0.8900	2.6700
Column sums		$1,000.00	1.0000	2.8334

Duration = 2.833 years

16-1

b. **YTM = 10%**

(1) Time until Payment (Years)	(2) Cash Flow	(3) PV of CF (Discount Rate = 10%)	(4) Weight	(5) Column (1) × Column (4)
1	$ 60.00	$ 54.55	0.0606	0.0606
2	60.00	49.59	0.0551	0.1102
3	1,060.00	796.39	0.8844	2.6532
Column sums		$900.53	1.0000	2.8240

Duration = 2.824 years, which is less than the duration at the YTM of 6%.

5. For a semiannual 6% coupon bond selling at par, we use the following parameters: coupon = 3% per half-year period, $y = 3\%$, T = 6 semiannual periods.

(1) Time until Payment (Years)	(2) Cash Flow	(3) PV of CF (Discount Rate = 3%)	(4) Weight	(5) Column (1) × Column (4)
1	$ 3.00	$ 2.913	0.02913	0.02913
2	3.00	2.828	0.02828	0.05656
3	3.00	2.745	0.02745	0.08236
4	3.00	2.665	0.02665	0.10662
5	3.00	2.588	0.02588	0.12939
6	103.00	86.261	0.86261	5.17565
Column sums		$100.000	1.00000	5.57971

D = 5.5797 half-year periods = 2.7899 years

If the bond's yield is 10%, use a semiannual yield of 5% and semiannual coupon of 3%:

(1) Time until Payment (Years)	(2) Cash Flow	(3) PV of CF (Discount Rate = 5%)	(4) Weight	(5) Column (1) × Column (4)
1	$ 3.00	$ 2.857	0.03180	0.03180
2	3.00	2.721	0.03029	0.06057
3	3.00	2.592	0.02884	0.08653
4	3.00	2.468	0.02747	0.10988
5	3.00	2.351	0.02616	0.13081
6	103.00	76.860	0.85544	5.13265
Column sums		$89.849	1.00000	5.55223

D = 5.5522 half-year periods = 2.7761 years

6. If the current yield spread between AAA bonds and Treasury bonds is too wide compared to historical yield spreads and is expected to narrow, you should shift from Treasury bonds into AAA bonds. As the spread narrows, the AAA bonds will outperform the Treasury bonds. This is an example of an intermarket spread swap.

7. D. Investors tend to purchase longer term bonds when they expect yields to fall so they can capture significant capital gains, and the lack of a coupon payment ensures the capital gain will be even greater.

8. a. Bond B has a higher yield to maturity than bond A since its coupon payments and maturity are equal to those of A, while its price is lower. (Perhaps the yield is higher because of differences in credit risk.) Therefore, the duration of Bond B must be shorter.

   b. Bond A has a lower yield and a lower coupon, both of which cause Bond A to have a longer duration than Bond B. Moreover, A cannot be called, so that its maturity is at least as long as that of B, which generally increases duration.

9. a.

(1) Time until Payment (Years)	(2) Cash Flow	(3) PV of CF (Discount Rate = 10%)	(4) Weight	(5) Column (1) × Column (4)
1	$10 million	$ 9.09 million	0.7857	0.7857
5	4 million	2.48 million	0.2143	1.0715
	Column sums	$11.57 million	1.0000	1.8572

$D = 1.8572$ years = required maturity of zero coupon bond.

   b. The market value of the zero must be $11.57 million, the same as the market value of the obligations. Therefore, the face value must be:

$$\$11.57 \text{ million} \times (1.10)^{1.8572} = \$13.81 \text{ million}$$

10. In each case, choose the longer-duration bond in order to benefit from a rate decrease.

   a. i. The Aaa-rated bond has the lower yield to maturity and therefore the longer duration.

   b. ii. The lower-coupon bond has the longer duration *and* greater de facto call protection.

   c. iii. The lower coupon bond has the longer duration.

11. The table below shows the holding period returns for each of the three bonds:

Maturity	1 Year	2 Years	3 Years
YTM at beginning of year	7.00%	8.00%	9.00%
Beginning of year prices	$1,009.35	$1,000.00	$974.69
Prices at year-end (at 9% YTM)	$1,000.00	$990.83	$982.41
Capital gain	−$9.35	−$9.17	$7.72
Coupon	$80.00	$80.00	$80.00
1-year total $ return	$70.65	$70.83	$87.72
1-year total rate of return	7.00%	7.08%	9.00%

You should buy the three-year bond because it provides a 9% holding-period return over the next year, which is greater than the return on either of the other bonds.

12. a. PV of the obligation = $10,000 × Annuity factor (8%, 2) = $17,832.65

(1)	(2)	(3)	(4)	(5)
Time until Payment (Years)	Cash Flow	PV of CF (Discount Rate = 8%)	Weight	Column (1) × Column (4)
1	$10,000.00	$ 9,259.259	0.51923	0.51923
2	10,000.00	8,573.388	0.48077	0.96154
	Column sums	$17,832.647	1.00000	1.48077

$D = 1.4808$ years

b. A zero-coupon bond maturing in 1.4808 years would immunize the obligation. Since the present value of the zero-coupon bond must be $17,832.65, the face value (i.e., the future redemption value) must be

$$\$17,832.65 \times 1.08^{1.4808} = \$19,985.26$$

c. If the interest rate increases to 9%, the zero-coupon bond would decrease in value to

$$\frac{\$19,985.26}{1.09^{1.4808}} = \$17,590.92$$

The present value of the tuition obligation would decrease to $17,591.11

The net position decreases in value by $0.19

If the interest rate decreases to 7%, the zero-coupon bond would increase in value to

$$\frac{\$19,985.26}{1.07^{1.4808}} = \$18,079.99$$

The present value of the tuition obligation would increase to $18,080.18

The net position decreases in value by $0.19

The reason the net position changes at all is that, as the interest rate changes, so does the duration of the stream of tuition payments.

13. a. PV of obligation = $2 million/0.16 = $12.5 million

Duration of obligation = 1.16/0.16 = 7.25 years

Call w the weight on the five-year maturity bond (which has duration of four years). Then

$$(w \times 4) + [(1 - w) \times 11] = 7.25 \Rightarrow w = 0.5357$$

Therefore: $0.5357 \times \$12.5 = \$6.7$ million in the 5-year bond and

$0.4643 \times \$12.5 = \$5.8$ million in the 20-year bond.

b. The price of the 20-year bond is

$[\$60 \times$ Annuity factor (16%, 20)$] + [\$1,000 \times$ PV factor (16%, 20)$] = \$407.12$

Alternatively, PMT = $60; N = 20; I = 16; FV = $1,000; solve for PV = $407.12.

Therefore, the bond sells for 0.4071 times its par value, and

Market value = Par value × 0.4071

$5.8 million = Par value × 0.4071 $\Rightarrow$ Par value = $14.25 million

Another way to see this is to note that each bond with par value $1,000 sells for $407.12. If total market value is $5.8 million, then you need to buy approximately 14,250 bonds, resulting in total par value of $14.25 million.

14. a. The duration of the perpetuity is: 1.05/0.05 = 21 years

Call w the weight of the zero-coupon bond. Then

$$(w \times 5) + [(1 - w) \times 21] = 10 \Rightarrow w = 11/16 = 0.6875$$

Therefore, the portfolio weights would be as follows: 11/16 invested in the zero and 5/16 in the perpetuity.

b. Next year, the zero-coupon bond will have a duration of 4 years and the perpetuity will still have a 21-year duration. To obtain the target duration of nine years, which is now the duration of the obligation, we again solve for w:

$$(w \times 4) + [(1 - w) \times 21] = 9 \Rightarrow w = 12/17 = 0.7059$$

So, the proportion of the portfolio invested in the zero increases to 12/17 and the proportion invested in the perpetuity falls to 5/17.

15. a.   The duration of the annuity *if* it were to start in one year would be

(1) Time until Payment (Years)	(2) Cash Flow	(3) PV of CF (Discount Rate = 10%)	(4) Weight	(5) Column (1) × Column (4)
1	$10,000	$ 9,090.909	0.14795	0.14795
2	10,000	8,264.463	0.13450	0.26900
3	10,000	7,513.148	0.12227	0.36682
4	10,000	6,830.135	0.11116	0.44463
5	10,000	6,209.213	0.10105	0.50526
6	10,000	5,644.739	0.09187	0.55119
7	10,000	5,131.581	0.08351	0.58460
8	10,000	4,665.074	0.07592	0.60738
9	10,000	4,240.976	0.06902	0.62118
10	10,000	3,855.433	0.06275	0.62745
Column sums		$61,445.671	1.00000	4.72546

$D = 4.7255$ years

Because the payment stream starts in five years, instead of one year, we add four years to the duration, so the duration is 8.7255 years.

b.   The present value of the deferred annuity is

$$\frac{10,000 \times \text{Annuity factor } (10\%, 10)}{1.10^4} = \$41,968$$

Alternatively, CF 0 = 0; CF 1 = 0; N = 4; CF 2 = $10,000; N = 10; I = 10; Solve for NPV = $41,968.

Call w the weight of the portfolio invested in the five-year zero. Then

$$(w \times 5) + [(1 - w) \times 20] = 8.7255 \Rightarrow w = 0.7516$$

The investment in the five-year zero is equal to

$$0.7516 \times \$41,968 = \$31,543$$

The investment in the 20-year zeros is equal to

$$0.2484 \times \$41,968 = \$10,423$$

These are the present or *market* values of each investment. The face values are equal to the respective future values of the investments. The face value of the five-year zeros is

$$\$31,543 \times (1.10)^5 = \$50,801$$

Therefore, between 50 and 51 zero-coupon bonds, each of par value $1,000, would be purchased. Similarly, the face value of the 20-year zeros is

$$\$10,425 \times (1.10)^{20} = \$70,123$$

16. Using a financial calculator, we find that the actual price of the bond as a function of yield to maturity is

Yield to Maturity	Price
7%	$1,620.45
8	1,450.31
9	1,308.21

(N = 30; PMT = $120; FV = $1,000, I = 7, 8, and 9; Solve for PV)

Using the duration rule, assuming yield to maturity falls to 7%

$$\text{Predicted price change} = \left(-\frac{D}{1+y}\right)\times\Delta y\times P_0$$

$$= \left(-\frac{11.54}{1.08}\right)\times(-0.01)\times\$1,450.31 = \$155.06$$

Therefore: predicted new price = $1,450.31 + $155.06 = $1,605.37

The actual price at a 7% yield to maturity is $1,620.45. Therefore

$$\% \text{ error} = \frac{\$1,605.37 - \$1,620.45}{\$1,620.45} = -0.0093 = -0.93\% \text{ (approximation is too low)}$$

Using the duration rule, assuming yield to maturity increases to 9%

$$\text{Predicted price change} = \left(-\frac{D}{1+y}\right)\times\Delta y\times P_0$$

$$= \left(-\frac{11.54}{1.08}\right)\times 0.01\times\$1,450.31 = -\$155.06$$

Therefore: predicted new price = $1,450.31 − $155.06 = $1,295.25

The actual price at a 9% yield to maturity is $1,308.21. Therefore

$$\% \text{ error} = \frac{\$1,295.25 - \$1,308.21}{\$1,308.21} = -0.0099 = -0.99\% \text{ (approximation is too low)}$$

Using duration-with-convexity rule, assuming yield to maturity falls to 7%

$$\text{Predicted price change} = \left\{\left[\left(-\frac{D}{1+y}\right)\times\Delta y\right]+\left[0.5\times\text{Convexity}\times(\Delta y)^2\right]\right\}\times P_0$$

$$= \left\{\left[\left(-\frac{11.54}{1.08}\right)\times(-0.01)\right]+\left[0.5\times192.4\times(-0.01)^2\right]\right\}\times\$1,450.31 = \$168.99$$

Therefore the predicted new price = $1,450.31 + $168.99 = $1,619.30.

The actual price at a 7% yield to maturity is $1,620.45. Therefore

$$\% \text{ error} = \frac{\$1,619.30 - \$1,620.45}{\$1,620.45} = -0.0007, \text{ or} -0.07\% \text{ (approximation is too low)}.$$

Using duration-with-convexity rule, assuming yield to maturity rises to 9%

$$\text{Predicted price change} = \left\{ \left[\left(-\frac{D}{1+y} \right) \times \Delta y \right] + \left[0.5 \times \text{Convexity} \times (\Delta y)^2 \right] \right\} \times P_0$$

$$= \left\{ \left[\left(-\frac{11.54}{1.08} \right) \times 0.01 \right] + \left[0.5 \times 192.4 \times (0.01)^2 \right] \right\} \times \$1,450.31 = -\$141.11$$

Therefore the predicted new price = $1,450.31 − $141.11 = $1,309.20.

The actual price at a 9% yield to maturity is $1,308.21. Therefore

$$\% \text{ error} = \frac{\$1,309.20 - \$1,308.21}{\$1,308.21} = 0.0008, \text{ or } 0.08\% \text{ (approximation is too high)}.$$

Conclusion: The duration-with-convexity rule provides more accurate approximations to the true change in price. In this example, the percentage error using convexity with duration is less than one-tenth the error using only duration to estimate the price change.

17. Shortening his portfolio duration makes the value of the portfolio less sensitive relative to interest rate changes. So if interest rates increase the value of the portfolio will decrease less.

18. Predicted price change:

$$= \left(-\frac{D}{1+y} \right) \times \Delta y \times P_0 = (-\$3.5851) \times .01 \times 100 = -\$3.59 \text{ decrease}$$

19. The maturity of the 30-year bond will fall to 25 years, and its yield is forecast to be 8%. Therefore, the price forecast for the bond is $893.25

[Using a financial calculator, enter the following: $n = 25$; $i = 8$; FV = 1000; PMT = 70]

At a 6% interest rate, the five coupon payments will accumulate to $394.60 after five years. Therefore, total proceeds will be: $394.60 + $893.25 = $1,287.85

Therefore, the five-year return is ($1,287.85/$867.42) − 1 = 0.4847.

This is a 48.47% five-year return, or 8.22% annually.

The maturity of the 20-year bond will fall to 15 years, and its yield is forecast to be 7.5%. Therefore, the price forecast for the bond is $911.73.

[Using a financial calculator, enter the following: $n = 15$; $i = 7.5$; FV = 1000; PMT = 65]

At a 6% interest rate, the five coupon payments will accumulate to $366.41 after five years. Therefore, total proceeds will be $366.41 + $911.73 = $1,278.14.

Therefore, the five-year return is: ($1,278.14/$879.50) − 1 = 0.4533

This is a 45.33% five-year return, or 7.76% annually. The 30-year bond offers the higher expected return.

20.

a.

	Period	Time until Payment (Years)	Cash Flow	PV of CF Discount Rate = 6% per Period	Weight	Years × Weight
A. 8% coupon bond	1	0.5	$ 40	$ 37.736	0.0405	0.0203
	2	1.0	40	35.600	0.0383	0.0383
	3	1.5	40	33.585	0.0361	0.0541
	4	2.0	1,040	823.777	0.8851	1.7702
Sum:				$930.698	1.0000	1.8829
B. Zero-coupon	1	0.5	$0	$ 0.000	0.0000	0.0000
	2	1.0	0	0.000	0.0000	0.0000
	3	1.5	0	0.000	0.0000	0.0000
	4	2.0	1,000	792.094	1.0000	2.0000
Sum:				$792.094	1.0000	2.0000

For the coupon bond, the weight on the last payment in the table above is less than it is in Spreadsheet 16.1 because the discount rate is higher; the weights for the first three payments are larger than those in Spreadsheet 16.1. Consequently, the duration of the bond falls. The zero coupon bond, by contrast, has a fixed weight of 1.0 for the single payment at maturity.

b.

	Period	Time until Payment (Years)	Cash Flow	PV of CF Discount Rate = 5% per Period	Weight	Years × Weight
A. 8% coupon bond	1	0.5	$ 60	$ 57.143	0.0552	0.0276
	2	1.0	60	54.422	0.0526	0.0526
	3	1.5	60	51.830	0.0501	0.0751
	4	2.0	1,060	872.065	0.8422	1.6844
Sum:				$1,035.460	1.0000	1.8396

Since the coupon payments are larger in the above table, the weights on the earlier payments are higher than in Spreadsheet 16.1, so duration decreases.

21.

a.

Time (t)	Cash Flow	PV(CF)	$t + t^2$	$(t + t^2) \times$ PV(CF)
1	$ 80	$ 72.727	2	145.455
2	80	66.116	6	396.694
3	80	60.105	12	721.262
4	80	54.641	20	1,092.822
5	1,080	670.595	30	20,117.851

Coupon = $80
YTM = 0.10
Maturity = 5
Price = $924.184

Price: $924.184

Sum: 22,474.083

Convexity = Sum/[Price $\times (1+y)^2$] = 20.097

b.

Time (t)	Cash Flow	PV(CF)	$t^2 + t$	$(t^2 + t) \times$ PV(CF)
1	$ 0	$ 0.000	2	0.000
2	0	0.000	6	0.000
3	0	0.000	12	0.000
4	0	0.000	20	0.000
5	1,000	620.921	30	18,627.640

Coupon = $0
YTM = 0.10
Maturity = 5
Price = $620.921

Price: $620.921

Sum: 18,627.640

Convexity = Sum/[Price $\times (1+y)^2$] = 24.793

22. **a.** The price of the zero-coupon bond ($1,000 face value) selling at a yield to maturity of 8% is $374.84 and the price of the coupon bond is $774.84.

At a YTM of 9%, the actual price of the zero-coupon bond is $333.28 and the actual price of the coupon bond is $691.79.

Zero-coupon bond:

Actual % loss $= \dfrac{\$333.28 - \$374.84}{\$374.84} = -0.1109 = 11.09\%$ loss

The percentage loss predicted by the duration-with-convexity rule is:

Predicted % loss $= [(-11.81) \times 0.01] + [0.5 \times 150.3 \times 0.01^2] = -0.1106 = 11.06\%$ loss

Coupon bond:

Actual % loss $= \dfrac{\$691.79 - \$774.84}{\$774.84} = -0.1072$, or 10.72% loss

The percentage loss predicted by the duration-with-convexity rule is:

Predicted % loss $= [(-11.79) \times 0.01] + [0.5 \times 231.2 \times 0.01^2] = -0.1063$, or 10.63% loss

b. Now assume yield to maturity falls to 7%. The price of the zero increases to $422.04, and the price of the coupon bond increases to $875.91.

Zero-coupon bond:

$$\text{Actual \% gain} = \frac{\$422.04 - \$374.84}{\$374.84} = 0.1259, \text{ or } 12.59\% \text{ gain}$$

The percentage gain predicted by the duration-with-convexity rule is:

$$\text{Predicted \% gain} = \left[(-11.81) \times (-0.01)\right] + \left[0.5 \times 150.3 \times 0.01^2\right] = 0.1256, \text{ or } 12.56\% \text{ gain}$$

Coupon bond:

$$\text{Actual \% gain} = \frac{\$875.91 - \$774.84}{\$774.84} = 0.1304, \text{ or } 13.04\% \text{ gain}$$

The percentage gain predicted by the duration-with-convexity rule is:

$$\text{Predicted \% gain} = \left[(-11.79) \times (-0.01)\right] + \left[0.5 \times 231.2 \times 0.01^2\right] = 0.1295, \text{ or } 12.95\% \text{ gain}$$

c. The 6% coupon bond, which has higher convexity, outperforms the zero regardless of whether rates rise or fall. This can be seen to be a general property using the duration-with-convexity formula: the duration effects on the two bonds due to any change in rates are equal (since the respective durations are virtually equal), but the convexity effect, which is always positive, always favors the higher convexity bond. Thus, if the yields on the bonds change by equal amounts, as we assumed in this example, the higher convexity bond outperforms a lower convexity bond with the same duration and initial yield to maturity.

d. This situation cannot persist. No one would be willing to buy the lower convexity bond if it always underperforms the other bond. The price of the lower convexity bond will fall and its yield to maturity will rise. Thus, the lower convexity bond will sell at a higher initial yield to maturity. That higher yield is compensation for lower convexity. If rates change only slightly, the higher yield–lower convexity bond will perform better; if rates change by a substantial amount, the lower yield–higher convexity bond will perform better.

23. a. The following spreadsheet shows that the convexity of the bond is 64.933. The present value of each cash flow is obtained by discounting at 7%. (Since the bond has a 7% coupon and sells at par, its YTM is 7%.)

Convexity equals: the sum of the last column (7,434.175) divided by:

$$[P \times (1 + y)^2] = 100 \times (1.07)^2 = 114.49$$

Time (t)	Cash Flow (CF)	PV(CF)	$t^2 + t$	$(t^2 + t) \times$ PV(CF)
1	7	6.542	2	13.084
2	7	6.114	6	36.684
3	7	5.714	12	68.569
4	7	5.340	20	106.805
5	7	4.991	30	149.727
6	7	4.664	42	195.905
7	7	4.359	56	244.118
8	7	4.074	72	293.333
9	7	3.808	90	342.678
10	107	54.393	110	5,983.271
	Sum:	100.000		7,434.175
			Convexity:	64.933

The duration of the bond is:

(1) Time until Payment (Years)	(2) Cash Flow	(3) PV of CF (Discount Rate = 7%)	(4) Weight	(5) Column (1) × Column (4)
1	$7	$ 6.542	0.06542	0.06542
2	7	6.114	0.06114	0.12228
3	7	5.714	0.05714	0.17142
4	7	5.340	0.05340	0.21361
5	$7	4.991	0.04991	0.24955
6	7	4.664	0.04664	0.27986
7	7	4.359	0.04359	0.30515
8	7	4.074	0.04074	0.32593
9	7	3.808	0.03808	0.34268
10	107	54.393	0.54393	5.43934
	Column sums	$100.000	1.00000	7.51523

D = 7.515 years

b. If the yield to maturity increases to 8%, the bond price will fall to 93.29% of par value, a percentage decrease of 6.71%.

c. The duration rule predicts a percentage price change of

$$\left(-\frac{D}{1.07}\right) \times 0.01 = \left(-\frac{7.515}{1.07}\right) \times 0.01 = -0.0702, \text{or} -7.02\%$$

This overstates the actual percentage decrease in price by 0.31%.

The price predicted by the duration rule is 7.02% less than face value, or 92.98% of face value.

d. The duration-with-convexity rule predicts a percentage price change of

$$\left[\left(-\frac{7.515}{1.07}\right)\times0.01\right]+\left[0.5\times64.933\times0.01^2\right]=-0.0670,\,or-6.70\%$$

The percentage error is 0.01%, which is substantially less than the error using the duration rule.

The price predicted by the duration with convexity rule is 6.70% less than face value, or 93.30% of face value.

24. a. The following spreadsheet shows that the convexity of the "bullet" bond is 28.2779. The present value of each cash flow is obtained by discounting at 3%. Convexity equals the sum of the last column (25,878.26) divided by

$$[P\times(1+y)^2]=862.61\times(1.03)^2=915.1416$$

Time (t)	Cash flow (CF)	PV(CF)	t^2+t	$(t^2+t)\times$ PV(CF)
1	0	0	2	0
2	0	0	6	0
3	0	0	12	0
4	0	0	20	0
5	1000	862.61	30	25,878.26
Sum:		862.61		25,878.26
Convexity:		28.2779		

The duration of the "bullet" is five years because of the single payment at maturity.

b.

Time (t)	Cash Flow (CF)	PV(CF)	$t+t^2$	$(t+t^2)$ x PV(CF)	t X PV(CF)/price
1	100	$97.09	2	$194.17	0.12
2	100	94.26	6	565.56	0.24
3	100	91.51	12	1,098.17	0.35
4	100	88.85	20	1,776.97	0.46
5	100	86.26	30	2,587.83	0.55
6	100	83.75	42	3,517.43	0.65
7	100	81.31	56	4,553.31	0.73
8	100	78.94	72	5,683.75	0.81
9	100	76.64	90	6,897.75	0.89
Sum		$778.61		$26,874.95	4.80
Convexity		32.53513991			

The present value of each cash flow is obtained by discounting at 3%. Convexity equals: the sum of the last column (26,874.95) divided by
$$[P \times (1 + y)^2] = 778.61 \times (1.03)^2 = 826.0283.$$ The duration is the sum of the last column. Notice the duration is close to that of the bullet bond.

c. The barbell has the greater convexity.

CFA PROBLEMS

1. a. The call feature provides a valuable option to the issuer, since it can buy back the bond at a specified call price even if the present value of the scheduled remaining payments is greater than the call price. The investor will demand, and the issuer will be willing to pay, a higher yield on the issue as compensation for this feature.

   b. The call feature reduces both the duration (interest rate sensitivity) and the convexity of the bond. If interest rates fall, the increase in the price of the callable bond will not be as large as it would be if the bond were noncallable. Moreover, the usual curvature that characterizes price changes for a straight bond is reduced by a call feature. The price-yield curve (see Figure 16.6) flattens out as the interest rate falls and the option to call the bond becomes more attractive. In fact, at very low interest rates, the bond exhibits negative convexity.

2. a. Bond price decreases by $80.00, calculated as follows:
   $$10 \times 0.01 \times 800 = 80.00$$

   b. $\frac{1}{2} \times 120 \times (0.015)^2 = 0.0135 = 1.35\%$

   c. $9/1.10 = 8.18$

   d. (i)

   e. (i)

   f. (iii)

3. a. $\text{Modified duration} = \frac{\text{Macaulay duration}}{1 + \text{YTM}} = \frac{10}{1.08} = 9.26 \text{ years}$

   b. For option-free coupon bonds, modified duration is a better measure of the bond's sensitivity to changes in interest rates. Maturity considers only the final cash flow, while modified duration includes other factors, such as the size and timing of coupon payments, and the level of interest rates (yield to maturity). Modified duration indicates the approximate percentage change in the bond price for a given change in yield to maturity.

c. (i) Modified duration increases as the coupon decreases.

(ii) Modified duration decreases as maturity decreases.

d. Convexity measures the curvature of the bond's price-yield curve. Such curvature means that the duration rule for bond price change (which is based only on the slope of the curve at the original yield) is only an approximation. Adding a term to account for the convexity of the bond increases the accuracy of the approximation. That convexity adjustment is the last term in the following equation:

$$\frac{\Delta P}{P} = (-D^* \times \Delta y) + \left[\frac{1}{2} \times \text{Convexity} \times (\Delta y)^2\right]$$

4. a. (i) Current yield = Coupon/Price = \$70/\$960 = 0.0729, or 7.29%

(ii) YTM = 3.993% semiannually or 7.986% annual bond equivalent yield. [Financial calculator: $n = 10$; PV = −960; FV = 1000; PMT = 35 Compute the interest rate.]

(iii) Horizon yield or realized compound yield is 4.166% (semiannually), or 8.332% annual bond equivalent yield. To obtain this value, first find the future value (FV) of reinvested coupons and principal. There will be six payments of \$35 each, reinvested semiannually at 3% per period. On a financial calculator, enter

PV = 0; PMT = \$35; $n = 6$; $i = 3$%. Compute: FV = \$226.39

Three years from now, the bond will be selling at the par value of \$1,000 because the yield to maturity is forecast to equal the coupon rate. Therefore, total proceeds in three years will be \$1,226.39.

Find the rate (y_{realized}) that makes the FV of the purchase price = \$1,226.39:

$$\$960 \times (1 + y_{\text{realized}})^6 = \$1,226.39 \Rightarrow y_{\text{realized}} = 4.166\% \text{ (semiannual)}$$

Alternatively, PV = −\$960; FV = \$1,226.39; N = 6; PMT = \$0; Solve for I = 4.16.

b. Shortcomings of each measure:

(i) Current yield does not account for capital gains or losses on bonds bought at prices other than par value. It also does not account for reinvestment income on coupon payments.

(ii) Yield to maturity assumes the bond is held until maturity and that all coupon income can be reinvested at a rate equal to the yield to maturity.

(iii) Horizon yield or realized compound yield is affected by the forecast of reinvestment rates, holding period, and yield of the bond at the end of the investor's holding period.

Note: This criticism of horizon yield is a bit unfair: while YTM can be calculated without *explicit* assumptions regarding future YTM and reinvestment rates, you *implicitly* assume that these values equal the current YTM if you use YTM as a measure of expected return.

5.   a.   (i)   The effective duration of the 4.75% Treasury security is:

$$-\frac{\Delta P / P}{\Delta r} = \frac{(116.887 - 86.372)/100}{0.02} = 15.2575$$

(ii)   The duration of the portfolio is the weighted average of the durations of the individual bonds in the portfolio:

Portfolio duration $= w_1 D_1 + w_2 D_2 + w_3 D_3 + \ldots + w_k D_k$

where

w_i = Market value of bond i/Market value of the portfolio
D_i = Duration of bond i
k = Number of bonds in the portfolio

The effective duration of the bond portfolio is calculated as follows:

[($48,667,680/$98,667,680) × 2.15] + [($50,000,000/$98,667,680) × 15.26]
= 8.79

b.   VanHusen's remarks would be correct if there were a small, parallel shift in yields. Duration is a first (linear) approximation only for small changes in yield. For larger changes in yield, the convexity measure is needed in order to approximate the change in price that is not explained by duration. Additionally, portfolio duration assumes that all yields change by the same number of basis points (parallel shift), so any nonparallel shift in yields would result in a difference in the price sensitivity of the portfolio compared to the price sensitivity of a single security having the same duration.

6.   a.   The Aa bond initially has a higher YTM (yield spread of 40 b.p. versus 31 b.p.), but it is expected to have a widening spread relative to Treasuries. This will reduce the rate of return. The Aaa spread is expected to be stable. Calculate comparative returns as follows:

Incremental return over Treasuries =

Incremental yield spread − (Change in spread × Duration)

Aaa bond: 31 bp − (0 × 3.1 years) = 31 bp

Aa bond: 40 bp − (10 bp × 3.1 years) = 9 bp

Therefore, choose the Aaa bond.

b.   Other variables to be considered:

- Potential changes in issue-specific credit quality: If the credit quality of the bonds changes, spreads relative to Treasuries will also change.

- Changes in relative yield spreads for a given bond rating: If quality spreads in the general bond market change because of changes in required risk premiums, the yield spreads of the bonds will change even if there is no change in the assessment of the credit quality of these *particular* bonds.

- Maturity effect: As bonds near their maturity, the effect of credit quality on spreads can also change. This can affect bonds of different initial credit quality differently.

7. a.   % price change = (−Effective duration) × Change in YTM (%)

    CIC: $(-7.35) \times (-0.50\%) = 3.675\%$

    PTR: $(-5.40) \times (-0.50\%) = 2.700\%$

    b.   Since we are asked to calculate horizon return over a period of only one coupon period, there is no reinvestment income.

    $$\text{Horizon return} = \frac{\text{Coupon payment} + \text{Year-end price} - \text{Initial Price}}{\text{Initial price}}$$

    CIC: $\dfrac{\$26.25 + \$1{,}055.50 - \$1{,}017.50}{\$1{,}017.50} = 0.06314, \text{or } 6.314\%$

    PTR: $\dfrac{\$31.75 + \$1{,}041.50 - \$1{,}017.50}{\$1{,}017.50} = 0.05479, \text{or } 5.479\%$

    c.   Notice that CIC is noncallable but PTR is callable. Therefore, CIC has positive convexity, while PTR has negative convexity. Thus, the convexity correction to the duration approximation will be positive for CIC and negative for PTR.

8. The economic climate is one of impending interest rate increases. Hence, we will seek to shorten portfolio duration.

    a.   Choose the short maturity (2014) bond.

    b.   The Arizona bond likely has lower duration. The Arizona coupons are slightly lower, but the Arizona yield is higher.

    c.   Choose the 9 3/8 % coupon bond. The maturities are approximately equal, but the 9 3/8 % coupon is much higher, resulting in a lower duration.

    d.   The duration of the Shell bond is lower if the effect of the earlier start of sinking fund redemption dominates its slightly lower coupon rate.

    e.   The floating rate note has a duration that approximates the adjustment period, which is only six months, thus choose the floating rate note.

9. a.   A manager who believes that the level of interest rates will change should engage in a rate anticipation swap, lengthening duration if rates are expected to fall, and shortening duration if rates are expected to rise.

    b.   A change in yield spreads across sectors would call for an intermarket spread swap, in which the manager buys bonds in the sector for which yields are expected to fall relative to other bonds and sells bonds in the sector for which yields are expected to rise relative to other bonds.

     c.   A belief that the yield spread on a particular instrument will change calls for a substitution swap in which that security is sold if its yield is expected to rise relative to the yield of other similar bonds, or is bought if its yield is expected to fall relative to the yield of other similar bonds.

10. a.   The advantages of a bond indexing strategy are

- Historically, the majority of active managers underperform benchmark indexes in most periods; indexing reduces the possibility of underperformance at a given level of risk.

- Indexed portfolios do not depend on advisor expectations and so have less risk of underperforming the market.

- Management advisory fees for indexed portfolios are dramatically less than fees for actively managed portfolios. Fees charged by active managers generally range from 15 to 50 basis points, while fees for indexed portfolios range from 1 to 20 basis points (with the highest of those representing enhanced indexing). Other nonadvisory fees (i.e., custodial fees) are also less for indexed portfolios.

- Plan sponsors have greater control over indexed portfolios because individual managers do not have as much freedom to vary from the parameters of the benchmark index. Some plan sponsors even decide to manage index portfolios with in-house investment staff.

- Indexing is essentially "buying the market." If markets are efficient, an indexing strategy should reduce unsystematic diversifiable risk and should generate maximum return for a given level of risk.

    The disadvantages of a bond indexing strategy are

- Indexed portfolio returns may match the bond index, but do not necessarily reflect optimal performance. In some time periods, many active managers may outperform an indexing strategy at the same level of risk.

- The chosen bond index and portfolio returns may not meet the client objectives or the liability stream.

- Bond indexing may restrict the fund from participating in sectors or other opportunities that could increase returns.

    b.   The stratified sampling, or cellular, method divides the index into cells, with each cell representing a different characteristic of the index. Common cells used in the cellular method combine (but are not limited to) duration, coupon, maturity, market sectors, credit rating, and call and sinking fund features. The index manager then selects one or more bond issues to represent the entire cell. The total market weight of issues held for each cell is based on the target index's composition of that characteristic.

    c.   Tracking error is defined as the discrepancy between the performance of an indexed portfolio and the benchmark index. When the amount invested is relatively small and the number of cells to be replicated is large, a significant source of tracking error with the cellular method occurs because of the need to buy odd lots of issues in order to accurately represent the required cells. Odd lots generally must be purchased at higher prices than round lots. On the other hand, reducing the number of cells to limit the required number of odd lots would potentially increase tracking error because of the mismatch with the target.

11. a. For an option-free bond, the effective duration and modified duration are approximately the same. Using the data provided, the duration is calculated as follows:

$$-\frac{\Delta P / P}{\Delta r} = \frac{(100.71 - 99.29)/100}{0.002} = 7.100$$

b. The total percentage price change for the bond is estimated as follows:

Percentage price change using duration = $-7.90 \times -0.02 \times 100 = 15.80\%$

Convexity adjustment = 1.66%

Total estimated percentage price change = 15.80% + 1.66% = 17.46%

c. The assistant's argument is incorrect. Because modified convexity does not recognize the fact that cash flows for bonds with an embedded option can change as yields change, modified convexity remains positive as yields move below the callable bond's stated coupon rate, just as it would for an option-free bond. Effective convexity, however, takes into account the fact that cash flows for a security with an embedded option can change as interest rates change. When yields move significantly below the stated coupon rate, the likelihood that the bond will be called by the issuer increases and the effective convexity turns negative.

12. $\Delta P/P = -D^* \, \Delta y$

For Strategy I:

5-year maturity: $\Delta P/P = -4.83 \times (-0.75\%) = 3.6225\%$

25-year maturity: $\Delta P/P = -23.81 \times 0.50\% = -11.9050\%$

Strategy I: $\Delta P/P = (0.5 \times 3.6225\%) + [0.5 \times (-11.9050\%)] = -4.1413\%$

For Strategy II:

15-year maturity: $\Delta P/P = -14.35 \times 0.25\% = -3.5875\%$

13. a. i. Strong economic recovery with rising inflation expectations. Interest rates and bond yields will most likely rise, and the prices of both bonds will fall. The probability that the callable bond will be called would decrease, and the callable bond will behave more like the noncallable bond. (Note that they have similar durations when priced to maturity). The slightly lower duration of the callable bond will result in somewhat better performance in the high interest rate scenario.

ii. Economic recession with reduced inflation expectations. Interest rates and bond yields will most likely fall. The callable bond is likely to be called. The relevant duration calculation for the callable bond is now modified duration to call. Price appreciation is limited as indicated by the lower duration. The noncallable bond, on the other hand, continues to have the same modified duration and hence has greater price appreciation.

b. Projected price change = (Modified duration) × (Change in YTM)

$$= (-6.80) \times (-0.75\%) = 5.1\%$$

Therefore, the price will increase to approximately $105.10 from its current level of $100.

c. For Bond A, the callable bond, bond life, and therefore bond cash flows are uncertain. If one ignores the call feature and analyzes the bond on a "to maturity" basis, all calculations for yield and duration are distorted. Durations are too long and yields are too high. On the other hand, if one treats the premium bond selling above the call price on a "to call" basis, the duration is unrealistically short and yields too low. The most effective approach is to use an option valuation approach. The callable bond can be decomposed into two separate securities: a noncallable bond and an option:

Price of callable bond = Price of noncallable bond − Price of option

Since the call option always has some positive value, the price of the callable bond is always less than the price of the noncallable security.

CHAPTER 17: MACROECONOMIC AND INDUSTRY ANALYSIS

PROBLEM SETS

1. Expansionary (looser) monetary policy to lower interest rates would stimulate both investment and expenditures on consumer durables. Expansionary fiscal policy (i.e., lower taxes, increased government spending, increased welfare transfers) would stimulate aggregate demand directly.

2. A depreciating dollar makes imported cars more expensive and American cars less expensive to foreign consumers. This should benefit the U.S. auto industry.

3. This exercise is left to the student; answers will vary. Successful students will likely discuss an industry's profitability, leverage, and growth opportunities, especially in relation to general macroeconomic conditions.

4. A top-down approach to security valuation begins with an analysis of the global and domestic economy. Analysts who follow a top-down approach then narrow their attention to an industry or sector likely to perform well, given the expected performance of the broader economy. Finally, the analysis focuses on specific companies within an industry or sector that has been identified as likely to perform well. A bottom-up approach typically emphasizes fundamental analysis of individual company stocks and is largely based on the belief that undervalued stocks will perform well regardless of the prospects for the industry or the broader economy. The major advantage of the top-down approach is that it provides a structured approach to incorporating the impact of economic and financial variables, at every level, into analysis of a company's stock. One would expect, for example, that prospects for a particular industry are highly dependent on broader economic variables. Similarly, the performance of an individual company's stock is likely to be greatly affected by the prospects for the industry in which the company operates.

5. Firms with greater sensitivity to business cycles are in industries that produce durable consumer goods or capital goods. Consumers of durable goods (e.g., automobiles, major appliances) are more likely to purchase these products during an economic expansion but can often postpone purchases during a recession. Business purchases of capital goods (e.g., purchases of manufacturing equipment by firms that produce their own products) decline during a recession because demand for the firms' end products declines during a recession.

6. a. **Gold Mining.** Gold traditionally is viewed as a hedge against inflation. Expansionary monetary policy may lead to increased inflation and thus could enhance the value of gold mining stocks.

b.   **Construction.** Expansionary monetary policy will lead to lower interest rates which ought to stimulate housing demand. The construction industry should benefit.

7.   Supply-side economists believe that a reduction in income tax rates will make workers more willing to work at current or even slightly lower (gross-of-tax) wages. Such an effect ought to mitigate cost pressures on the inflation rate.

8.   a.   When both fiscal and monetary policies are expansive, the yield curve is sharply upward sloping (i.e. short-term rates are lower than long-term rates) and the economy is likely to expand in the future.

9.   a.   When wealth is redistributed through the government's tax policy, economic inefficiency is created. Tax policies should promote economic growth as much as possible.

10. a.   The robotics process entails higher fixed costs and lower variable (labor) costs. Therefore, this firm will perform better in a boom and worse in a recession. For example, costs will rise less rapidly than revenue when sales volume expands during a boom.

     b.   Because its profits are more sensitive to the business cycle, the robotics firm will have the higher beta.

11. a.   Housing construction (cyclical but interest-rate sensitive): (iii) Healthy expansion

     b.   Health care (a noncyclical industry): (i) Deep recession

     c.   Gold mining (counter-cyclical): (iv) Stagflation

     d.   Steel production (cyclical industry): (ii) Superheated economy

12. a.   Oil well equipment: Relative decline (Environmental pressures, decline in easily developed new oil fields)

     b.   Computer hardware: Consolidation

     c.   Computer software: Consolidation

     d.   Genetic engineering: Start-up

     e.   Railroads: Relative decline

13. a.   General Autos. Pharmaceuticals are less of a discretionary purchase than automobiles.

    b.   Friendly Airlines. Travel expenditure is more sensitive to the business cycle than movie consumption.

14.   The index of consumer expectations is a useful leading economic indicator because, if consumers are optimistic about the future, they will be more willing to spend money, especially on consumer durables, which will increase aggregate demand and stimulate the economy.

15.   Labor cost per unit is a useful lagging indicator because wages typically start rising only well into an economic expansion. At the beginning of an expansion, there is considerable slack in the economy and output can expand without employers bidding up the price of inputs or the wages of employees. By the time wages start increasing due to high demand for labor, the boom period has already progressed considerably.

16.   The expiration of the patent means that General Weedkillers will soon face considerably greater competition from its competitors. We would expect prices and profit margins to fall and total industry sales to increase somewhat as prices decline. The industry will probably enter the consolidation stage in which producers are forced to compete more extensively on the basis of price.

17. a.   Expected profit = Revenues − Fixed costs − Variable costs

$$= \$120,000 - \$30,000 - [(1/3) \times \$120,000] = \$50,000$$

    b. $$\text{DOL} = 1 + \frac{\text{Fixed costs}}{\text{Profits}} = 1 + \frac{\$30,000}{\$50,000} = 1.60$$

    c.   If sales are only $108,000, profit will fall to:

$$\$108,000 - \$30,000 - [(1/3) \times \$108,000] = \$42,000$$

    This is a 16% decline from the forecasted value.

    d.   The decrease in profit is 16% = DOL × 10% drop in sales.

    e.   Profit must drop more than 100% to turn negative. For profit to fall 100%, revenue must fall by:

$$\frac{100\%}{\text{DOL}} = \frac{100\%}{1.60} = 62.5\%$$

    Therefore, revenue would be only 37.5% of the original forecast. At this level, revenue will be: $0.375 \times \$120,000 = \$45,000$

    f.   If revenue is $45,000, profit will be:

$$\$45,000 - \$30,000 - (1/3) \times \$45,000 = \$0$$

18.   Equity prices are positively correlated with job creation or longer work weeks, as each new dollar earned means more will likely be spent. High confidence presages well for spending and stock prices.

19.   a.   Stock prices are one of the leading indicators. One possible explanation is that stock prices anticipate future interest rates, corporate earnings, and dividends. Another possible explanation is that stock prices react to changes in the other leading economic indicators, such as changes in the money supply or the spread between long-term and short-term interest rates.

20.   a.   Industrial production is a coincident indicator; the others are leading.

21.   b.   If historical returns are used, the arithmetic and geometric means of returns are available. The geometric mean is preferred for multiperiod horizons to observe long-term trends. An alternative to the equity risk premium is to use a moving average of recent historical market returns. This will reveal a low expected equity risk premium when times have been bad, which is contrary to investor expectations. When using historical data, there is a trade-off between long and short time spans. Short time spans are helpful to reduce the impact of regime changes. Long time spans provide better statistical data that are less sensitive.

22.   a.   Foreign exchange rates can significantly affect the competitiveness and profitability for a given industry. For industries that derive a significant proportion of sales via exports, an appreciating currency is usually bad news because it makes the industry less competitive overseas. Here, the appreciating French currency makes French imports more expensive in England.

23.   Determinants of buyer power include buyer concentration, buyer volume, buyer information, available substitutes, switching costs, brand identity, and product differences. Point 1 addresses available substitutes, Point 2 addresses buyer information, and Point 4 addresses buyer volume and buyer concentration. Point 3, which addresses the number of competitors in the industry, and Point 5, new entrants, may be factual statements but do not support the conclusion that consumers have strong bargaining power.

24.   a.   Product differentiation can be based on the product itself, the method of delivery, or the marketing approach.

25. A firm with a strategic planning process not guided by its generic competitive strategy usually makes one or more of the following mistakes:

    1. The strategic plan is a list of unrelated action items that do not lead to a sustainable competitive advantage.

    2. Price and cost forecasts are based on current market conditions and fail to take into account how industry structure will influence future long-term industry profitability.

    3. Business units are placed into categories such as build, hold, and harvest; with businesses failing to realize that these are not business strategies, but rather the means to achieve the strategy.

    4. The firm focuses on market share as a measure of competitive position, failing to realize that market share is the result and not the cause of a sustainable competitive position.

    Smith's observations 2 and 3 describe two of these mistakes and therefore do not support the conclusion that the North Winery's strategic planning process is guided and informed by their generic competitive strategy.

CFA PROBLEMS

1. a. Lowering reserve requirements would allow banks to lend out a higher fraction of deposits and thus increase the money supply.

    b. The Fed would buy Treasury securities, thereby increasing the money supply.

    c. The discount rate would be reduced, allowing banks to borrow additional funds at a lower rate.

2. a. Expansionary monetary policy is likely to increase the inflation rate, either because it may overstimulate the economy or ultimately because the end result of more money in the economy is higher prices.

    b. Real output and employment should increase in response to the expansionary policy, at least in the short run.

    c. The real interest rate should fall, at least in the short-run, as the supply of funds to the economy has increased.

    d. The nominal interest rate could either increase or decrease. On the one hand, the real rate might fall [see part (c)], but the inflation premium might rise [see part (a)]. The nominal rate is the sum of these two components.

3.   a.   The concept of an industrial life cycle refers to the tendency of most industries to go through various stages of growth. The rate of growth, the competitive environment, profit margins and pricing strategies tend to shift as an industry moves from one stage to the next, although it is generally difficult to identify precisely when one stage has ended and the next begun.

           The start-up stage is characterized by perceptions of a large potential market and by a high level of optimism for potential profits. However, this stage usually demonstrates a high rate of failure. In the second stage, often called *stable growth* or *consolidation*, growth is high and accelerating, the markets are broadening, unit costs are declining, and quality is improving. In this stage, industry leaders begin to emerge. The third stage, usually called *slowing growth* or *maturity*, is characterized by decelerating growth caused by factors such as maturing markets and/or competitive inroads by other products. Finally, an industry reaches a stage of relative decline in which sales slow or even decline.

           Product pricing, profitability, and industry competitive structure often vary by stage. Thus, for example, the first stage usually encompasses high product prices, high costs (R&D, marketing, etc.) and a (temporary) monopolistic industry structure. In stage two (stable growth), new entrants begin to appear and costs fall rapidly due to the learning curve. Prices generally do not fall as rapidly, however, allowing profit margins to increase. In stage three (slowing growth), growth begins to slow as the product or service begins to saturate the market, and margins are eroded by significant price reductions. In the final stage, industry cumulative production is so high that production costs have stopped declining, profit margins are thin (assuming competition exists), and the fate of the industry depends on replacement demand and the existence of substitute products/services.

     b.   The passenger car business in the United States has probably entered the final stage in the industrial life cycle because normalized growth is quite low. The information processing business, on the other hand, is undoubtedly earlier in the cycle. Depending on whether or not growth is still accelerating, it is either in the second or third stage.

     c.   Cars: In the final stages of the life cycle, demand tends to be price sensitive. Thus, Universal cannot raise prices without losing volume. Moreover, given the industry's maturity, cost structures are likely to be similar across all competitors, and any price cuts can be matched immediately. Thus, Universal's car business is boxed in: Product pricing is determined by the market, and the company is a "price-taker."

           Idata: Idata should have much more pricing flexibility given its earlier stage in the industrial life cycle. Demand is growing faster than supply, and depending on the presence and/or actions of an industry leader, Idata may set prices high to maximize current profits and generate cash for product development or set prices low in an effort to gain market share.

4.   a.   A basic premise of the business cycle approach to investment timing is that stock prices anticipate fluctuations in the business cycle. For example, there is evidence that stock prices tend to move about six months ahead of the economy. In fact, stock prices are a leading indicator for the economy.

Over the course of a business cycle, this approach to investing would work roughly as follows. As the investor perceives that the top of a business cycle is approaching, stocks purchased should not be vulnerable to a recession. When the investor perceives that a downturn is at hand, stock holdings should be lightened with proceeds invested in fixed-income securities. Once the recession has matured to some extent, and interest rates fall, bond prices will rise. As the investor perceives that the recession is about to end, profits should be taken in the bonds and reinvested in stocks, particularly those in cyclical industries with a high beta.

Generally, abnormal returns can be earned only if these asset allocation switches are timed better than those of other investors. Switches made after the turning points may not lead to excess returns.

   b.   Based on the business cycle approach to investment timing, the ideal time to invest in a cyclical stock such as a passenger car company would be just before the end of a recession. If the recovery is already underway, Adam's recommendation would be too late. The equities market generally anticipates the changes in the economic cycle. Therefore, since the "recovery is underway," the price of Universal Auto should already reflect the anticipated improvements in the economy.

5.   a.   • The industrywide ROE is leveling off, indicating that the industry may be approaching a later stage of the life cycle.

   • Average P/E ratios are declining, suggesting that investors are becoming less optimistic about growth prospects.

   • Dividend payout is increasing, suggesting that the firm sees less reason to reinvest earnings in the firm. There may be fewer growth opportunities in the industry.

   • Industry dividend yield is also increasing, even though market dividend yield is decreasing.

   b.   • Industry growth rate is still forecast at 10% to 15%, higher than would be true of a mature industry.

   • Non-U.S. markets are still untapped, and some firms are now entering these markets.

   • Mail order sale segment is growing at 40% a year.

   • Niche markets are continuing to develop.

   • New manufacturers continue to enter the market.

6.   a.   Relevant data from the table supporting the conclusion that the retail auto parts industry as a whole is in the maturity stage of the industry life cycle are:

   • The population of 18–29 year olds, a major customer base for the industry, is gradually declining.

- The number of households with income less than $35,000, another important consumer base, is not expanding.
- The number of cars 5 to 15 years old, an important end market, has experienced low annual growth (or actual decline in some years), so the number of units that potentially need parts is not growing.
- Automotive aftermarket industry retail sales have been growing slowly for several years.
- Consumer expenditures on automotive parts and accessories have grown slowly for several years.
- Average operating margins of all retail autoparts companies have steadily declined.

b. (i) Relevant data from the table supporting the conclusion that Wigwam Autoparts Heaven, Inc. (WAH) and its principal competitors are in the consolidation stage of their life cycle are:

- Sales growth of retail autoparts companies with 100 or more stores have been growing rapidly and at an increasing rate.
- Market share of retail autoparts stores with 100 or more stores has been increasing but is still less than 20 percent, leaving room for much more growth.
- Average operating margins for retail autoparts companies with 100 or more stores are high and rising.

(ii) Because of industry fragmentation (i.e., most of the market share is distributed among many companies with only a few stores), the retail autoparts industry apparently is undergoing marketing innovation and consolidation. The industry is moving toward the "category killer" format, in which a few major companies control large market shares through proliferation of outlets. The evidence suggests that a new "industry within an industry" is emerging in the form of the "category killer" large chain-store company. This industry subgroup is in its consolidation stage (i.e., rapid growth with high operating profit margins and emerging market leaders) despite the fact that the industry is in the maturity stage of its life cycle.

7. a. (iii)

   b. All of the above

   c. (iii)

CHAPTER 18: EQUITY VALUATION MODELS

PROBLEM SETS

1. Theoretically, dividend discount models can be used to value the stock of rapidly growing companies that do not currently pay dividends; in this scenario, we would be valuing expected dividends in the relatively more distant future. However, as a practical matter, such estimates of payments to be made in the more distant future are notoriously inaccurate, rendering dividend discount models problematic for valuation of such companies; free cash flow models are more likely to be appropriate. At the other extreme, one would be more likely to choose a dividend discount model to value a mature firm paying a relatively stable dividend.

2. It is most important to use multistage dividend discount models when valuing companies with temporarily high growth rates. These companies tend to be companies in the early phases of their life cycles, when they have numerous opportunities for reinvestment, resulting in relatively rapid growth and relatively low dividends (or, in many cases, no dividends at all). As these firms mature, attractive investment opportunities are less numerous so that growth rates slow.

3. The intrinsic value of a share of stock is the individual investor's assessment of the true worth of the stock. The market capitalization rate is the market consensus for the required rate of return for the stock. If the intrinsic value of the stock is equal to its price, then the market capitalization rate is equal to the expected rate of return. On the other hand, if the individual investor believes the stock is underpriced (i.e., intrinsic value > price), then that investor's expected rate of return is greater than the market capitalization rate.

4. First estimate the amount of each of the next two dividends and the terminal value. The current value is the sum of the present value of these cash flows, discounted at 8.5%.

5. The required return is 9%. $k = \dfrac{\$1.22 \times (1.05)}{\$32.03} + 0.05 = .09,$ or 9%

6. The Gordon DDM uses the dividend for period ($t+1$) which would be 1.05.

$$\$35 = \frac{\$1.05}{(k - 0.05)}$$

$$k = \frac{\$1.05}{\$35} + 0.05 = 0.08 = 8\%$$

7. The PVGO is $0.56:

$$PVGO = \$41 - \frac{\$3.64}{0.09} = \$0.56$$

8. a. $k = \dfrac{D_1}{P_0} + g$

$$0.16 = \frac{\$2}{\$50} + g \Rightarrow g = 0.12, \text{ or } 12\%$$

   b. $P_0 = \dfrac{D_1}{k-g} = \dfrac{\$2}{0.16 - 0.05} = \$18.18$

The price falls in response to the more pessimistic dividend forecast. The forecast for *current* year earnings, however, is unchanged. Therefore, the P/E ratio falls. The lower P/E ratio is evidence of the diminished optimism concerning the firm's growth prospects.

9. a. $g = \text{ROE} \times b = 16\% \times 0.5 = 8\%$

$$D_1 = \$2 \times (1-b) = \$2 \times (1-0.5) = \$1$$

$$P_0 = \frac{D_1}{k-g} = \frac{\$1}{0.12 - 0.08} = \$25.00$$

   b. $P_3 = P_0(1+g)^3 = \$25(1.08)^3 = \$31.49$

10. a. $k = r_f + \beta \times [E(r_m) - r_f] = 6\% + 1.25 \times (14\% - 6\%) = 16\%$

$$g = \frac{2}{3} \times 9\% = 6\%$$

$$D_1 = E_0 \times (1+g) \times (1-b) = \$3 \times (1.06) \times \frac{1}{3} = \$1.06$$

$$P_0 = \frac{D_1}{k-g} = \frac{\$1.06}{0.16 - 0.06} = \$10.60$$

   b. Leading $P_0/E_1 = \$10.60/\$3.18 = 3.33$

   Trailing $P_0/E_0 = \$10.60/\$3.00 = 3.53$

   c. $PVGO = P_0 - \dfrac{E_1}{k} = \$10.60 - \dfrac{\$3.18}{0.16} = -\$9.275$

The low P/E ratios and negative PVGO are due to a poor ROE (9%) that is less than the market capitalization rate (16%).

d. Now, you revise b to 1/3, g to $1/3 \times 9\% = 3\%$, and D_1 to:

$$E_0 \times (1 + g) \times (2/3)$$

$$\$3 \times 1.03 \times (2/3) = \$2.06$$

Thus:

$$V_0 = \$2.06/(0.16 - 0.03) = \$15.85$$

V_0 increases because the firm pays out more earnings instead of reinvesting a poor ROE. This information is not yet known to the rest of the market.

11. a. $$P_0 = \frac{D_1}{k-g} = \frac{\$8}{0.10-0.05} = \$160$$

b. The dividend payout ratio is $8/12 = 2/3$, so the plowback ratio is $b = 1/3$. The implied value of ROE on future investments is found by solving:

$$g = b \times \text{ROE with } g = 5\% \text{ and } b = 1/3 \Rightarrow \text{ROE} = 15\%$$

c. Assuming ROE = k, price is equal to:

$$P_0 = \frac{E_1}{k} = \frac{\$12}{0.10} = \$120$$

Therefore, the market is paying $40 per share ($160 − $120) for growth opportunities.

12. a. $k = D_1/P_0 + g$

$D_1 = 0.5 \times \$2 = \$1$

$g = b \times \text{ROE} = 0.5 \times 0.20 = 0.10$

Therefore: $k = (\$1/\$10) + 0.10 = 0.20$, or 20%

b. Since $k = \text{ROE}$, the NPV of future investment opportunities is zero:

$$PVGO = P_0 - \frac{E_1}{k} = \$10 - \$10 = 0$$

c. Since $k = \text{ROE}$, the stock price would be unaffected by cutting the dividend and investing the additional earnings.

13. a. $k = r_f + \beta \, [E(r_M) - r_f] = 8\% + 1.2(15\% - 8\%) = 16.4\%$

$g = b \times \text{ROE} = 0.6 \times 20\% = 12\%$

$$V_0 = \frac{D_0(1+g)}{k-g} = \frac{\$4 \times 1.12}{0.164 - 0.12} = \$101.82$$

b. $P_1 = V_1 = V_0(1 + g) = \$101.82 \times 1.12 = \$114.04$

$$E(r) = \frac{D_1 + P_1 - P_0}{P_0} = \frac{\$4.48 + \$114.04 - \$100}{\$100} = 0.1852, \text{ or } 18.52\%$$

14.

Time:	0	1	5	6
E_t	\$10.000	\$12.000	\$24.883	\$27.123
D_t	\$ 0.000	\$ 0.000	\$ 0.000	\$10.849
b	1.00	1.00	1.00	0.60
g	20.0%	20.0%	20.0%	9.0%

The year-6 earnings estimate is based on growth rate of $0.15 \times (1-.0.40) = 0.09$.

a. $V_5 = \dfrac{D_6}{k-g} = \dfrac{\$10.85}{0.15 - 0.09} = \$180.82 \Rightarrow$

$V_0 = \dfrac{V_5}{(1+k)^5} = \dfrac{\$180.82}{1.15^5} = \$89.90$

b. The price should rise by 15% per year until year 6: because there is no dividend, the entire return must be in capital gains.

c. The payout ratio would have no effect on intrinsic value because ROE = k.

15. a. The solution is shown in the Excel spreadsheet below:

Inputs			Year	Dividend	Div growth	erm value	nvestor CF	
beta	0.95		2012	0.78			0.78	
mkt_prem	0.08		2013	0.85			0.85	
rf	0.02		2014	0.93			0.93	
k_equity	0.0960		2015	1.00			1.00	
plowback	0.75		2016	1.09	0.0863		1.09	
roe	0.09		2017	1.18	0.0845		1.18	
term_gwt	0.068		2018	1.28	0.0826		1.28	
			2019	1.38	0.0807		1.38	
			2020	1.49	0.0788		1.49	
			2021	1.60	0.0769		1.60	
Value line			2022	1.72	0.0750		1.72	
forecasts of			2023	1.85	0.0732		1.85	
annual dividends			2024	1.98	0.0713		1.98	
			2025	2.12	0.0694		2.12	
			2026	2.26	0.0675		2.26	
Transitional period			2027	2.41	0.0675	90.33	92.75	
with slowing dividend								
growth							31.21	= PV of CF
	Beginning of constant			E17 * (1+ F17)/(B5 - F17)				
	growth period						NPV(B5,H2:H17)	

b., c. Using the Excel spreadsheet, we find that the intrinsic values are $33.80 and $32.80, respectively.

16. The solutions derived from Spreadsheet 18.2 are as follows:

	Intrinsic Value: FCFF	Intrinsic Value: FCFE	Intrinsic Value per Share: FCFF	Intrinsic Value per Share: FCFE
a.	100,000	75,128	38.89	41.74
b.	109,422	81,795	44.12	45.44
c.	89,693	66,014	33.16	36.67

17.

Time:	0	1	2	3
D_t	$1.0000	$1.2500	$1.5625	$1.953
g	25.0%	25.0%	25.0%	5.0%

a. The dividend to be paid at the end of year 3 is the first installment of a dividend stream that will increase indefinitely at the constant growth rate of 5%. Therefore, we can use the constant growth model as of the end of year 2 in order to calculate intrinsic value by adding the present value of the first two dividends plus the present value of the price of the stock at the end of year 2.

The expected price 2 years from now is:

$P_2 = D_3/(k - g) = \$1.953125/(0.20 - 0.05) = \$13.02$

The PV of this expected price is $13.02/1.20^2 = \$9.04$

The PV of expected dividends in years 1 and 2 is

$$\frac{\$1.25}{1.20} + \frac{\$1.5625}{1.20^2} = \$2.13$$

Thus the current price should be: $9.04 + $2.13 = $11.17

b. Expected dividend yield = $D_1/P_0 = \$1.25/\$11.17 = 0.112$, or 11.2%

c. The expected price one year from now is the PV at that time of P_2 and D_2:

$P_1 = (D_2 + P_2)/1.20 = (\$1.5625 + \$13.02)/1.20 = \$12.15$

The implied capital gain is

$(P_1 - P_0)/P_0 = (\$12.15 - \$11.17)/\$11.17 = 0.088 = 8.8\%$

The sum of the implied capital gains yield and the expected dividend yield is equal to the market capitalization rate. This is consistent with the DDM.

18.

Time:	0	1	4	5
E_t	$5.000	$6.000	$10.368	$10.368
D_t	$0.000	$0.000	$0.000	$10.368

Dividends = 0 for the next four years, so $b = 1.0$ (100% plowback ratio).

a. $P_4 = \dfrac{D_5}{k} = \dfrac{\$10.368}{0.15} = \$69.12$

(Since k=ROE, knowing the plowback rate is unnecessary)

$V_0 = \dfrac{P_4}{(1+k)^4} = \dfrac{\$69.12}{1.15^4} = \$39.52$

b. Price should increase at a rate of 15% over the next year, so that the HPR will equal k.

19.
Before-tax cash flow from operations	$2,100,000
Depreciation	210,000
Taxable Income	1,890,000
Taxes (@ 35%)	661,500
After-tax unleveraged income	1,228,500
After-tax cash flow from operations	
(After-tax unleveraged income + depreciation)	1,438,500
New investment (20% of cash flow from operations)	420,000
Free cash flow	
(After-tax cash flow from operations − new investment)	$1,018,500

The value of the firm (i.e., debt plus equity) is:

$V_0 = \dfrac{C_1}{k-g} = \dfrac{\$1,018,500}{0.12-0.05} = \$14,550,000$

Since the value of the debt is $4 million, the value of the equity is $10,550,000.

20. a. $g = \text{ROE} \times b = 20\% \times 0.5 = 10\%$

$P_0 = \dfrac{D_1}{k-g} = \dfrac{D_0(1+g)}{k-g} = \dfrac{\$0.50 \times 1.10}{0.15-0.10} = \$11$

b.

Time	EPS	Dividend	Comment
0	$1.0000	$0.5000	
1	1.1000	0.5500	$g = 10\%$, plowback = 0.50
2	1.2100	0.7260	EPS has grown by 10% based on last year's earnings plowback and ROE; this year's earnings plowback ratio now falls to 0.40 and payout ratio = 0.60
3	$1.2826	$0.7696	EPS grows by (0.4)(15%) = 6% and payout ratio = 0.60

At time 2: $P_2 = \dfrac{D_3}{k-g} = \dfrac{\$0.7696}{0.15-0.06} = \$8.551$

At time 0: $V_0 = \dfrac{\$0.55}{1.15} + \dfrac{\$0.726 + \$8.551}{(1.15)^2} = \$7.493$

c. $P_0 = \$11$ and $P_1 = P_0(1 + g) = \$12.10$

(Because the market is unaware of the changed competitive situation, it believes the stock price should grow at 10% per year.)

$P_2 = \$8.551$ *after* the market becomes aware of the changed competitive situation.

$P_3 = \$8.551 \times 1.06 = \$9.064$ (The new growth rate is 6%.)

Year	Return
1	$\dfrac{(\$12.10 - \$11) + \$0.55}{\$11} = 0.150, \text{ or } 15.0\%$
2	$\dfrac{(\$8.551 - \$12.10) + \$0.726}{\$12.10} = -0.233, \text{ or } -23.3\%$
3	$\dfrac{(\$9.064 - \$8.551) + \$0.7696}{\$8.551} = 0.150, \text{ or } 15.0\%$

Moral: In normal periods when there is no special information, the stock return = k = 15%. When special information arrives, all the abnormal return accrues *in that period*, as one would expect in an efficient market.

CFA PROBLEMS

1. a. This director is confused. In the context of the constant growth model [i.e., $P_0 = D_1 / k - g)$], it is true that price is higher when dividends are higher *holding everything else including dividend growth constant*. But everything else will not be constant. If the firm increases the dividend payout rate, the growth rate g will fall, and stock price will not necessarily rise. In fact, if ROE > k, price will fall.

   b. (i) An increase in dividend payout will reduce the sustainable growth rate as less funds are reinvested in the firm. The sustainable growth rate

      (i.e. ROE × plowback) will fall as plowback ratio falls.

      (ii) The increased dividend payout rate will reduce the growth rate of book value for the same reason – less funds are reinvested in the firm.

2. Using a two-stage dividend discount model, the current value of a share of Sundanci is calculated as follows.

$$V_0 = \frac{D_1}{(1+k)^1} + \frac{D_2}{(1+k)^2} + \frac{\dfrac{D_3}{(k-g)}}{(1+k)^2}$$

$$= \frac{\$0.3770}{1.14^1} + \frac{\$0.4976}{1.14^2} + \frac{\dfrac{\$0.5623}{(0.14-0.13)}}{1.14^2} = \$43.98$$

where:

$E_0 = \$0.952$

$D_0 = \$0.286$

$E_1 = E_0 (1.32)^1 = \$0.952 \times 1.32 = \$1.2566$

$D_1 = E_1 \times 0.30 = \$1.2566 \times 0.30 = \$0.3770$

$E_2 = E_0 (1.32)^2 = \$0.952 \times (1.32)^2 = \$1.6588$

$D_2 = E_2 \times 0.30 = \$1.6588 \times 0.30 = \$0.4976$

$E_3 = E_0 \times (1.32)^2 \times 1.13 = \$0.952 \times (1.32)^2 \times 1.13 = \$1.8744$

$D_3 = E_3 \times 0.30 = \$1.8743 \times 0.30 = \$0.5623$

3. a. Free cash flow to equity (FCFE) is defined as the cash flow remaining after meeting all financial obligations (including debt payment) and after covering capital expenditure and working capital needs. The FCFE is a measure of how much the firm can afford to pay out as dividends but, in a given year, may be more or less than the amount actually paid out.

Sundanci's FCFE for the year 2008 is computed as follows:

FCFE = Earnings + Depreciation − Capital expenditures − Increase in NWC

= $80 million + $23 million − $38 million − $41 million = $24 million

$$\text{FCFE per share} = \frac{FCFE}{\text{\# of shares outstanding}} = \frac{\$24 \text{ million}}{84 \text{ million shares}} = \$0.286$$

At this payout ratio, Sundanci's FCFE per share equals dividends per share.

b. The FCFE model requires forecasts of FCFE for the high growth years (2012 and 2013) plus a forecast for the first year of stable growth (2014) in order to allow for an estimate of the terminal value in 2013 based on perpetual growth. Because all of the components of FCFE are expected to grow at the same rate, the values can be obtained by projecting the FCFE at the common rate. (Alternatively, the components of FCFE can be projected and aggregated for each year.)

This table shows the process for estimating the current per share value:

FCFE Base Assumptions

Shares outstanding: 84 million, $k = 14\%$

	Total	Per Share	Actual 2011	Projected 2012	Projected 2013	Projected 2014
Growth rate (g)				27%	27%	13%
Earnings after tax	$80	$0.952		$1.2090	$ 1.5355	$1.7351
Plus: Depreciation expense	23	0.274		0.3480	0.4419	$0.4994
Less: Capital expenditures	38	0.452		0.5740	0.7290	$0.8238
Less: Increase in net working capital	41	0.488		0.6198	0.7871	$0.8894
Equals: FCFE	24	0.286		0.3632	0.4613	$0.5213
Terminal value					$52.1300*	
Total cash flows to equity				$0.3632	$52.5913†	
Discounted value				$0.3186‡	$40.4673‡	
Current value per share					$40.7859§	

*Projected 2013 terminal value = (Projected 2014 FCFE)/$(r - g)$

†Projected 2013 Total cash flows to equity =

  Projected 2013 FCFE + Projected 2013 terminal value

‡Discounted values obtained using $k = 14\%$

§Current value per share=Sum of discounted projected 2012 and 2013 total FCFE

  c. i. The DDM uses a strict definition of cash flows to equity, i.e. the expected dividends on the common stock. In fact, taken to its extreme, the DDM cannot be used to estimate the value of a stock that pays no dividends. The FCFE model expands the definition of cash flows to include the balance of residual cash flows after all financial obligations and investment needs have been met. Thus the FCFE model explicitly recognizes the firm's investment and financing policies as well as its dividend policy. In instances of a change of corporate control, and therefore the possibility of changing dividend policy, the FCFE model provides a better estimate of value. The DDM is biased toward finding low P/E ratio stocks with high dividend yields to be undervalued and conversely, high P/E ratio stocks with low dividend yields to be overvalued. It is considered a conservative model in that it tends to identify fewer undervalued firms as market prices rise relative to fundamentals. The DDM does not allow for the potential tax disadvantage of high dividends relative to the capital gains achievable from retention of earnings.

  ii. Both two-stage valuation models allow for two distinct phases of growth, an initial finite period where the growth rate is abnormal, followed by a stable growth period that is expected to last indefinitely. These two-stage models share the same limitations with respect to the growth assumptions. First, there is the difficulty of defining the duration of the extraordinary growth period. For example, a longer period of high growth will lead to a higher valuation, and there is the temptation to assume an unrealistically long period of extraordinary growth. Second, the assumption of a sudden shift from high growth to lower, stable growth is unrealistic. The transformation is more likely to occur gradually, over a period of time. Given that the assumed total horizon does not shift (i.e., is infinite), the timing of the shift from high to stable growth is a critical determinant of the valuation estimate. Third, because the value is quite sensitive to the steady-state growth assumption, over- or underestimating this rate can lead to large errors in value. The two models share other limitations as well, notably difficulties in accurately forecasting required rates of return, in dealing with the distortions that result from substantial and/or volatile debt ratios, and in accurately valuing assets that do not generate any cash flows.

4.   a.   The formula for calculating a price earnings ratio (P/E) for a stable growth firm is the dividend payout ratio divided by the difference between the required rate of return and the growth rate of dividends. If the P/E is calculated based on trailing earnings (year 0), the payout ratio is increased by the growth rate. If the P/E is calculated based on next year's earnings (year 1), the numerator is the payout ratio.

                P/E on trailing earnings:

$$P/E = [\text{payout ratio} \times (1 + g)]/(k - g) = [0.30 \times 1.13]/(0.14 - 0.13) = 33.9$$

                P/E on next year's earnings:

$$P/E = \text{payout ratio}/(k - g) = 0.30/(0.14 - 0.13) = 30.0$$

      b.   The P/E ratio is a decreasing function of riskiness; as risk increases, the P/E ratio decreases. Increases in the riskiness of Sundanci stock would be expected to lower the P/E ratio.

              The P/E ratio is an increasing function of the growth rate of the firm; the higher the expected growth, the higher the P/E ratio. Sundanci would command a higher P/E if analysts increase the expected growth rate.

              The P/E ratio is a decreasing function of the market risk premium. An increased market risk premium increases the required rate of return, lowering the price of a stock relative to its earnings. A higher market risk premium would be expected to lower Sundanci's P/E ratio.

5.   a.   The sustainable growth rate is equal to:

              Plowback ratio × Return on equity = b × ROE

$$\text{where } b = \frac{\text{Net income} - (\text{Dividends per share} \times \text{Shares outstanding})}{\text{Net income}}$$

              ROE = Net income/Beginning of year equity

CHAPTER 18: EQUITY VALUATION MODELS

In 2010:

$$b = [208 - (0.80 \times 100)]/208 = 0.6154$$

$$ROE = 208/1380 = 0.1507$$

Sustainable growth rate = $0.6154 \times 0.1507 = 9.3\%$

In 2013:

$$b = [275 - (0.80 \times 100)]/275 = 0.7091$$

$$ROE = 275/1836 = 0.1498$$

Sustainable growth rate = $0.7091 \times 0.1498 = 10.6\%$

b. i. The increased retention ratio increased the sustainable growth rate.

$$\text{Retention ratio} = \frac{[\text{Net income} - (\text{Dividend per share} \times \text{Shares outstanding})]}{\text{Net income}}$$

Retention ratio increased from 0.6154 in 2010 to 0.7091 in 2013.

This increase in the retention ratio directly increased the sustainable growth rate because the retention ratio is one of the two factors determining the sustainable growth rate.

ii. The decrease in leverage reduced the sustainable growth rate.

Financial leverage = (Total assets/Beginning of year equity)

Financial leverage decreased from 2.34 (3230/1380) at the beginning of 2010 to 2.10 at the beginning of 2013 (3856/1836)

This decrease in leverage directly decreased ROE (and thus the sustainable growth rate) because financial leverage is one of the factors determining ROE (and ROE is one of the two factors determining the sustainable growth rate).

6. a. The formula for the Gordon model is

$$V_0 = \frac{D_0 \times (1+g)}{k-g}$$

where:

D_0 = Dividend paid at time of valuation

g = Annual growth rate of dividends

k = Required rate of return for equity

In the above formula, P_0, the market price of the common stock, substitutes for V_0 and g becomes the dividend growth rate implied by the market:

$$P_0 = [D_0 \times (1+g)]/(k-g)$$

Substituting, we have:

$$58.49 = [0.80 \times (1+g)]/(0.08 - g) \Rightarrow g = 6.54\%$$

    b.   Use of the Gordon growth model would be inappropriate to value Dynamic's common stock, for the following reasons:

        i.   The Gordon growth model assumes a set of relationships about the growth rate for dividends, earnings, and stock values. Specifically, the model assumes that dividends, earnings, and stock values will grow at the same constant rate. In valuing Dynamic's common stock, the Gordon growth model is inappropriate because management's dividend policy has held dividends constant in dollar amount although earnings have grown, thus reducing the payout ratio. This policy is inconsistent with the Gordon model assumption that the payout ratio is constant.

        ii.   It could also be argued that use of the Gordon model, given Dynamic's current dividend policy, violates one of the general conditions for suitability of the model, namely that the company's dividend policy bears an understandable and consistent relationship with the company's profitability.

7.   a.   The industry's estimated P/E can be computed using the following model:

$$\frac{P_0}{E_1} = \frac{\text{Payout ratio}}{k - g}$$

However, since k and g are not explicitly given, they must be computed using the following formulas:

$$g_{ind} = \text{ROE} \times \text{Retention rate} = 0.25 \times 0.40 = 0.10$$

$$k_{ind} = \text{Government bond yield} + (\text{Industry beta} \times \text{Equity risk premium})$$

$$= 0.06 + (1.2 \times 0.05) = 0.12$$

Therefore: $$\frac{P_0}{E_1} = \frac{0.60}{0.12 - 0.10} = 30.0$$

    b. i.   Forecast growth in real GDP would cause P/E ratios to be generally higher for Country A. Higher expected growth in GDP implies higher earnings growth and a higher P/E.

        ii.   Government bond yield would cause P/E ratios to be generally higher for Country B. A lower government bond yield implies a lower risk-free rate and therefore a higher P/E.

        iii.   Equity risk premium would cause P/E ratios to be generally higher for Country B. A lower equity risk premium implies a lower required return and a higher P/E.

8.   a. $k = r_f + \beta (k_M - r_f) = 4.5\% + 1.15(14.5\% - 4.5\%) = 16\%$

    b.

Year		Dividend
2009		$1.72
2010	$1.72 \times 1.12 =$	$1.93
2011	$1.72 \times 1.12^2 =$	$2.16
2012	$1.72 \times 1.12^3 =$	$2.42
2013	$1.72 \times 1.12^3 \times 1.09 =$	$2.63

Present value of dividends paid in 2010 – 2012:

Year	PV of Dividend	
2010	$1.93/1.16^1 =$	$1.66
2011	$2.16/1.16^2 =$	$1.61
2012	$2.42/1.16^3 =$	$1.55
	Total =	$4.82

$$\text{Price at year-end } 2012 = \frac{D_{2013}}{k-g} = \frac{\$2.63}{0.16-0.09} = \$37.57$$

$$\text{PV in 2009 of this stock price} = \frac{\$37.57}{1.16^3} = \$24.07$$

Intrinsic value of stock = $4.82 + $24.07 = $28.89

c. The data in the problem indicate that Quick Brush is selling at a price substantially below its intrinsic value, while the calculations above demonstrate that SmileWhite is selling at a price somewhat above the estimate of its intrinsic value. Based on this analysis, Quick Brush offers the potential for considerable abnormal returns, while SmileWhite offers slightly below-market risk-adjusted returns.

d. Strengths of two-stage versus constant growth DDM:
- Two-stage model allows for separate valuation of two distinct periods in a company's future. This can accommodate life-cycle effects. It also can avoid the difficulties posed by initial growth that is higher than the discount rate.
- Two-stage model allows for initial period of above-sustainable growth. It allows the analyst to make use of her expectations regarding when growth might shift from off-trend to a more sustainable level.

A weakness of all DDMs is that they are very sensitive to input values. Small changes in k or g can imply large changes in estimated intrinsic value. These inputs are difficult to measure.

9. a. The value of a share of Rio National equity using the Gordon growth model and the capital asset pricing model is $22.40, as shown below.
Calculate the required rate of return using the capital asset pricing model:

$$k = r_f + \beta \times (k_M - r_f) = 4\% + 1.8 \times (9\% - 4\%) = 13\%$$

Calculate the share value using the Gordon growth model:

$$P_0 = \frac{D_o \times (1+g)}{k-g} = \frac{\$0.20 \times (1+0.12)}{0.13-0.12} = \$22.40$$

b. The sustainable growth rate of Rio National is 9.97%, calculated as follows:

$$g = b \times \text{ROE} = \text{Earnings retention rate} \times \text{ROE} = (1 - \text{Payout ratio}) \times \text{ROE} =$$

$$\left(1 - \frac{\text{Dividends}}{\text{Net income}}\right) \times \frac{\text{Net income}}{\text{Beginning equity}} = \left(1 - \frac{\$3.20}{\$30.16}\right) \times \frac{\$30.16}{\$270.35} = 0.0997 = 9.97\%$$

10. a. To obtain free cash flow to equity (FCFE), the two adjustments that Shaar should make to cash flow from operations (CFO) are:

   1. Subtract investment in fixed capital: CFO does not take into account the investing activities in long-term assets, particularly plant and equipment. The cash flows corresponding to those necessary expenditures are not available to equity holders and therefore should be subtracted from CFO to obtain FCFE.

   2. Add net borrowing: CFO does not take into account the amount of capital supplied to the firm by lenders (e.g., bondholders). The new borrowings, net of debt repayment, are cash flows available to equity holders and should be added to CFO to obtain FCFE.

   b. *Note 1*: Rio National had $75 million in capital expenditures during the year.

   Adjustment: negative $75 million

   The cash flows required for those capital expenditures (−$75 million) are no longer available to the equity holders and should be subtracted from net income to obtain FCFE.

   Note 2: A piece of equipment that was originally purchased for $10 million was sold for $7 million at year-end, when it had a net book value of $3 million. Equipment sales are unusual for Rio National.

   Adjustment: positive $3 million

   In calculating FCFE, only cash flow investments in fixed capital should be considered. The $7 million sale price of equipment is a cash inflow now available to equity holders and should be added to net income. However, the gain over book value that was realized when selling the equipment ($4 million) is already included in net income. Because the total sale is cash, not just the gain, the $3 million net book value must be added to net income. Therefore, the adjustment calculation is:

   $7 million in cash received −$4 million of gain recorded in net income =

   $3 million additional cash received added to net income to obtain FCFE.

   Note 3: The decrease in long-term debt represents an unscheduled principal repayment; there was no new borrowing during the year.

   Adjustment: negative $5 million

   The unscheduled debt repayment cash flow (−$5 million) is an amount no longer available to equity holders and should be subtracted from net income to determine FCFE.

   Note 4: On January 1, 2013, the company received cash from issuing 400,000 shares of common equity at a price of $25 per share.

   No adjustment

   Transactions between the firm and its shareholders do not affect FCFE. To calculate FCFE, therefore, no adjustment to net income is required with respect to the issuance of new shares.

Note 5: A new appraisal during the year increased the estimated market value of land held for investment by $2 million, which was not recognized in 2013 income.

No adjustment

The increased market value of the land did not generate any cash flow and was not reflected in net income. To calculate FCFE, therefore, no adjustment to net income is required.

c. Free cash flow to equity (FCFE) is calculated as follows:

FCFE = NI + NCC − FCINV − WCINV + Net borrowing

where:

        NCC = Noncash charges

        FCINV = Investment in fixed capital

        WCINV = Investment in working capital

	Million $	Explanation
NI =	$30.16	From Table 18G
NCC =	+$67.17	$71.17 (depreciation and amortization from Table 18G) − $4.00* (gain on sale from Note 2)
FCINV =	−$68.00	$75.00 (capital expenditures from Note 1) − $7.00* (cash on sale from Note 2)
WCINV =	−$24.00	−$3.00 (increase in accounts receivable from Table 18F) + −$20.00 (increase in inventory from Table 18F) + −$1.00 (decrease in accounts payable from Table 18F)
Net borrowing =	+(−$5.00)	−$5.00 (decrease in long-term debt from Table 18F)
FCFE =	$0.33	

*Supplemental Note 2 in Table 18H affects both NCC and FCINV.

11. Rio National's equity is relatively undervalued compared to the industry on a P/E-to-growth (PEG) basis. Rio National's PEG ratio of 1.33 is below the industry PEG ratio of 1.66. The lower PEG ratio is attractive because it implies that the growth rate at Rio National is available at a relatively lower price than is the case for the industry. The PEG ratios for Rio National and the industry are calculated below:

Rio National

Current price = $25.00

Normalized earnings per share = $1.71

Price-to-earnings ratio = $25/$1.71 = 14.62

Growth rate (as a percentage) = 11

PEG ratio = 14.62/11 = 1.33

Industry

Price-to-earnings ratio = 19.90

Growth rate (as a percentage) = 12

PEG ratio = 19.90/12 = 1.66

CHAPTER 19: FINANCIAL STATEMENT ANALYSIS

PROBLEM SETS

1. The major difference in approach of international financial reporting standards and U.S. GAAP accounting stems from the difference between principles and rules. U.S. GAAP accounting is rules-based, with extensive detailed rules to be followed in the preparation of financial statements; many international standards, European Union adapted IFRS, allow much greater flexibility, as long as conformity with general principles is demonstrated. Even though U.S. GAAP is generally more detailed and specific, issues of comparability still arise among U.S. companies. Comparability problems are still greater among companies in foreign countries.

2. Earnings management should not matter in a truly efficient market, where all publicly available information is reflected in the price of a share of stock. Investors can see through attempts to manage earnings so that they can determine a company's true profitability and, hence, the intrinsic value of a share of stock. However, if firms do engage in earnings management, then the clear implication is that managers do not view financial markets as efficient.

3. Both credit rating agencies and stock market analysts are likely to be more or less interested in all of the ratios discussed in this chapter (as well as many other ratios and forms of analysis). Since the Moody's and Standard and Poor's ratings assess bond default risk, these agencies are most interested in leverage ratios. A stock market analyst would be most interested in profitability and market price ratios.

4. $ROA = ROS \times ATO$

   The only way that Crusty Pie can have an ROS higher than the industry average and an ROA equal to the industry average is for its ATO to be lower than the industry average.

5. ABC's asset turnover must be above the industry average.

6. $ROE = (1 - \text{Tax rate})[ROA + (ROA - \text{Interest rate})\dfrac{\text{Debt}}{\text{Equity}}]$

   $ROE_A > ROE_B$

   Firms A and B have the same ROA. Assuming the same tax rate and assuming that ROA > interest rate, then Firm A must have either a lower interest rate or a higher debt ratio.

7.
$$\text{ROE} = \frac{\text{Net income}}{\text{Equity}} = \frac{\text{Net income}}{\text{Sales}} \times \frac{\text{Sales}}{\text{Assets}} \times \frac{\text{Assets}}{\text{Equity}}$$

$= \text{Net profit margin} \times \text{Asset turnover} \times \text{Leverage ratio}$

$= 5.5\% \times 2.0 \times 2.2 = 24.2\%$

8. a.   Lower bad debt expense will result in higher operating income.

   b.   Lower bad debt expense will have no effect on operating cash flow until Galaxy actually collects receivables.

9.   A. Certain GAAP rules can be exploited by companies in order to achieve specific goals, while still remaining within the letter of the law. Aggressive assumptions, such as lengthening the depreciable life of an asset (which are utilized to boost earnings) result in a lower quality of earnings.

10. A. Off-balance-sheet financing through the use of operating leases is acceptable when used appropriately. However, companies can use them too aggressively in order to reduce their perceived leverage. A comparison among industry peers and their practices may indicate improper use of accounting methods.

11. A. A warning sign of accounting manipulation is abnormal inventory growth as compared to sales growth. By overstating inventory, the cost of goods sold is lower, leading to higher profitability.

12.
$$\text{ROE} = (1-t) \times [\text{ROA} + (\text{ROA-Interest rate}) \times \frac{\text{Debt}}{\text{Equity}}]$$

$0.03 = (0.65) \times [\text{ROA} + (\text{ROA} - 0.06) \times 0.5]$

$0.03 = 0.975 \times \text{ROA} - 0.0195$

$0.975 \times \text{ROA} = 0.0495$

$\text{ROA} = 0.0508 = 5.08\%$

Alternatively,
$0.03 = 0.65 \times [\text{ROA} + (\text{ROA} - 0.06) \times 0.5]$
$0.0462 = [\text{ROA} + (\text{ROA} - 0.06) \times 0.5]$
$0.0462 = \text{ROA} + 0.5\text{ROA} - 0.03$
$0.0762 = \text{ROA} + 0.5\text{ROA}$
$0.0762 = 1.5\text{ROA}$
$0.0508 = \text{ROA}$

13. $\text{ROE} = \dfrac{\text{Net income}}{\text{Equity}} = \dfrac{\text{Net income}}{\text{Taxable income}} \times \dfrac{\text{Taxable income}}{\text{EBIT}} \times \dfrac{\text{EBIT}}{\text{Sales}} \times \dfrac{\text{Sales}}{\text{Assets}} \times \dfrac{\text{Assets}}{\text{Equity}}$

$\text{ROE} = 0.75 \times 0.6 \times 0.1 \times 2.40 \times 1.25 = .135 = 13.5\%$

14.

a. Cash flows from investing activities

Sale of old equipment	$72,000
Purchase of bus	(33,000)
Net cash used in investing activities	39,000

b. Cash flows from financing activities

Repurchase of stock	$(55,000)
Cash dividend	(80,000)
Net cash used in financing activities	(135,000)

c. Cash flows from operating activities

Cash collections from customers	$300,000
Cash payments to suppliers	(95,000)
Cash payments for interest	(25,000)
Net cash provided by operating activities	$180,000
Net increase in cash	$ 84,000

15. a. The total capital of the firms must first be calculated by adding their respective debt and equity together. The total capital for Acme is $100 + 50 = 150$, and the total capital for Apex is $450 + 150 = 600$. The economic value added will be the spread between the ROC and cost of capital multiplied by the total capital of the firm. Acme's EVA thus equals $(17\% - 9\%) \times 150 = 12$ (million). Apex's EVA equals $(15\% - 10\%) \times 600 = 30$ (mil). Notice that even though Apex's spread is smaller, their larger capital stock allows them more economic value added.

b. However, since Apex has a larger capital stock, it's EVA per dollar invested in capital is smaller at $30/600 = .05$ compared to Acme's $12/150 = .08$.

CFA PROBLEMS

1. SmileWhite has higher quality of earnings for the following reasons:

- SmileWhite amortizes its goodwill over a shorter period than does QuickBrush. SmileWhite therefore presents more conservative earnings because it has greater goodwill amortization expense.

- SmileWhite depreciates its property, plant and equipment using an accelerated depreciation method. This results in recognition of depreciation expense sooner and also implies that its income is more conservatively stated.

- SmileWhite's bad debt allowance is greater as a percentage of receivables. SmileWhite is recognizing greater bad-debt expense than QuickBrush. If actual collection experience will be comparable, then SmileWhite has the more conservative recognition policy.

2. a. $$ROE = \frac{Net\ profits}{Equity} = \frac{Net\ profits}{Sales} \times \frac{Sales}{Assets} \times \frac{Assets}{Equity}$$

   $$= Net\ profit\ margin \times Total\ asset\ turnover \times Assets/equity$$

   $$\frac{Net\ profits}{Sales} = \frac{475}{4750} = 0.100 = 10\% \qquad \frac{Sales}{Assets} = \frac{4,750}{2,950} = 1.61$$

   $$\frac{Assets}{Equity} = \frac{2,950}{2,100} = 1.40$$

   b. $$ROE = \frac{475}{4,750} \times \frac{4,750}{2,950} \times \frac{2,950}{2,100} = 10\% \times 1.61 \times 1.40 = .2262,\ or\ 22.62\%$$

   c. $$g = ROE \times Plowback = 22.62\% \times \frac{1.79 - 0.55}{1.79} = 15.67\%$$

3. a. CF from operating activities = $260 − $85 − $12 − $35 = $128

   b. CF from investing activities = −$8 + $30 − $40 = −$18

   c. CF from financing activities = −$32 − $37 = −$69

4. a. QuickBrush has had higher sales and earnings growth (per share) than SmileWhite. Margins are also higher. But this does not mean that QuickBrush is necessarily a better investment. SmileWhite has a higher ROE, which has been stable, while QuickBrush's ROE has been declining. We can see the source of the difference in ROE using DuPont analysis:

Component	Definition	QuickBrush	SmileWhite
Tax burden $(1 - t)$	Net profits/pretax profits	67.4%	66.0%
Interest burden	Pretax profits/EBIT	1.000	0.955
Profit margin	EBIT/Sales	8.5%	6.5%
Asset turnover	Sales/Assets	1.42	3.55
Leverage	Assets/Equity	1.47	1.48
ROE	Net profits/Equity	12.0%	21.4%

While tax burden, interest burden, and leverage are similar, profit margin and asset turnover differ. Although SmileWhite has a lower profit margin, it has a far higher asset turnover.

Sustainable growth = ROE × Plowback ratio

	ROE	Plowback Ratio	Sustainable Growth Rate	Ludlow's Estimate of Growth Rate
QuickBrush	12.0%	1.00	12.0%	30%
SmileWhite	21.4	0.34	7.3	10

Ludlow has overestimated the sustainable growth rate for both companies. QuickBrush has little ability to increase its sustainable growth—plowback already equals 100%. SmileWhite could increase its sustainable growth by increasing its plowback ratio.

b. QuickBrush's recent EPS growth has been achieved by increasing book value per share, not by achieving greater profits per dollar of equity. A firm can increase EPS even if ROE is declining as is true of QuickBrush. QuickBrush's book value per share has more than doubled in the last two years.

Book value per share can increase either by retaining earnings or by issuing new stock at a market price greater than book value. QuickBrush has been retaining all earnings, but the increase in the number of outstanding shares indicates that it has also issued a substantial amount of stock.

5. a. ROE = Operating margin × Interest burden × Asset turnover × Leverage × Tax burden
ROE for Eastover (EO) and for Southampton (SHC) in 2013 is found as follows:

$$\text{Profit margin} = \frac{\text{EBIT}}{\text{Sales}}$$
SHC: 145/1,793 = 8.1%
EO: 795/7,406 = 10.7%

$$\text{Interest burden} = \frac{\text{Pretax profits}}{\text{EBIT}}$$
SHC: 137/145 = 0.94
EO: 600/795 = 0.75

$$\text{Asset turnover} = \frac{\text{Sales}}{\text{Assets}}$$
SHC: 1,793/2,104 = 0.85
EO: 7,406/8,265 = 0.90

$$\text{Leverage} = \frac{\text{Assets}}{\text{Equity}}$$
SHC: 2,104/1,167 = 1.80
EO: 8,265/3,864 = 2.14

$$\text{Tax burden} = \frac{\text{Net profits}}{\text{Pretax profits}}$$
SHC: 91/137 = 0.66
EO: 394/600 = 0.66

ROE
SHC: 7.8%
EO: 10.2%

b. The differences in the components of ROE for Eastover and Southampton are:

Profit margin   EO has a higher margin.

Interest burden   EO has a higher interest burden because its pretax profits are a lower percentage of EBIT.

Asset turnover   EO is more efficient at turning over its assets.

Leverage   EO has higher financial leverage.

Tax burden   No major difference here between the two companies ROE. EO has a higher ROE than SHC, but this is only in part due to higher margins and a better asset turnover. Greater financial leverage also plays a part.

c.   The sustainable growth rate can be calculated as ROE times plowback ratio. The sustainable growth rates for Eastover and Southampton are as follows:

	ROE	Plowback Ratio*	Sustainable Growth Rate
Eastover	10.2%	0.36	3.7%
Southampton	7.8	0.58	4.5

*Plowback = (1 − Payout ratio)

EO: Plowback = (1 − 0.64) = 0.36

SHC: Plowback = (1 − 0.42) = 0.58

The sustainable growth rates derived in this manner are not likely to be representative of future growth because 2013 was probably not a "normal" year. For Eastover, earnings had not yet recovered to 2010–2011 levels; earnings retention of only 0.36 seems low for a company in a capital intensive industry. Southampton's earnings fell by over 50 percent in 2013 and its earnings retention will probably be higher than 0.58 in the future. There is a danger, therefore, in basing a projection on one year's results, especially for companies in a cyclical industry such as forest products.

6.   a.   The formula for the constant growth discounted dividend model is

$$P_0 = \frac{D_0(1+g)}{k-g}$$

For Eastover:

$$P_0 = \frac{\$1.20 \times 1.08}{0.11-0.08} = \$43.20$$

This compares with the current stock price of $28. On this basis, it appears that Eastover is undervalued.

b.   The formula for the two-stage discounted dividend model is

$$P_0 = \frac{D_1}{(1+k)^1} + \frac{D_2}{(1+k)^2} + \frac{D_3}{(1+k)^3} + \frac{P_3}{(1+k)^3}$$

For Eastover: $g_1 = 0.12$ and $g_2 = 0.08$

$D_0 = 1.20$

$D_1 = D_0 (1.12)^1 = \$1.34$

$D_2 = D_0 (1.12)^2 = \$1.51$

$D_3 = D_0 (1.12)^3 = \$1.69$

$$D_4 = D_0 (1.12)^3 (1.08) = \$1.82$$

$$P_3 = \frac{D_4}{k - g_2} = \frac{\$1.82}{0.11 - 0.08} = \$60.67$$

$$P_0 = \frac{\$1.34}{(1.11)^1} + \frac{\$1.51}{(1.11)^2} + \frac{\$1.69}{(1.11)^3} + \frac{\$60.67}{(1.11)^3} = \$48.03$$

Alternatively, CF 0 = $0; CF 1 = $1.34; CF 2 = $1.51; CF 3 = $1.69 + $60.67; I = 11; Solve for NPV = $48.03.

This approach makes Eastover appear even more undervalued than was the case using the constant growth approach.

c. Advantages of the constant growth model include: (1) logical, theoretical basis; (2) simple to compute; (3) inputs can be estimated.

Disadvantages include: (1) very sensitive to estimates of growth; (2) g and k difficult to estimate accurately; (3) only valid for $g < k$; (4) constant growth is an unrealistic assumption; (5) assumes growth will never slow down; (6) dividend payout must remain constant; (7) not applicable for firms not paying dividends.

Improvements offered by the two-stage model include:

(1) The two-stage model is more realistic. It accounts for low, high, or zero growth in the first stage, followed by constant long-term growth in the second stage.

(2) The model can be used to determine stock value when the growth rate in the first stage exceeds the required rate of return.

7. a. In order to determine whether a stock is undervalued or overvalued, analysts often compute price-earnings ratios (P/Es) and price-book ratios (P/Bs); then, these ratios are compared to benchmarks for the market, such as the S&P 500 index. The formulas for these calculations are:

$$\text{Relative P/E} = \frac{\text{P/E of specific company}}{\text{P/E of S\&P 500}}$$

$$\text{Relative P/B} = \frac{\text{P/B of specific company}}{\text{P/B of S\&P 500}}$$

To evaluate EO and SHC using a relative P/E model, Mulroney can calculate the five-year average P/E for each stock and divide that number by the five-year average P/E for the S&P 500 (shown in the last column of Table 19E). This gives the historical average relative P/E. Mulroney can then compare the average historical relative P/E to the current relative P/E (i.e., the current P/E on each stock, using the estimate of this year's earnings per share in Table 19F, divided by the current P/E of the market).

For the price/book model, Mulroney should make similar calculations, i.e., divide the five-year average price-book ratio for a stock by the five year average price/book for the S&P 500, and compare the result to the current relative price/book (using current book value). The results are as follows:

P/E model	EO	SHC	S&P500
5-year average P/E	16.56	11.94	15.20
Relative 5-year P/E	1.09	0.79	
Current P/E	17.50	16.00	20.20
Current relative P/E	0.87	0.79	

Price/Book model	EO	SHC	S&P500
5-year average price/book	1.52	1.10	2.10
Relative 5-year price/book	0.72	0.52	
Current price/book	1.62	1.49	2.60
Current relative price/book	0.62	0.57	

From this analysis, it is evident that EO is trading at a discount to its historical five-year relative P/E ratio, whereas Southampton is trading right at its historical five-year relative P/E. With respect to price/book, Eastover is trading at a discount to its historical relative price/book ratio, whereas SHC is trading modestly above its five-year relative price/book ratio. As noted in the preamble to the problem (see CFA Problem 5), Eastover's book value is understated due to the very low historical cost basis for its timberlands. The fact that Eastover is trading below its five-year average relative price to book ratio, even though its book value is understated, makes Eastover seem especially attractive on a price/book basis.

b. Disadvantages of the relative P/E model include: (1) the relative P/E measures only relative, rather than absolute, value; (2) the accounting earnings estimate for the next year may not equal sustainable earnings; (3) accounting practices may not be standardized; (4) changing accounting standards may make historical comparisons difficult.

Disadvantages of the relative P/B model include: (1) book value may be understated or overstated, particularly for a company like Eastover, which has valuable assets on its books carried at low historical cost; (2) book value may not be representative of earning power or future growth potential; (3) changing accounting standards make historical comparisons difficult.

8. The following table summarizes the valuation and ROE for Eastover and Southampton:

	Eastover	Southampton
Stock price	$28.00	$48.00
Constant-growth model	$43.20	$29.00
2-stage growth model	$48.03	$35.50
Current P/E	17.50	16.00
Current relative P/E	0.87	0.79
5-year average P/E	16.56	11.94
Relative 5 year P/E	1.09	0.79
Current P/B	1.62	1.49
Current relative P/B	0.62	0.57
5-year average P/B	1.52	1.10

Relative 5 year P/B	0.72	0.52
Current ROE	10.2%	7.8%
Sustainable growth rate	3.7%	4.5%

Eastover seems to be undervalued according to each of the discounted dividend models. Eastover also appears to be cheap on both a relative P/E and a relative P/B basis. Southampton, on the other hand, looks overvalued according to each of the discounted dividend models and is slightly overvalued using the relative price/book model. On a relative P/E basis, SHC appears to be fairly valued. Southampton does have a slightly higher sustainable growth rate, but not appreciably so, and its ROE is less than Eastover's.

The current P/E for Eastover is based on relatively depressed current earnings, yet the stock is still attractive on this basis. In addition, the price/book ratio for Eastover is overstated due to the low historical cost basis used for the timberland assets. This makes Eastover seem all the more attractive on a price/book basis. Based on this analysis, Mulroney should select Eastover over Southampton.

9. a. Net income can increase even while cash flow from operations decreases. This can occur if there is a buildup in net working capital—for example, increases in accounts receivable or inventories, or reductions in accounts payable. Lower depreciation expense will also increase net income but can reduce cash flow through the impact on taxes owed.

    b. Cash flow from operations might be a good indicator of a firm's quality of earnings because it shows whether the firm is actually generating the cash necessary to pay bills and dividends without resorting to new financing. Cash flow is less susceptible to arbitrary accounting rules than net income is.

10. $1,200

    Cash flow from operations = Sales − Cash expenses − Increase in A/R

    Ignore depreciation because it is a noncash item and its impact on taxes is already accounted for.

11. Both current assets and current liabilities will decrease by equal amounts. But this is a larger percentage decrease for current liabilities because the initial current ratio is above 1.0. So the current ratio increases. Total assets are lower, so turnover increases.

12. Considering the components of after-tax ROE, there are several possible explanations for a stable after-tax ROE despite declining operating income:

    1. Declining operating income could have been offset by an increase in nonoperating income (i.e., from discontinued operations, extraordinary gains, gains from changes in accounting policies) because both are components of profit margin (net income/sales).

    2. Another offset to declining operating income could have been declining interest rates on any interest rate obligations, which would have decreased interest expense while allowing pretax margins to remain stable.

3. Leverage could have increased as a result of a decline in equity from: (a) writing down an equity investment; (b) stock repurchases, (c) losses; or (d) selling new debt. The effect of the increased leverage could have offset a decline in operating income.

4. An increase in asset turnover could also offset a decline in operating income. Asset turnover could increase as a result of a sales growth rate that exceeds the asset growth rate, or from the sale or write-off of assets.

5. If the effective tax rate declined, the resulting increase in earnings after tax could offset a decline in operating income. The decline in effective tax rates could result from increased tax credits, the use of tax loss carry-forwards, or a decline in the statutory tax rate.

13. **a.**

		2010	2014
(1) Operating margin =	$\dfrac{\text{Operating income - Depreciation}}{\text{Sales}}$	$\dfrac{38-3}{542} = 6.5\%$	$\dfrac{76-9}{979} = 6.8\%$
(2) Asset turnover =	$\dfrac{\text{Sales}}{\text{Total assets}}$	$\dfrac{542}{245} = 2.21$	$\dfrac{979}{291} = 3.36$
(3) Interest burden =	$\dfrac{[\text{Op Inc} - \text{Dep}] - \text{Int Expense}}{\text{Operating Income} - \text{Depreciation}}$	$\dfrac{38-3-3}{38-3} = 0.914$	1.0
(4) Financial leverage =	$\dfrac{\text{Total assets}}{\text{Shareholders' equity}}$	$\dfrac{245}{159} = 1.54$	$\dfrac{291}{220} = 1.32$
(5) Income tax rate =	$\dfrac{\text{Income taxes}}{\text{Pretax income}}$	$\dfrac{13}{32} = 40.63\%$	$\dfrac{37}{67} = 55.22\%$

Using the Du Pont formula:

ROE = [1.0 – (5)] × (3) × (1) × (2) × (4)

ROE(2007) = 0.5937 × 0.914 × 0.065 × 2.21 × 1.54 = 0.120 = 12.0%

ROE(2011) = 0.4478 × 1.0 × 0.068 × 3.36 × 1.32 = 0.135 = 13.5%

Because of rounding error, these results differ slightly from those obtained by directly calculating ROE as net income/equity.)

b. Asset turnover measures the ability of a company to minimize the level of assets (current or fixed) to support its level of sales. The asset turnover increased substantially over the period, thus contributing to an increase in the ROE.

Financial leverage measures the amount of financing other than equity, including short- and long-term debt. Financial leverage declined over the period, thus adversely affecting the ROE. Since asset turnover rose substantially more than financial leverage declined, the net effect was an increase in ROE.

CHAPTER 20: OPTIONS MARKETS: INTRODUCTION

PROBLEM SETS

1. Options provide numerous opportunities to modify the risk profile of a portfolio. The simplest example of an option strategy that increases risk is investing in an 'all options' portfolio of at the money options (as illustrated in the text). The leverage provided by options makes this strategy very risky, and potentially very profitable. An example of a risk-reducing options strategy is a protective put strategy. Here, the investor buys a put on an existing stock or portfolio, with exercise price of the put near or somewhat less than the market value of the underlying asset. This strategy protects the value of the portfolio because the minimum value of the stock-plus-put strategy is the exercise price of the put.

2. Buying a put option on an existing portfolio provides *portfolio insurance,* which is protection against a decline in the value of the portfolio. In the event of a decline in value, the minimum value of the put-plus-stock strategy is the exercise price of the put. As with any insurance purchased to protect the value of an asset, the trade-off an investor faces is the cost of the put versus the protection against a decline in value. The cost of the protection is the cost of acquiring the protective put, which reduces the profit that results should the portfolio increase in value.

3. An investor who writes a call on an existing portfolio takes a *covered call* position. If, at expiration, the value of the portfolio exceeds the exercise price of the call, the writer of the covered call can expect the call to be exercised, so that the writer of the call must sell the portfolio at the exercise price. Alternatively, if the value of the portfolio is less than the exercise price, the writer of the call keeps both the portfolio and the premium paid by the buyer of the call. The trade-off for the writer of the covered call is the premium income received versus forfeit of any possible capital appreciation above the exercise price of the call.

4. An option is out of the money when exercise of the option would be unprofitable. A call option is out of the money when the market price of the underlying stock is less than the exercise price of the option. If the stock price is substantially less than the exercise price, then the likelihood that the option will be exercised is low, and fluctuations in the market price of the stock have relatively little impact on the value of the option. This sensitivity of the option price to changes in the price of the stock is called the option's delta, which is discussed in detail in Chapter 21. For options that are far out of the money, delta is close to zero. Consequently, there is generally little to be gained or lost by buying or writing a call that is far out of the money. (A similar result applies to a put option that is far out of the money, with stock price substantially greater than exercise price.)

A call is in the money when the market price of the stock is greater than the exercise price of the option. If stock price is substantially greater than exercise price, then the price of the option approaches the order of magnitude of the price of the stock. Also, since such an option is very likely to be exercised, the sensitivity of the option price to changes in stock price approaches one, indicating that a $1 increase in the price of the stock results in a $1 increase in the price of the option. Under these circumstances, the buyer of an option loses the benefit of the leverage provided by options that are near the money. Consequently, there is little interest in options that are far in the money.

5.

		Cost	Payoff	Profit
a.	Call option, $X = \$190.00$	$6.75	$5.00	-$1.75
b.	Put option, $X = \$190.00$	3.00	0.00	-3.00
c.	Call option, $X = \$195.00$	3.65	0.00	-3.65
d.	Put option, $X = \$195.00$	5.00	0.00	-5.00
e.	Call option, $X = \$200.00$	1.61	0.00	-1.61
f.	Put option, $X = \$200.00$	8.09	5.00	-3.09

6. In terms of dollar returns, based on a $10,000 investment:

	Price of Stock 6 Months from Now			
Stock Price	$ 80	$ 100	$ 110	$ 120
All stocks (100 shares)	8,000	10,000	11,000	12,000
All options (1,000 options)	0	0	10,000	20,000
Bills + 100 options	9,360	9,360	10,360	11,360

In terms of rate of return, based on a $10,000 investment:

	Price of Stock 6 Months from Now			
Stock Price	$80	$100	$110	$120
All stocks (100 shares)	-20%	0%	10%	20%
All options (1,000 options)	-100	-100	0	100
Bills + 100 options	-6.4	-6.4	3.6	13.6

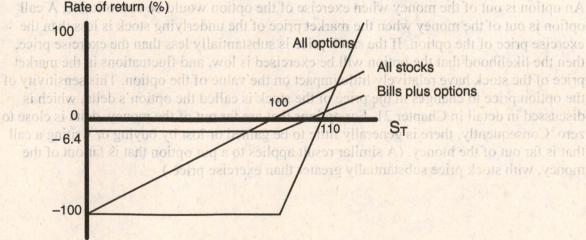

7. a. From put-call parity:

$$P = C - S_0 + \frac{X}{(1+r_f)^T} = 10 - 100 + \frac{100}{1.10^{.25}} = \$7.65$$

   b. Purchase a straddle, i.e., both a put and a call on the stock. The total cost of the straddle is $10 + $7.65 = $17.65

---

8. a. From put-call parity:

$$C = P + S_0 - \frac{X}{(1+r_f)^T} = 4 + 50 - \frac{50}{1.10^{.25}} = \$5.18$$

   b. Sell a straddle, i.e., sell a call and a put, to realize premium income of

   $5.18 + $4 = $9.18

   If the stock ends up at $50, both of the options will be worthless and your profit will be $9.18. This is your maximum possible profit since, at any other stock price, you will have to pay off on either the call or the put. The stock price can move by $9.18 in either direction before your profits become negative.

   c. Buy the call, sell (write) the put, lend $50/(1.10)^{1/4}$

   The payoff is as follows:

Position	Immediate CF	CF in 3 months	
		$S_T \leq X$	$S_T > X$
Call (long)	$C = 5.18$	0	$S_T - 50$
Put (short)	$-P = 4.00$	$-(50 - S_T)$	0
Lending position	$\dfrac{50}{1.10^{1/4}} = 48.82$	50	50
Total	$C - P + \dfrac{50}{1.10^{1/4}} = 50.00$	S_T	S_T

   By the put-call parity theorem, the initial outlay equals the stock price:

   $S_0 = \$50$

   In either scenario, you end up with the same payoff as you would if you bought the stock itself.

9. a. i. A long straddle produces gains if prices move up or down and limited losses if prices do not move. A short straddle produces significant losses if prices move significantly up or down. A bullish spread produces limited gains if prices move up.

   b. i. Long put positions gain when stock prices fall and produce very limited losses if prices instead rise. Short calls also gain when stock prices fall but create losses if prices instead rise. The other two positions will not protect the portfolio should prices fall.

10. Note that the price of the put equals the revenue from writing the call, net initial cash outlays = $38.00. The

Position	$S_T < 35$	$35 \le S_T \le 40$	$40 < S_T$
Buy stock	S_T	S_T	S_T
Write call ($40)	0	0	$40 - S_T$
Buy put ($35)	$35 - S_T$	0	0
Total	$35	S_T	$40

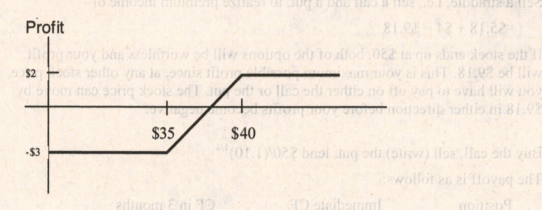

11. Answers may vary. For $5,000 initial outlay, buy 5,000 puts, write 5,000 calls:

Position	$S_T = \$30$	$S_T = \$40$	$S_T = \$50$
Stock portfolio	$150,000	$200,000	$250,000
Write call(X=$45)	0	0	−$ 25,000
Buy put (X=$35)	$ 25,000	0	0
Initial outlay	−$5,000	−$ 5,000	−$ 5,000
Portfolio value	$170,000	$195,000	$220,000

Compare this to just holding the portfolio:

Position	$S_T = \$30$	$S_T = \$40$	$S_T = \$50$
Stock portfolio	$150,000	$200,000	$250,000
Portfolio value	$150,000	$200,000	$250,000

12. a.

Outcome	$S_T \leq X$	$S_T > X$
Stock	$S_T + D$	$S_T + D$
Put	$X - S_T$	0
Total	$X + D$	$S_T + D$

b.

Outcome	$S_T \leq X$	$S_T > X$
Call	0	$S_T - X$
Zeros	$X + D$	$X + D$
Total	$X + D$	$S_T + D$

The total payoffs for the two strategies are equal regardless of whether S_T exceeds X.

c. The cost of establishing the stock-plus-put portfolio is: $S_0 + P$
The cost of establishing the call-plus-zero portfolio is: $C + PV(X + D)$
Therefore:

$$S_0 + P = C + PV(X + D)$$

This result is identical to equation 20.2.

13. a.

Position	$S_T < X_1$	$X_1 \leq S_T \leq X_2$	$X_2 < S_T \leq X_3$	$X_3 < S_T$
Long call (X_1)	0	$S_T - X_1$	$S_T - X_1$	$S_T - X_1$
Short 2 calls (X_2)	0	0	$-2(S_T - X_2)$	$-2(S_T - X_2)$
Long call (X_3)	0	0	0	$S_T - X_3$
Total	0	$S_T - X_1$	$2X_2 - X_1 - S_T$	$(X_2 - X_1) - (X_3 - X_2) = 0$

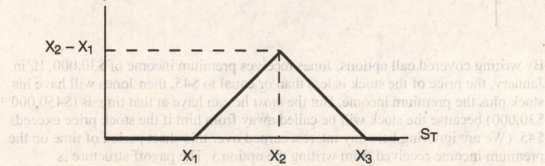

b.

Position	$S_T < X_1$	$X_1 \leq S_T \leq X_2$	$X_2 < S_T$
Buy call (X_2)	0	0	$S_T - X_2$
Buy put (X_1)	$X_1 - S_T$	0	0
Total	$X_1 - S_T$	0	$S_T - X_2$

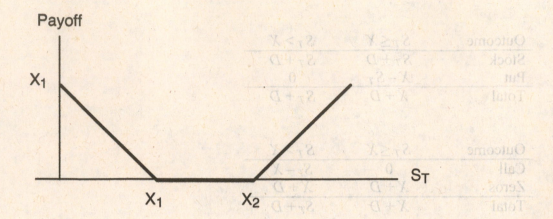

14.

Position	$S_T < X_1$	$X_1 \leq S_T \leq X_2$	$X_2 < S_T$
Buy call (X_2)	0	0	$S_T - X_2$
Sell call (X_1)	0	$-(S_T - X_1)$	$-(S_T - X_1)$
Total	0	$X_1 - S_T$	$X_1 - X_2$

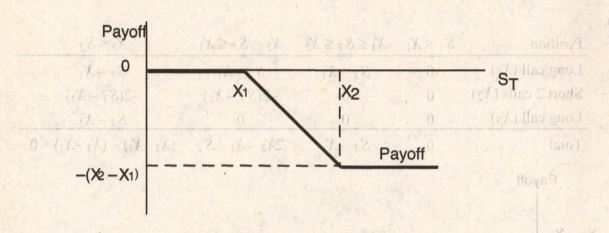

15. a. By writing covered call options, Jones receives premium income of $30,000. If, in January, the price of the stock is less than or equal to $45, then Jones will have his stock plus the premium income. But the *most* he can have at that time is ($450,000 + $30,000) because the stock will be called away from him if the stock price exceeds $45. (We are ignoring here any interest earned over this short period of time on the premium income received from writing the option.) The payoff structure is

Stock price	Portfolio value
less than $45	10,000 times stock price + $30,000
greater than $45	$450,000 + $30,000 = $480,000

This strategy offers some extra premium income but leaves Jones subject to substantial downside risk. At an extreme, if the stock price fell to zero, Jones would be left with only $30,000. This strategy also puts a cap on the final value at $480,000, but this is more than sufficient to purchase the house.

b. By buying put options with a $35 strike price, Jones will be paying $30,000 in premiums in order to ensure a minimum level for the final value of his position. That minimum value is ($35 × 10,000) – $30,000 = $320,000.

This strategy allows for upside gain, but exposes Jones to the possibility of a moderate loss equal to the cost of the puts. The payoff structure is:

Stock price	Portfolio value
less than $35	$350,000 – $30,000 = $320,000
greater than $35	10,000 times stock price – $30,000

c. The net cost of the collar is zero. The value of the portfolio will be as follows:

Stock price	Portfolio value
less than $35	$350,000
between $35 and $45	10,000 times stock price
greater than $45	$450,000

If the stock price is less than or equal to $35, then the collar preserves the $350,000 principal. If the price exceeds $45, then Jones gains up to a cap of $450,000. In between $35 and $45, his proceeds equal 10,000 times the stock price.

The best strategy in this case would be (c) since it satisfies the two requirements of preserving the $350,000 in principal while offering a chance of getting $450,000. Strategy (a) should be ruled out since it leaves Jones exposed to the risk of substantial loss of principal.

Our ranking would be: (1) strategy c; (2) strategy b; (3) strategy a.

16. Using Excel, with Profit Diagram on next page.

Stock Prices						Price	Profit
Beginning Market Price	116.5					**Price**	**Profit**
Ending Market Price	130					**Ending**	**Straddle**
Buying Options:						50	42.80
Call Options Strike	**Price**	**Payoff**	**Profit**	**Return %**		60	32.80
110	22.80	20.00	–2.80	–12.28%		70	22.80
120	16.80	10.00	–6.80	–40.48%		80	12.80
130	13.60	0.00	–13.60	–100.00%		90	2.80
140	10.30	0.00	–10.30	–100.00%		100	–7.20

Put Options Strike	Price	Payoff	Profit	Return %
110	12.60	0.00	−12.60	−100.00%
120	17.20	0.00	−17.20	−100.00%
130	23.60	0.00	−23.60	−100.00%
140	30.50	10.00	−20.50	−67.21%

Straddle	Price	Payoff	Profit	Return %
110	35.40	20.00	−15.40	−43.50%
120	34.00	10.00	−24.00	−70.59%
130	37.20	0.00	−37.20	−100.00%
140	40.80	10.00	−30.80	−75.49%

Selling Options:

Call Options Strike	Price	Payoff	Profit	Return %
110	22.80	−20	2.80	12.28%
120	16.80	−10	6.80	40.48%
130	13.60	0	13.60	100.00%
140	10.30	0	10.30	100.00%

Put Options Strike	Price	Payoff	Profit	Return %
110	12.60	0	12.60	100.00%
120	17.20	0	17.20	100.00%
130	23.60	0	23.60	100.00%
140	30.50	10	40.50	132.79%

Money Spread	Price	Payoff	Profit
Bullish Spread			
Purchase 120 Call	16.80	10.00	−6.80
Sell 130 Call	13.60	0	13.60
Combined Profit		10.00	6.80

(Stock Price)	Bullish Spread
110	−17.20
120	−27.20
130	−37.20
140	−27.20
150	−17.20
160	−7.20
170	2.80
180	12.80
190	22.80
200	32.80
210	42.80

Ending Stock Price	Bullish Spread
50	−3.2
60	−3.2
70	−3.2
80	−3.2
90	−3.2
100	−3.2
110	−3.2
120	−3.2
130	6.8
140	6.8
150	6.8
160	6.8
170	6.8
180	6.8
190	6.8
200	6.8
210	6.8

Profit diagram for problem 16:

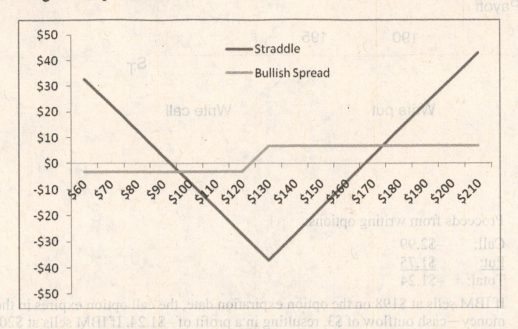

17. The farmer has the option to sell the crop to the government for a guaranteed minimum price if the market price is too low. If the support price is denoted P_S and the market price P_m then the farmer has a put option to sell the crop (the asset) at an exercise price of P_S even if the price of the underlying asset (P_m) is less than P_S.

18. The bondholders have, in effect, made a loan that requires repayment of B dollars, where B is the face value of bonds. If, however, the value of the firm (V) is less than B, the loan is satisfied by the bondholders taking over the firm. In this way, the bondholders are forced to "pay" B (in the sense that the loan is cancelled) in return for an asset worth only V. It is as though the bondholders wrote a put on an asset worth V with exercise price B. Alternatively, one might view the bondholders as giving the right to the equity holders to reclaim the firm by paying off the B dollar debt. The bondholders have issued a call to the equity holders.

19. The manager receives a bonus if the stock price exceeds a certain value and receives nothing otherwise. This is the same as the payoff to a call option.

20. a.

Position	$S_T < 190$	$190 \leq S_T \leq 195$	$S_T > 195$
Write call, $X = \$195$	0	0	$-(S_T - 195)$
Write put, $X = \$190$	$-(190 - S_T)$	0	0
Total	$S_T - 190$	0	$195 - S_T$

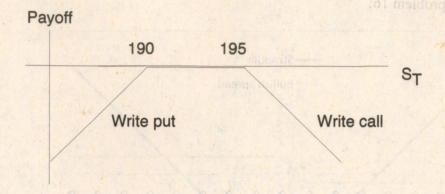

b.   Proceeds from writing options:

Call: −$2.99
<u>Put:</u>   <u>$1.75</u>
Total: −$1.24

If IBM sells at $198 on the option expiration date, the call option expires in the money—cash outflow of $3, resulting in a profit of −$1.24. If IBM sells at $208 on the option expiration date, the call written results in a cash outflow of $10 at expiration and an overall profit of: −$1.24 − $10.00 = −$11.24

c.   You break even when either the put or the call results in a cash outflow of −$1.24. For the put, this requires that:

$$-\$1.24 = \$190.00 - S_T \Rightarrow S_T = \$191.24$$

For the call, this requires that:

$$-\$1.24 = S_T - \$195.00 \Rightarrow S_T = \$193.76$$

d.   The investor is betting that IBM stock price will have low volatility. This position is similar to a straddle.

21.   The put with the higher exercise price must cost more. Therefore, the net outlay to establish the portfolio is positive.

Position	$S_T < 90$	$90 \le S_T \le 95$	$S_T > 95$
Write put, $X = \$90$	$-(90 - S_T)$	0	0
Buy put, $X = \$95$	$95 - S_T$	$95 - S_T$	0
Total	5	$95 - S_T$	0

The payoff and profit diagram is:

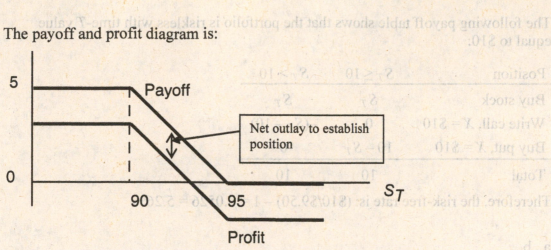

22. Buy the $X = 62$ put (which should cost more but does not) and write the $X = 60$ put. Since the options have the same price, your net outlay is zero. Your proceeds at expiration may be positive, but cannot be negative.

Position	$S_T < 60$	$60 \leq S_T \leq 62$	$S_T > 62$
Buy put, $X = \$62$	$62 - S_T$	$62 - S_T$	0
Write put, $X = \$60$	$-(60 - S_T)$	0	0
Total	2	$62 - S_T$	0

Payoff = Profit (because net investment = 0)

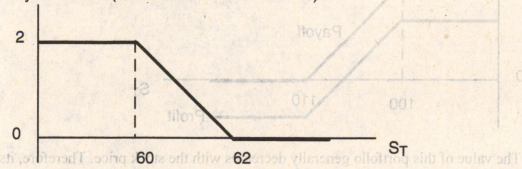

23. Put-call parity states that: $P = C - S_0 + PV(X) + PV(\text{Dividends})$

Solving for the price of the call option: $C = S_0 - PV(X) - PV(\text{Dividends}) + P$

$$C = \$100 - \frac{\$100}{(1.05)} - \frac{\$2}{(1.05)} + \$7$$

$$= \$9.86$$

24. The following payoff table shows that the portfolio is riskless with time-T value equal to $10:

Position	$S_T \leq 10$	$S_T > 10$
Buy stock	S_T	S_T
Write call, $X = \$10$	0	$-(S_T - 10)$
Buy put, $X = \$10$	$10 - S_T$	0
Total	10	10

Therefore, the risk-free rate is: ($10/$9.50) − 1 = 0.0526 = 5.26%

25. a., b.

Position	$S_T < 100$	$100 \leq S_T \leq 110$	$S_T > 110$
Buy put, $X = \$110$	$110 - S_T$	$110 - S_T$	0
Write put, $X = \$100$	$-(100 - S_T)$	0	0
Total	10	$110 - S_T$	0

The net outlay to establish this position is positive. The put you buy has a higher exercise price than the put you write, and therefore must cost more than the put that you write. Therefore, net profits will be less than the payoff at time T.

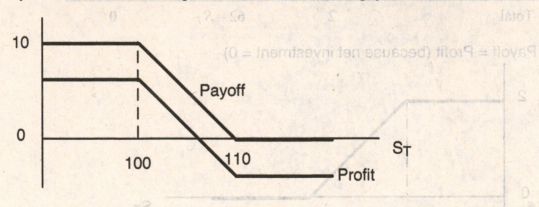

c. The value of this portfolio generally decreases with the stock price. Therefore, its beta is negative.

26. a. <u>Joe's strategy</u>

Position	Cost	Payoff	
		$S_T \leq 1,200$	$S_T > 1,200$
Stock index	1,200	S_T	S_T
Put option, $X = \$1200$	60	$1,200 - S_T$	0
Total	−1,260	1,200	S_T
Profit = payoff − $1260		−60	$S_T - 1,260$

<u>Sally's strategy</u>

Position	Cost	Payoff	
		$S_T \le 1,170$	$S_T > 1,170$
Stock index	1,200	S_T	S_T
Put option, $X = \$1,270$	45	$1,170 - S_T$	0
Total	1,245	1,245	S_T
Profit = Payoff – $1,245		–76	$S_T - 1,245$

b. Sally does better when the stock price is high, but worse when the stock price is low.

c. Sally's strategy has greater systematic risk. Profits are more sensitive to the value of the stock index.

27. a., b. (See graph)

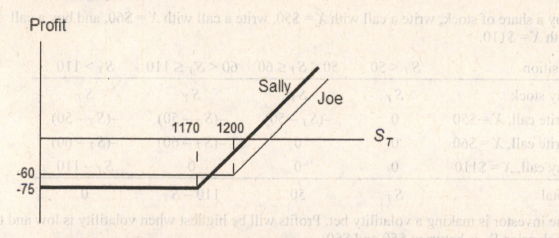

This strategy is a bear spread. Initial proceeds = $9 – $3 = $6

The payoff is either negative or zero:

Position	$S_T < 50$	$50 \le S_T \le 60$	$S_T > 60$
Buy call, $X = \$60$	0	0	$S_T - 60$
Write call, $X = \$50$	0	$-(S_T - 50)$	$-(S_T - 50)$
Total	0	$-(S_T - 50)$	–10

c. Breakeven occurs when the payoff offsets the initial proceeds of $6, which occurs at stock price $S_T = \$56$. The investor must be bearish: the position does worse when the stock price increases.

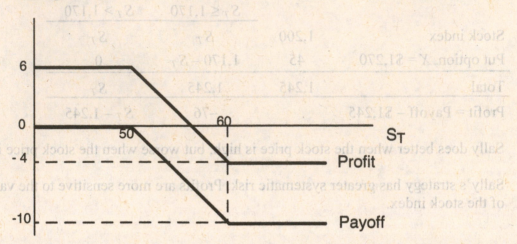

28. Buy a share of stock, write a call with $X = \$50$, write a call with $X = \$60$, and buy a call with $X = \$110$.

Position	$S_T < 50$	$50 \leq S_T \leq 60$	$60 < S_T \leq 110$	$S_T > 110$
Buy stock	S_T	S_T	S_T	S_T
Write call, $X = \$50$	0	$-(S_T - 50)$	$-(S_T - 50)$	$-(S_T - 50)$
Write call, $X = \$60$	0	0	$-(S_T - 60)$	$-(S_T - 60)$
Buy call, $X = \$110$	0	0	0	$S_T - 110$
Total	S_T	50	$110 - S_T$	0

The investor is making a volatility bet. Profits will be highest when volatility is low and the stock price S_T is between $50 and $60.

29. a.

Position	$S_T \leq 1,179$	$S_T > 1,170$
Buy stock	S_T	S_T
Buy put	$1,170 - S_T$	0
Total	1,170	S_T

Position	$S_T \leq 1,260$	$S_T > 1,260$
Buy call	0	$S_T - 1,260$
Buy T-bills	1,260	1,260
Total	1,260	S_T

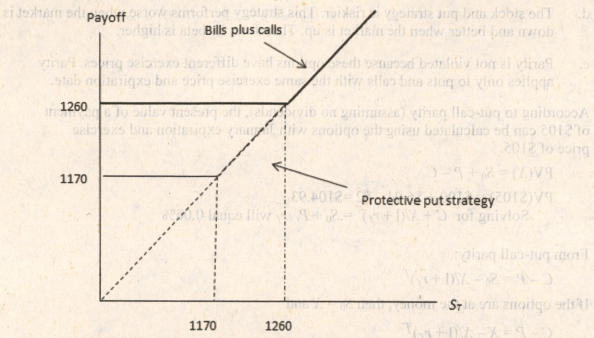

b. The bills plus call strategy has a greater payoff for some values of S_T and never a lower payoff. Since its payoffs are always at least as attractive and sometimes greater, it must be more costly to purchase.

c. The initial cost of the stock plus put position is $1,350 + $9 = $1,359
The initial cost of the bills plus call position is: $1,215 + $180 = $1,395

	$S_T = 1,000$	$S_T = 1,260$	$S_T = 1,350$	$S_T = 1,440$
Stock	1,000	1,260	1,350	1,440
+ Put	170	0	0	0
Payoff	1,170	1,260	1,350	1,440
Profit	−189	−99	−9	81
Bill	1,260	1,260	1,260	1,260
+ Call	0	0	90	180
Payoff	1,260	1,260	1,350	1,440
Profit	−135	−135	−45	+45

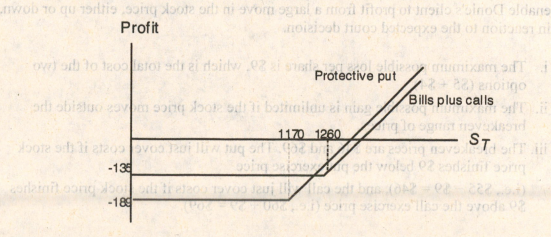

d. The stock and put strategy is riskier. This strategy performs worse when the market is down and better when the market is up. Therefore, its beta is higher.

e. Parity is not violated because these options have different exercise prices. Parity applies only to puts and calls with the same exercise price and expiration date.

30. According to put-call parity (assuming no dividends), the present value of a payment of $105 can be calculated using the options with January expiration and exercise price of $105.

$$PV(X) = S_0 + P - C$$

PV($105) = $100 + $6.94 − $2 =$104.93

Solving for $C + X/(1 + r_f)^T = S_0 + P$, r_f will equal 0.06%

31. From put-call parity:

$$C - P = S_0 - X/(1 + r_f)^T$$

If the options are at the money, then $S_0 = X$ and

$$C - P = X - X/(1 + r_f)^T$$

The right-hand side of the equation is positive, and we conclude that $C > P$.

CFA PROBLEMS

1. a. Donie should choose the long strangle strategy. A long strangle option strategy consists of buying a put and a call with the same expiration date and the same underlying asset, but different exercise prices. In a strangle strategy, the call has an exercise price above the stock price and the put has an exercise price below the stock price. An investor who buys (goes long) a strangle expects that the price of the underlying asset (TRT Materials in this case) will either move substantially below the exercise price on the put or above the exercise price on the call. With respect to TRT, the long strangle investor buys both the put option and the call option for a total cost of $9 and will experience a profit if the stock price moves more than $9 above the call exercise price or more than $9 below the put exercise price. This strategy would enable Donie's client to profit from a large move in the stock price, either up or down, in reaction to the expected court decision.

    b. i.   The maximum possible loss per share is $9, which is the total cost of the two options ($5 + $4).

        ii. The maximum possible gain is unlimited if the stock price moves outside the breakeven range of prices.

        iii. The breakeven prices are $46 and $69. The put will just cover costs if the stock price finishes $9 below the put exercise price

             (i.e., $55 − $9 = $46), and the call will just cover costs if the stock price finishes $9 above the call exercise price (i.e., $60 + $9 = $69).

2. i.   Equity index-linked note: Unlike traditional debt securities that pay a scheduled rate of coupon interest on a periodic basis and the par amount of principal at maturity, the equity index-linked note typically pays little or no coupon interest; at maturity, however, a unit holder receives the original issue price plus a supplemental redemption amount, the value of which depends on where the equity index settled relative to a predetermined initial level.

    ii. Commodity-linked bear bond: Unlike traditional debt securities that pay a scheduled rate of coupon interest on a periodic basis and the par amount of principal at maturity, the commodity-linked bear bond allows an investor to participate in a decline in a commodity's price. In exchange for a lower than market coupon, buyers of a bear tranche receive a redemption value that exceeds the purchase price if the commodity price has declined by the maturity date.

3. i.   Conversion value of a convertible bond is the value of the security if it is converted immediately. That is:

    Conversion value = Market price of the common stock × Conversion ratio

    = $40 × 22

    = $880

    ii. Market conversion price is the price that an investor effectively pays for the common stock if the convertible bond is purchased:

    Market conversion price = Market price of the convertible bond/Conversion ratio

    = $1,050/22

    = $47.73

4. a. i.   The current market conversion price is computed as follows:

    Market conversion price = Market price of the convertible bond/Conversion ratio = $980/25

    = $39.20

    ii. The expected one-year return for the Ytel convertible bond is

    Expected return = [(End of year price + Coupon)/Current price] – 1

    = [($1,125 + $40)/$980] – 1

    = 0.1888, or 18.88%

    iii. The expected one-year return for the Ytel common equity is:

    Expected return = [(End of year price + Dividend)/Current price] – 1

    = ($45/$35) – 1 = 0.2857, or 28.57%

b. The two components of a convertible bond's value are

1. The straight bond value, which is the convertible bond's value as a bond.
2. The option value, which is the value from a potential conversion to equity.

(i) In response to the increase in Ytel's common equity price, the straight bond value should stay the same and the option value should increase.

The increase in equity price does not affect the straight bond value component of the Ytel convertible. The increase in equity price increases the option value component significantly, because the call option becomes deep "in the money" when the $51 per share equity price is compared to the convertible's conversion price of: $1,000/25 = $40 per share.

(ii) In response to the increase in interest rates, the straight bond value should decrease and the option value should increase.

The increase in interest rates decreases the straight bond value component (bond values decline as interest rates increase) of the convertible bond and increases the value of the equity call option component (call option values increase as interest rates increase). This increase may be small or even unnoticeable when compared to the change in the option value resulting from the increase in the equity price.

5. a. (i) [Profit = $40 – $25 + $2.50 – $4.00]

b. (ii) The most the put writer can lose occurs when the stock price drops completely to $0. This is a $40 loss less the $2 premium. The call writer will keep the premium of $3.50 if the option finishes out of the money.

CHAPTER 21: OPTION VALUATION

PROBLEM SETS

1. The value of a put option also increases with the volatility of the stock. We see this from the put–call parity theorem as follows:

    $$P = C - S_0 + PV(X) + PV(\text{Dividends})$$

    Given a value for S and a risk-free interest rate, then, if C increases because of an increase in volatility, P must also increase in order to maintain the equality of the parity relationship.

2. A $1 increase in a call option's exercise price would lead to a decrease in the option's value of less than $1. The change in the call price would equal $1 only if: (a) there is a 100% probability that the call would be exercised, and (b) the interest rate is zero.

3. Holding firm-specific risk constant, higher beta implies higher total stock volatility. Therefore, the value of the put option increases as beta increases.

4. Holding beta constant, the stock with a lot of firm-specific risk has higher total volatility. The option on the stock with higher firm-specific risk is worth more.

5. A call option with a high exercise price has a lower hedge ratio. This call option is less in the money. Both d_1 and $N(d_1)$ are lower when X is higher.

6. a. Put A must be written on the stock with the lower price. Otherwise, given the lower volatility of Stock A, Put A would sell for less than Put B.

    b. Put B must be written on the stock with the lower price. This would explain its higher price.

    c. Call B must have the lower time to expiration. Despite the higher price of Stock B, Call B is cheaper than Call A. This can be explained by a lower time to expiration.

    d. Call B must be written on the stock with higher volatility. This would explain its higher price.

    e. Call A must be written on the stock with higher volatility. This would explain its higher price.

7.

Exercise Price	Hedge Ratio
120	0/30 = 0.000
110	10/30 = 0.333
100	20/30 = 0.667
90	30/30 = 1.000

As the option becomes more in the money, the hedge ratio increases to a maximum of 1.0.

8.

S	d_1	$N(d_1)$
45	−0.2768	0.3910
50	0.2500	0.5987
55	0.7266	0.7662

9. a. $uS_0 = 130 \Rightarrow P_u = 0$

$dS_0 = 80 \Rightarrow P_d = 30$

The hedge ratio is: $H = \dfrac{P_u - P_d}{uS_0 - dS_0} = \dfrac{0 - 30}{130 - 80} = -\dfrac{3}{5}$

b.

Riskless Portfolio	$S_T = 80$	$S_T = 130$
Buy 3 shares	240	390
Buy 5 puts	150	0
Total	390	390

Present value = $390/1.10 = \$354.545$

c.   The portfolio cost is: $3S + 5P = 300 + 5P$

The value of the portfolio is: $\$354.545$

Therefore: $300 + 5P = \$354.545 \rightarrow P = \$54.545/5 = \$10.91$

10. The hedge ratio for the call is: $H = \dfrac{C_u - C_d}{uS_0 - dS_0} = \dfrac{20 - 0}{130 - 80} = \dfrac{2}{5}$

Riskless Portfolio	$S = 80$	$S = 130$
Buy 2 shares	160	260
Write 5 calls	0	–100
Total	160	160

Present value = $160/1.10 = $145.455

The portfolio cost is: $2S - 5C = $200 - 5C$

The value of the portfolio is $145.455

Therefore: $C = $54.545/5 = 10.91

Does $P = C + PV(X) - S$?

$10.91 = 10.91 + 110/1.10 - 100 = 10.91$

11. $d_1 = 0.2192 \Rightarrow N(d_1) = 0.5868$

$d_2 = -0.1344 \Rightarrow N(d_2) = 0.4465$

$Xe^{-rT} = 49.2556$

$C = $50 \times 0.5868 - 49.2556 \times 0.4465 = 7.34

12. $P = 6.60

This value is derived from our Black-Scholes spreadsheet, but note that we could have derived the value from put-call parity:

$P = C + PV(X) - S_0 = $7.34 + $49.26 - $50 = 6.60

13. a. C falls to $5.1443

b. C falls to $3.8801

c. C falls to $5.4043

d. C rises to $10.5356

e. C rises to $7.5636

14. According to the Black-Scholes model, the call option should be priced at:

$[\$55 \times N(d_1)] - [50 \times N(d_2)] = (\$55 \times 0.6) - (\$50 \times 0.5) = \$8$

Since the option actually sells for more than $8, implied volatility is greater than 0.30.

15. A straddle is a call and a put. The Black-Scholes value would be:

$C + P = S_0 \times N(d_1) - Xe^{-rT} \times N(d_2) + Xe^{-rT} \times [1 - N(d_2)] - S_0 [1 - N(d_1)]$

$= S_0 \times [2N(d_1) - 1] + Xe^{-rT} \times [1 - 2N(d_2)]$

On the Excel spreadsheet (Spreadsheet 21.1), the valuation formula would be:

=B5*(2*E4 − 1) + B6*EXP(−B4*B3)*(1 − 2*E5)

16. A. A delta-neutral portfolio is perfectly hedged against small price changes in the underlying asset. This is true both for price increases and decreases. That is, the portfolio value will not change significantly if the asset price changes by a small amount. However, large changes in the underlying asset will cause the hedge to become imperfect. This means that overall portfolio value can change by a significant amount if the price change in the underlying asset is large.

17. A. Delta is the change in the option price for a given instantaneous change in the stock price. The change is equal to the slope of the option price diagram.

18. The best estimate for the change in price of the option is

Change in asset price × Delta = −$6 × (−0.65) = $3.90

19. The number of call options necessary to delta hedge is $\dfrac{51,750}{0.69} = 75,000$ options, or 750 options contracts, each covering 100 shares. Since these are call options, the options should be sold short.

20. The number of calls needed to create a delta-neutral hedge is inversely proportional to the delta. The delta decreases when stock price decreases. Therefore the number of calls necessary would increase if the stock price falls.

21. A delta-neutral portfolio can be created with any of the following combinations: long stock and short calls, long stock and long puts, short stock and long calls, and short stock and short puts.

22.   The rate of return of a call option on a long-term Treasury bond should be more sensitive to changes in interest rates than is the rate of return of the underlying bond. The option elasticity exceeds 1.0. In other words, the option is effectively a levered investment and the rate of return on the option is more sensitive to interest rate swings.

23.   Implied volatility has increased. If not, the call price would have fallen as a result of the decrease in stock price.

24.   Implied volatility has increased. If not, the put price would have fallen as a result of the decreased time to expiration.

25.   The hedge ratio approaches one. As S increases, the probability of exercise approaches 1.0. $N(d_1)$ approaches 1.0.

26.   The hedge ratio approaches 0. As X decreases, the probability of exercise approaches 0. $[N(d_1) - 1]$ approaches 0 as $N(d_1)$ approaches 1.

27.   A straddle is a call and a put. The hedge ratio of the straddle is the sum of the hedge ratios of the individual options: $0.4 + (-0.6) = -0.2$

28.   a.   The spreadsheet appears as follows:

INPUTS		OUTPUTS	
Standard deviation (annual)	0.3213	$d1$	0.0089
Expiration (in years)	0.5	$d2$	−0.2183
Risk-free rate (annual)	0.05	$N(d1)$	0.5036
Stock price	100	$N(d2)$	0.4136
Exercise price	105	B/S call value	8.0000
Dividend yield (annual)	0	B/S put value	10.4076

The standard deviation is: 0.3213

b.   The spreadsheet below shows the standard deviation has increased to: 0.3568

INPUTS		OUTPUTS	
Standard deviation (annual)	0.3568	$d1$	0.0318
Expiration (in years)	0.5	$d2$	−0.2204
Risk-free rate (annual)	0.05	$N(d1)$	0.5127
Stock price	100	$N(d2)$	0.4128
Exercise price	105	B/S call value	9.0000
Dividend yield (annual)	0	B/S put value	11.4075

Implied volatility has increased because the value of an option increases with greater volatility.

c. Implied volatility increases to 0.4087 when expiration decreases to four months. The shorter expiration decreases the value of the option; therefore, in order for the option price to remain unchanged at $8, implied volatility must increase.

INPUTS		OUTPUTS	
Standard deviation (annual)	0.4087	$d1$	−0.0182
Expiration (in years)	0.33333	$d2$	−0.2541
Risk-free rate (annual)	0.05	$N(d1)$	0.4928
Stock price	100	$N(d2)$	0.3997
Exercise price	105	B/S call value	8.0001
Dividend yield (annual)	0	B/S put value	11.2646

d. Implied volatility decreases to 0.2406 when exercise price decreases to $100. The decrease in exercise price increases the value of the call, so that, in order for the option price to remain at $8, implied volatility decreases.

INPUTS		OUTPUTS	
Standard deviation (annual)	0.2406	$d1$	0.2320
Expiration (in years)	0.5	$d2$	0.0619
Risk-free rate (annual)	0.05	$N(d1)$	0.5917
Stock price	100	$N(d2)$	0.5247
Exercise price	100	B/S call value	8.0010
Dividend yield (annual)	0	B/S put value	5.5320

e. The decrease in stock price decreases the value of the call. In order for the option price to remain at $8, implied volatility increases.

INPUTS		OUTPUTS	
Standard deviation (annual)	0.3566	$d1$	−0.0484
Expiration (in years)	0.5	$d2$	−0.3006
Risk-free rate (annual)	0.05	$N(d1)$	0.4807
Stock price	98	$N(d2)$	0.3819
Exercise price	105	B/S call value	8.0000
Dividend yield (annual)	0	B/S put value	12.4075

29. a. The delta of the collar is calculated as follows:

Position	Delta
Buy stock	1.0
Buy put, $X = \$45$	$N(d_1) - 1 = -0.40$
Write call, $X = \$55$	$-N(d_1) = -0.35$
Total	0.25

If the stock price increases by $1, then the value of the collar increases by $0.25. The stock will be worth $1 more, the loss on the purchased put will be $0.40, and the call written represents a *liability* that increases by $0.35.

b. If S becomes very large, then the delta of the collar approaches zero. Both $N(d_1)$ terms approach 1. Intuitively, for very large stock prices, the value of the portfolio is simply the (present value of the) exercise price of the call, and is unaffected by small changes in the stock price.

As S approaches zero, the delta also approaches zero: both $N(d_1)$ terms approach 0. For very small stock prices, the value of the portfolio is simply the (present value of the) exercise price of the put and is unaffected by small changes in the stock price.

30.

Put	X	Delta
A	10	−0.1
B	20	−0.5
C	30	−0.9

31. a. Choice A: Calls have higher elasticity than shares. For equal dollar investments, a call's capital gain potential is greater than that of the underlying stock.

   b. Choice B: Calls have hedge ratios less than 1.0, so the shares have higher profit potential. For an equal number of shares controlled, the dollar exposure of the shares is greater than that of the calls, and the profit potential is therefore greater.

32. a. $uS_0 = 110 \Rightarrow P_u = 0$

   $dS_0 = 90 \Rightarrow P_d = 10$

   The hedge ratio is $H = \dfrac{P_u - P_d}{uS_0 - dS_0} = \dfrac{0 - 10}{110 - 90} = -\dfrac{1}{2}$

   A portfolio comprised of one share and two puts provides a guaranteed payoff of $110, with present value: $110/1.05 = $104.76

   Therefore:

   $S + 2P = \$104.76$

   $\$100 + 2P = \$104.76 \Rightarrow P = \$2.38$

   b. Cost of protective put portfolio with a $100 guaranteed payoff:

   $= \$100 + \$2.38 = \$102.38$

c.   Our goal is a portfolio with the same exposure to the stock as the hypothetical protective put portfolio. Since the put's hedge ratio is -0.5, the portfolio consists of $(1 - 0.5) = 0.5$ shares of stock, which costs $50, and the remaining funds ($52.38) invested in T-bills, earning 5% interest.

Portfolio	$S = 90$	$S = 110$
Buy 0.5 shares	45	55
Invest in T-bills	55	55
Total	100	110

This payoff is identical to that of the protective put portfolio. Thus, the stock plus bills strategy replicates both the cost and payoff of the protective put.

33.   The put values in the second period are:

$P_{uu} = 0$

$P_{ud} = P_{du} = 110 - 104.50 = 5.50$

$P_{dd} = 110 - 90.25 = 19.75$

To compute P_u, first compute the hedge ratio:

$$H = \frac{P_{uu} - P_{ud}}{uuS_0 - udS_0} = \frac{0 - 5.50}{121 - 104.50} = -\frac{1}{3}$$

Form a riskless portfolio by buying one share of stock and buying three puts.

The cost of the portfolio is: $S + 3P_u = \$110 + 3P_u$

The payoff for the riskless portfolio equals $121:

Riskless Portfolio	$S = 104.50$	$S = 121$
Buy 1 share	104.50	121.00
Buy 3 puts	16.50	0.00
Total	121.00	121.00

Therefore, find the value of the put by solving:

$\$110 + 3P_u = \$121/1.05 \Rightarrow P_u = \$1.746$

To compute P_d, compute the hedge ratio:

$$H = \frac{P_{du} - P_{dd}}{duS_0 - ddS_0} = \frac{5.50 - 19.75}{104.50 - 90.25} = -1.0$$

Form a riskless portfolio by buying one share and buying one put.

The cost of the portfolio is: $S + P_d = \$95 + P_d$

(continued on next page)

The payoff for the riskless portfolio equals $110:

Riskless Portfolio	$S = 90.25$	$S = 104.50$
Buy 1 share	90.25	104.50
Buy 1 put	19.75	5.50
Total	110.00	110.00

Therefore, find the value of the put by solving:

$$\$95 + P_d = \$110/1.05 \Rightarrow P_d = \$9.762$$

To compute P, compute the hedge ratio:

$$H = \frac{P_u - P_d}{uS_0 - dS_0} = \frac{1.746 - 9.762}{110 - 95} = -0.5344$$

Form a riskless portfolio by buying 0.5344 of a share and buying one put. The cost of the portfolio is: $0.5344S + P = \$53.44 + P$

The payoff for the riskless portfolio equals $60.53:

Riskless Portfolio	$S = 95$	$S = 110$
Buy 0.5344 share	50.768	58.784
Buy 1 put	9.762	1.746
Total	60.530	60.530

Therefore, find the value of the put by solving:

$$\$53.44 + P = \$60.53/1.05 \Rightarrow P = \$4.208$$

Finally, we verify this result using put-call parity. Recall from Example 21.1 that:

$$C = \$4.434$$

Put-call parity requires that:

$$P = C + \text{PV}(X) - S$$

$$\$4.208 = \$4.434 + (\$110/1.05^2) - \$100$$

Except for minor rounding error, put-call parity is satisfied.

34. If $r = 0$, then one should never exercise a put early. There is no "time value cost" to waiting to exercise, but there is a "volatility benefit" from waiting. To show this more rigorously, consider the following portfolio: lend $X and short one share of stock. The cost to establish the portfolio is $(X - S_0)$. The payoff at time T (with zero interest earnings on the loan) is $(X - S_T)$. In contrast, a put option has a payoff at time T of $(X - S_T)$ if that value is positive, and zero otherwise. The put's payoff is at least as large as the portfolio's, and therefore, the put must cost at least as much as the portfolio to purchase. Hence, $P \geq (X - S_0)$, and the put can be sold for more than the proceeds from immediate exercise. We conclude that it doesn't pay to exercise early.

35. a. Xe^{-rT}

    b. X

    c. 0

    d. 0

    e. It is optimal to exercise immediately a put on a stock whose price has fallen to zero. The value of the American put equals the exercise price. Any delay in exercise lowers value by the time value of money.

36. Step 1: Calculate the option values at expiration. The two possible stock prices and the corresponding call values are:

$uS_0 = 120 \Rightarrow C_u = 20$

$dS_0 = 80 \Rightarrow C_d = 0$

Step 2: Calculate the hedge ratio.

$$H = \frac{C_u - C_d}{uS_0 - dS_0} = \frac{20 - 0}{120 - 80} = \frac{1}{2}$$

Therefore, form a riskless portfolio by buying one share of stock and writing two calls. The cost of the portfolio is $S - 2C = 100 - 2C$

Step 3: Show that the payoff for the riskless portfolio equals $80:

Riskless Portfolio	$S = 80$	$S = 120$
Buy 1 share	80	120
Write 2 calls	0	−40
Total	80	80

Therefore, find the value of the call by solving

$100 − 2C = \$80/1.10 \Rightarrow C = \$13.636$

Notice that we did not use the probabilities of a stock price increase or decrease. These are not needed to value the call option.

37. The two possible stock prices and the corresponding call values are:

$$uS_0 = 130 \Rightarrow C_u = 30$$

$$dS_0 = 70 \Rightarrow C_d = 0$$

The hedge ratio is $H = \dfrac{C_u - C_d}{uS_0 - dS_0} = \dfrac{30 - 0}{130 - 70} = \dfrac{1}{2}$

Form a riskless portfolio by buying one share of stock and writing two calls. The cost of the portfolio is: $S - 2C = 100 - 2C$

The payoff for the riskless portfolio equals \$70:

Riskless Portfolio	$S = 70$	$S = 130$
Buy 1 share	70	130
Write 2 calls	0	−60
Total	70	70

Therefore, find the value of the call by solving

$$\$100 - 2C = \$70/1.10 \Rightarrow C = \$18.182$$

Here, the value of the call is greater than the value in the lower-volatility scenario.

38. The two possible stock prices and the corresponding put values are:

$$uS_0 = 120 \Rightarrow P_u = 0$$

$$dS_0 = 80 \Rightarrow P_d = 20$$

The hedge ratio is $H = \dfrac{P_u - P_d}{uS_0 - dS_0} = \dfrac{0 - 20}{120 - 80} = -\dfrac{1}{2}$

Form a riskless portfolio by buying one share of stock and buying two puts. The cost of the portfolio is: $S + 2P = 100 + 2P$

The payoff for the riskless portfolio equals \$120:

Riskless Portfolio	$S = 80$	$S = 120$
Buy 1 share	80	120
Buy 2 puts	40	0
Total	120	120

Therefore, find the value of the put by solving

$$\$100 + 2P = \$120/1.10 \Rightarrow P = \$4.545$$

According to put-call parity $P + S = C + PV(X)$

Our estimates of option value satisfy this relationship:

$$\$4.545 + \$100 = \$13.636 + \$100/1.10 = \$104.545$$

39. If we assume that the only possible exercise date is just prior to the ex-dividend date, then the relevant parameters for the Black-Scholes formula are:

$S_0 = 60$

$r = 0.5\%$ per month

$X = 55$

$\sigma = 7\%$

$T = 2$ months

In this case: $C = \$6.04$

If instead, one commits to foregoing early exercise, then we reduce the stock price by the present value of the dividends. Therefore, we use the following parameters:

$S_0 = 60 - 2e^{-(0.005 \times 2)} = 58.02$

$r = 0.5\%$ per month

$X = 55$

$\sigma = 7\%$

$T = 3$ months

In this case, $C = \$5.05$

The pseudo-American option value is the higher of these two values: $6.04

40. True. The call option has an elasticity greater than 1.0. Therefore, the call's percentage rate of return is greater than that of the underlying stock. Hence the GM call responds more than proportionately when the GM stock price changes in response to broad market movements. Therefore, the beta of the GM call is greater than the beta of GM stock.

41. False. The elasticity of a call option is higher the more out of the money is the option. (Even though the delta of the call is lower, the value of the call is also lower. The proportional response of the call price to the stock price increases. You can confirm this with numerical examples.) Therefore, the rate of return of the call with the higher exercise price responds more sensitively to changes in the market index, and therefore it has the higher beta.

42. As the stock price increases, conversion becomes increasingly more assured. The hedge ratio approaches 1.0. The price of the convertible bond will move one-for-one with changes in the price of the underlying stock.

43. Goldman Sachs believes that the market assessment of volatility is too high. It should sell options because the analysis suggests the options are overpriced with respect to true volatility. The delta of the call is 0.6, while the put is $0.6 - 1 = -0.4$. Therefore, Goldman should sell puts and calls in the ratio of 0.6 to 0.4. For example, if Goldman sells 2 calls and 3 puts, the position will be delta neutral:

$$\text{Delta} = (2 \times 0.6) + [3 \times (-0.4)] = 0$$

44. If the stock market index increases 1%, the 1 million shares of stock on which the options are written would be expected to increase by
$$0.75\% \times \$5 \times 1 \text{ million} = \$37,500$$

The options would increase by:
$$\text{Delta} \times \$37,500 = 0.8 \times \$37,500 = \$30,000$$

In order to hedge your market exposure, you must sell \$3,000,000 of the market index portfolio so that a 1% change in the index would result in a \$30,000 change in the value of the portfolio.

45. $S = 100$; current value of portfolio

$X = 100$; floor promised to clients (0% return)

$\sigma = 0.25$; volatility

$r = 0.05$; risk-free rate

$T = 4$ years; horizon of program

a. Using the Black-Scholes formula, we find that

$$d_1 = 0.65, N(d_1) = 0.7422, d_2 = 0.15, N(d_2) = 0.5596$$

Put value = \$10.27

Therefore, total funds to be managed equals \$110.27 million: \$100 million portfolio value plus the \$10.27 million fee for the insurance program.

The put delta is $N(d_1) - 1 = 0.7422 - 1 = -0.2578$

Therefore, sell off 25.78% of the equity portfolio, placing the remaining funds in T-bills. The amount of the portfolio in equity is therefore \$74.22 million, while the amount in T-bills is: \$110.27 million − \$74.22 million = \$36.06 million

b. At the new portfolio value of 97, the put delta is
$$N(d_1) - 1 = 0.7221 - 1 = -0.2779$$

This means that you must reduce the delta of the portfolio by
$$0.2779 - 0.2578 = 0.0201$$

You should sell an additional 2.01% of the equity position and use the proceeds to buy T-bills. Since the stock price is now at only 97% of its original value, you need to sell

$$\$97 \text{ million} \times 0.0201 = \$1.946 \text{ million of stock}$$

46. Using the true volatility (32%) and time to expiration T = 0.25 years, the hedge ratio for ExxonMobil is $N(d_1) = 0.5945$. Because you believe the calls are underpriced (selling at an implied volatility that is too low), you will buy calls and short 0.5945 shares for each call you buy.

47. The calls are cheap (implied $\sigma = 0.30$) and the puts are expensive (implied $\sigma = 0.34$). Therefore, buy calls and sell puts. Using the "true" volatility of $\sigma = 0.32$, the call delta is 0.5945 and the put delta is $0.5945 - 1.0 = -0.4055$. Therefore, for each call purchased, buy $0.5945/0.4055 = 1.466$ puts.

48. a. To calculate the hedge ratio, suppose that the market index increases by 1%. Then the stock portfolio would be expected to increase by:

    $1\% \times 1.5 = 1.5\%$ or $0.015 \times \$1,250,000 = \$18,750$

    Given the option delta of 0.8, the option portfolio would increase by

    $\$18,750 \times 0.8 = \$15,000$

    JP Morgan Chase's liability from writing these options would increase by the same amount. The market index portfolio would increase in value by 1%. Therefore, JP Morgan should purchase \$1,500,000 of the market index portfolio in order to hedge its position so that a 1% change in the index would result in a \$15,000 change in the value of the portfolio.

    b. The delta of a put option is

    $0.8 - 1 = -0.2$

    Therefore, for every 1% the market increases, the index will rise by 10 points and the value of the put option contract will change by

    Delta $\times$ 10 $\times$ Contract multiplier $= -0.2 \times 10 \times 100 = -\$200$

    Therefore, JP Morgan should write $\$15,000/\$200 = 75$ put contracts

49. a,b,c

Subperiods	$\Delta t = T/n$	$u = \exp(\sigma\sqrt{\Delta t})$	$d = \exp(-\sigma\sqrt{\Delta t})$
1	1/1=1	1.4918	0.6703
4	1/4=.25	1.2214	0.8187
12	1/12=.0833	1.1224	0.8909

50. Since the spread between u and d reflects the volatility of the rate of return and u and d depend on that volatility, next year's rate of return should increase accordingly by the $\sigma\sqrt{\Delta t}$

51. $P = C - S_0 + \text{PV}(X)$. When at-the-money, $X = S_0$. $\text{PV}(X)$ will always be less than S_0 and due to discounting $\text{PV}(X)$ can never be large enough to raise P over the price of C. If $X = X(1+r)^T$ then $X = S_0$ and $P = C$.

52. Using the risk-neutral shortcut, we must first calculate the risk-neutral probability p.

$$p = \frac{1+rf-d}{u-d} = \frac{1+.1-.8}{1.2-.8} = .75$$

After one year, the stock price will have either a 75% chance of rising to $120 (a $20 payoff) or a 25% chance of falling to $80 ($0 payoff). Discounting the weighted average of these payoffs by the risk-free rate gives us

$$\frac{.75 \times 20 + .25 \times 0}{(1+.10)^1} = 13.636$$

which is exactly equal to the two-state approach.

53. If the stock price rises, the payoff will be zero as profit from a put is only made when the stock price is less than the exercise price. If the stock price falls, it falls below the $100 exercise price and the payoff will be the difference between the two. Using the risk-neutral shortcut

$$p = \frac{1+rf-d}{u-d} = \frac{1+.1-.8}{1.2-.8} = .75$$

After one year, the stock price will have either a 75% chance of rising to $120 (a $0 payoff) or a 25% chance of falling to $80 ($20 payoff). Discounting the weighted average of these payoffs by the risk-free rate gives us

$$\frac{.75 \times 0 + .25 \times 20}{(1+.10)^1} = 4.545$$

Equal to the two-stage approach.

CFA PROBLEMS

1. Statement a: The hedge ratio (determining the number of futures contracts to sell) ought to be adjusted by the beta of the equity portfolio, which is 1.20. The correct hedge ratio would be

$$\frac{\$100 \text{ million}}{\$100 \times 250} \times \beta = 4,000 \times \beta = 4,000 \times 1.2 = 4,800$$

Statement b: The portfolio will be hedged and should therefore earn the risk-free rate, not zero, as the consultant claims. Given a futures price of 100 and an equity price of 99, the rate of return over the three-month period is

$$(100 - 99)/99 = 1.01\% = \text{approximately } 4.1\% \text{ annualized}$$

2. a. The value of the call option decreases if underlying stock price volatility decreases. The less volatile the underlying stock price, the less the chance of extreme price movements—the lower the probability that the option expires in the money. This makes the participation feature on the upside less valuable.

    The value of the call option is expected to increase if the time to expiration of the option increases. The longer the time to expiration, the greater the chance that the option will expire in the money resulting in an increase in the time premium component of the option's value.

   b. i. When European options are out of the money, investors are essentially saying that they are willing to pay a premium for the right, but not the obligation, to buy or sell the underlying asset. The out-of-the-money option has no intrinsic value, but, since options require little capital (just the premium paid) to obtain a relatively large potential payoff, investors are willing to pay that premium even if the option may expire worthless. The Black-Scholes model does not reflect investors' demand for any premium above the time value of the option. Hence, if investors are willing to pay a premium for an out-of-the-money option above its time value, the Black-Scholes model does not value that excess premium.

      ii. With American options, investors have the right, but not the obligation, to exercise the option prior to expiration, even if they exercise for noneconomic reasons. This increased flexibility associated with American options has some value but is not considered in the Black-Scholes model because the model only values options to their expiration date (European options).

3. a. American options should cost more (have a higher premium). American options give the investor greater flexibility than European options since the investor can *choose* whether to exercise early. When the stock pays a dividend, the option to exercise a call early can be valuable. But regardless of the dividend, a European option (put or call) never sells for more than an otherwise-identical American option.

b. $C = S_0 + P - PV(X) = \$43 + \$4 - \$45/1.055 = \$4.346$

Note: we assume that Abaco does not pay any dividends.

c.   i.   An increase in short-term interest rate $\Rightarrow$ PV(exercise price) is lower, and call value increases.

ii.   An increase in stock price volatility $\Rightarrow$ the call value increases.

iii.   A decrease in time to option expiration $\Rightarrow$ the call value decreases.

4.   a.   The two possible values of the index in the first period are:

$$uS_0 = 1.20 \times 50 = 60$$
$$dS_0 = 0.80 \times 50 = 40$$

The possible values of the index in the second period are:

$$uuS_0 = (1.20)^2 \times 50 = 72$$
$$udS_0 = 1.20 \times 0.80 \times 50 = 48$$
$$duS_0 = 0.80 \times 1.20 \times 50 = 48$$
$$ddS_0 = (0.80)^2 \times 50 = 32$$

b.   The call values in the second period are:

$$C_{uu} = 72 - 60 = 12$$
$$C_{ud} = C_{du} = C_{dd} = 0$$

Since $C_{ud} = C_{du} = 0$, then $C_d = 0$.

To compute C_u, first compute the hedge ratio:

$$H = \frac{C_{uu} - C_{ud}}{uuS_0 - udS_0} = \frac{12 - 0}{72 - 48} = \frac{1}{2}$$

Form a riskless portfolio by buying one share of stock and writing two calls.

The cost of the portfolio is: $S - 2C_u = \$60 - 2C_u$

The payoff for the riskless portfolio equals $48:

Riskless Portfolio	$S = 48$	$S = 72$
Buy 1 share	48	72
Write 2 calls	0	−24
Total	48	48

Therefore, find the value of the call by solving:

$$\$60 - 2C_u = \$48/1.06 \Rightarrow C_u = \$7.358$$

(continued on next page)

To compute C, compute the hedge ratio:

$$H = \frac{C_u - C_d}{uS_0 - dS_0} = \frac{7.358 - 0}{60 - 40} = 0.3679$$

Form a riskless portfolio by buying 0.3679 of a share and writing one call. The cost of the portfolio is $0.3679S - C = \$18.395 - C$

The payoff for the riskless portfolio equals $14.716:

Riskless Portfolio	$S = 40$	$S = 60$
Buy 0.3679 share	14.716	22.074
Write 1 call	0.000	−7.358
Total	14.716	14.716

Therefore, find the value of the call by solving:

$$\$18.395 - C = \$14.716/1.06 \Rightarrow C = \$4.512$$

c. The put values in the second period are:

$$P_{uu} = 0$$

$$P_{ud} = P_{du} = 60 - 48 = 12$$

$$P_{dd} = 60 - 32 = 28$$

To compute P_u, first compute the hedge ratio:

$$H = \frac{P_{uu} - P_{ud}}{uuS_0 - udS_0} = \frac{0 - 12}{72 - 48} = -\frac{1}{2}$$

Form a riskless portfolio by buying one share of stock and buying two puts. The cost of the portfolio is: $S + 2P_u = \$60 + 2P_u$

The payoff for the riskless portfolio equals $72:

Riskless Portfolio	$S = 48$	$S = 72$
Buy 1 share	48	72
Buy 2 puts	24	0
Total	72	72

Therefore, find the value of the put by solving:

$$\$60 + 2P_u = \$72/1.06 \Rightarrow P_u = \$3.962$$

(continued on next page)

To compute P_d, compute the hedge ratio:

$$H = \frac{P_{du} - P_{dd}}{duS_0 - ddS_0} = \frac{12-28}{48-32} = -1.0$$

Form a riskless portfolio by buying one share and buying one put.
The cost of the portfolio is: $S + P_d = \$40 + P_d$
The payoff for the riskless portfolio equals $60:

Riskless Portfolio	$S = 32$	$S = 48$
Buy 1 share	32	48
Buy 1 put	28	12
Total	60	60

Therefore, find the value of the put by solving

$$\$40 + P_d = \$60/1.06 \Rightarrow P_d = \$16.604$$

To compute P, compute the hedge ratio:

$$H = \frac{P_u - P_d}{uS_0 - dS_0} = \frac{3.962-16.604}{60-40} = -0.6321$$

Form a riskless portfolio by buying 0.6321 of a share and buying one put.
The cost of the portfolio is: $0.6321S + P = \$31.605 + P$

The payoff for the riskless portfolio equals $41.888:

Riskless Portfolio	$S = 40$	$S = 60$
Buy 0.6321 share	25.284	37.926
Buy 1 put	16.604	3.962
Total	41.888	41.888

Therefore, find the value of the put by solving:

$$\$31.605 + P = \frac{\$41.888}{1.06} \Rightarrow P = \$7.912$$

d.   According to put-call-parity:

$$C = S_0 + P - PV(X) = \$50 + \$7.912 - \frac{\$60}{1.06^2} = \$4.512$$

This is the value of the call calculated in part (b) above.

5.   a.   (i)   Index increases to 1,193. The combined portfolio will suffer a loss. The written calls expire in the money; the protective put purchased expires worthless. Let's analyze the outcome on a per-share basis. The payout for each call option is $43, for a total cash outflow of $86. The stock is worth $1,190. The portfolio will thus be worth:

$$\$1,190 - \$86 = \$1,104.00$$

The net cost of the portfolio when the option positions are established is:

$$\$1,136 + \$16.10 \text{ (put)} - [2 \times \$8.60] \text{ (calls written)} = \$1,134.90$$

The portfolio experiences a small loss of $30.90

           (ii)   Index remains at 1,136. Both options expire out of the money. The portfolio will thus be worth $1,136 (per share), compared to an initial cost 30 days earlier of $1,134.90. The portfolio experiences a very small gain of $1.10.

           (iii)   Index declines to 1,080. The calls expire worthless. The portfolio will be worth $1,130, the exercise price of the protective put. This represents a very small loss of $4.90 compared to the initial cost 30 days earlier of $1,134.90

    b.   (i)   Index increases to 1,193. The delta of the call approaches 1.0 as the stock goes deep into the money, while expiration of the call approaches and exercise becomes essentially certain. The put delta approaches zero.

           (ii)   Index remains at 1,136. Both options expire out of the money. Delta of each approaches zero as expiration approaches and it becomes certain that the options will not be exercised.

           (iii)   Index declines to 1,080. The call is out of the money as expiration approaches. Delta approaches zero. Conversely, the delta of the put approaches -1.0 as exercise becomes certain.

    c.   The call sells at an implied volatility (22.00%) that is less than recent historical volatility (23.00%); the put sells at an implied volatility (24.00%) that is greater than historical volatility. The call seems relatively cheap; the put seems expensive.

CHAPTER 22: FUTURES MARKETS

PROBLEM SETS

1. There is little hedging or speculative demand for cement futures, since cement prices are fairly stable and predictable. The trading activity necessary to support the futures market would not materialize. Only those commodities and financial securities with significant volatility tend to have futures contracts available for hedgers and speculators.

2. The ability to buy on margin is one advantage of futures. Another is the ease with which one can alter one's holdings of the asset. This is especially important if one is dealing in commodities, for which the futures market is far more liquid than the spot market.

3. Short selling results in an immediate cash inflow, whereas the short futures position does not:

Action	Initial CF	Final CF
Short sale	$+P_0$	$-P_T$
Short futures	0	$F_0 - P_T$

4. a. False. For any given level of the stock index, the futures price will be lower when the dividend yield is higher. This follows from spot-futures parity:
    $$F_0 = S_0 (1 + r_f - d)^T$$

    b. False. The parity relationship tells us that the futures price is determined by the stock price, the interest rate, and the dividend yield; it is not a function of beta.

    c. True. The short futures position will profit when the S&P 500 Index falls. This is a negative beta position.

5. The futures price is the agreed-upon price for deferred delivery of the asset. If that price is fair, then the value of the agreement ought to be zero; that is, the contract will be a zero-NPV agreement for each trader. Over time, however, the price of the underlying asset will change and this will affect the value of the contract.

6. Because long positions equal short positions, futures trading must entail a "canceling out" of bets on the asset. Moreover, no cash is exchanged at the inception of futures trading. Thus, there should be minimal impact on the spot market for the asset, and futures trading should not be expected to reduce capital available for other uses.

7.   a.   The closing futures price for the March contract was 1,491.80, which has a dollar value of:

$$\$250 \times 1,491.80 = \$372,950$$

Therefore, the required margin deposit is: $37,295

    b.   The futures price increases by: $1,498.00 − 1,491.80 = $6.2

The credit to your margin account would be: 6.2 × $250 = $1,550

This is a percent gain of: $1,550/$37,295 = 0.04 = 4%

Note that the futures price itself increased by only 0.42%.

    c.   Following the reasoning in part (b), any change in F is magnified by a ratio of (1 /margin requirement). This is the leverage effect. The return will be −10%.

8.   a. $F_0 = S_0(1 + r_f) = \$150 \times 1.03 = \$154.50$

    b. $F_0 = S_0(1 + r_f)^3 = \$150 \times 1.03^3 = \$163.91$

    c. $F_0 = 150 \times 1.06^3 = \$178.65$

9.   a.   Take a short position in T-bond futures, to offset interest rate risk. If rates increase, the loss on the bond will be offset to some extent by gains on the futures.

    b.   Again, a short position in T-bond futures will offset the interest rate risk.

    c.   You want to protect your cash outlay when the bond is purchased. If bond prices increase, you will need extra cash to purchase the bond. Thus, you should take a long futures position that will generate a profit if prices increase.

10. $F_0 = S_0 \times (1 + r_f - d) = 1,400 \times (1 + 0.03 - 0.02) = 1,414$

If the T-bill rate is less than the dividend yield, then the futures price should be less than the spot price.

11.   The put-call parity relation states that: But spot-futures parity tells us that:

$$C = P + S_0 - \frac{X}{(1+r_f)^T} \qquad\qquad F = S_0 \times (1+r_f)^T$$

Substituting, we find that:

$$P = C - S_0 + \frac{[S_0 \times (1+r_f)^T]}{(1+r_f)^T} = C - S_0 + S_0 = C$$

12. According to the parity relation, the proper price for December futures is:

$$F_{Dec} = F_{June}(1 + r_f)^{1/2} = 1500 \times 1.02^{1/2} = 1,514.93$$

The actual futures price for December is low relative to the June price. You should take a long position in the December contract and short the June contract.

13. a. $120 \times 1.06 = \$127.20$

     b. The stock price falls to: $120 \times (1 - 0.03) = \$116.40$

         The futures price falls to: $116.4 \times 1.06 = \$123.384$

         The investor loses: $(127.20 - 123.384) \times 1,000 = \$3,816$

     c. The percentage loss is: $\$3,816/\$12,000 = 0.318 = 31.8\%$

14. a. The initial futures price is $F_0 = 1300 \times (1 + 0.005 - 0.002)^{12} = \$1,347.58$

         In one month, the futures price will be:

         $$F_0 = 1320 \times (1 + 0.005 - 0.002)^{11} = \$1,364.22$$

         The increase in the futures price is 16.64, so the cash flow will be:

         $$16.64 \times \$250 = \$4,160.00$$

     b. The holding period return is: $\$4,160.00/\$13,000 = 0.3200 = 32.00\%$

15. The treasurer would like to buy the bonds today but cannot. As a proxy for this purchase, T-bond futures contracts can be purchased. If rates do in fact fall, the treasurer will have to buy back the bonds for the sinking fund at prices higher than the prices at which they could be purchased today. However, the gains on the futures contracts will offset this higher cost to some extent.

16. The parity value of F is: $1,550 \times (1 + 0.04 - 0.01) = 1,597$

     The actual futures price is 1,550, too low by 47.

Arbitrage Portfolio	CF now	CF in 1 year
Short index	1,500	$-S_T - (0.01 \times 1,500)$
Buy futures	0	$S_T - 1,550$
Lend	−1,500	$1,500 \times 1.04$
Total	0	47

17. a.   Futures prices are determined from the spreadsheet as follows:

Spot Futures Parity and Time Spreads			
Spot price	1,500		
Income yield (%)	1.5	Futures prices versus maturity	
Interest rate (%)	3.0		
Today's date	1/1/2013	Spot price	1,500.00
Maturity date 1	2/14/2013	Futures 1	1,502.67
Maturity date 2	5/21/2013	Futures 2	1,508.71
Maturity date 3	11/18/2013	Futures 3	1,519.79
Time to maturity 1	0.12		
Time to maturity 2	0.39		
Time to maturity 3	0.88		
		LEGEND:	
		Enter data	
		Value calculated	
		See comment	

    b.   The spreadsheet demonstrates that the futures prices now decrease with increased income yield:

Spot Futures Parity and Time Spreads			
Spot price	1,500		
Income yield (%)	4.0	Futures prices versus maturity	
Interest rate (%)	3.0		
Today's date	1/1/2013	Spot price	1,500.00
Maturity date 1	2/14/2013	Futures 1	1,498.20
Maturity date 2	5/21/2013	Futures 2	1,494.15
Maturity date 3	11/18/2013	Futures 3	1,486.78
Time to maturity 1	0.12		
Time to maturity 2	0.39		
Time to maturity 3	0.88		
		LEGEND:	
		Enter data	
		Value calculated	
		See comment	

18. a.   The current yield for Treasury bonds (coupon divided by price) plays the role of the dividend yield.

    b.   When the yield curve is upward sloping, the current yield exceeds the short rate. Hence, T-bond futures prices on more distant contracts are lower than those on near-term contracts.

19. a.

	Cash Flows		
Action	Now	T_1	T_2
Long futures with maturity T_1	0	$P_1 - F(T_1)$	0
Short futures with maturity T_2	0	0	$F(T_2) - P_2$
Buy asset at T_1, sell at T_2	0	$-P_1$	P_2
At T_1, borrow $F(T_1)$	0	$F(T_1)$	$-F(T_1) \times (1+r_f)^{(T_2-T_1)}$
Total	0	0	$F(T_2) - F(T_1) \times (1+r_f)^{(T_2-T_1)}$

b. Since the T_2 cash flow is riskless and the net investment was zero, then any profits represent an arbitrage opportunity.

c. The zero-profit no-arbitrage restriction implies that

$$F(T_2) = F(T_1) \times (1+r_f)^{(T_2-T_1)}$$

CFA PROBLEMS

1. a. The strategy that would take advantage of the arbitrage opportunity is a "reverse cash and carry." A reverse cash and carry opportunity results when the following relationship does not hold true:

$$F_0 \geq S_0 (1+C)$$

If the futures price is less than the spot price plus the cost of carrying the goods to the futures delivery date, then an arbitrage opportunity exists. A trader would be able to sell the asset short, use the proceeds to lend at the prevailing interest rate, and then buy the asset for future delivery. At the future delivery, the trader would then collect the proceeds of the loan with interest, accept delivery of the asset, and cover the short position in the commodity.

b.

	Cash Flows	
Action	Now	One year from now
Sell the spot commodity short	+$120.00	-$125.00
Buy the commodity futures expiring in 1 year	$0.00	$0.00
Contract to lend $120 at 8% for 1 year	-$120.00	+$129.60
Total cash flow	$0.00	+$4.60

2. a. The call option is distinguished by its asymmetric payoff. If the Swiss franc rises in value, then the company can buy francs for a given number of dollars to service its debt and thereby put a cap on the dollar cost of its financing. If the franc falls, the company will benefit from the change in the exchange rate. The futures and forward contracts have symmetric payoffs. The dollar cost of the financing is locked in regardless of whether the franc appreciates or depreciates. The major difference from the firm's perspective between futures and forwards is in the mark-to-market feature of futures. The consequence of this is that the firm must be ready for the cash management issues surrounding cash inflows or outflows as the currency values and futures prices fluctuate.

    b. The call option gives the company the ability to benefit from depreciation in the franc but at a cost equal to the option premium. Unless the firm has some special expertise in currency speculation, it seems that the futures or forward strategy, which locks in a dollar cost of financing without an option premium, may be the better strategy.

3. The important distinction between a futures contract and an options contract is that the futures contract is an obligation. When an investor purchases or sells a futures contract, the investor has an obligation to either accept or deliver, respectively, the underlying commodity on the expiration date. In contrast, the buyer of an option contract is not obligated to accept or deliver the underlying commodity but instead has the right, or choice, to accept delivery (for call holders) or make delivery (for put holders) of the underlying commodity anytime during the life of the contract.

    Futures and options modify a portfolio's risk in different ways. Buying or selling a futures contract affects a portfolio's upside risk and downside risk by a similar magnitude. This is commonly referred to as *symmetrical impact*. On the other hand, the addition of a call or put option to a portfolio does not affect a portfolio's upside risk and downside risk to a similar magnitude. Unlike futures contracts, the impact of options on the risk profile of a portfolio is asymmetric.

4. a. The investor should sell the forward contract to protect the value of the bond against rising interest rates during the holding period. Because the investor intends to take a long position in the underlying asset, the hedge requires a short position in the derivative instrument.

    b. The value of the forward contract on expiration date is equal to the spot price of the underlying asset on expiration date minus the forward price of the contract:

    $978.40 - $1,024.70 = -$46.30

    The contract has a negative value. This is the value to the holder of a long position in the forward contract. In this example, the investor should be *short* the forward contract, so that the value to this investor would be +$46.30 since this is the cash flow the investor expects to receive.

c.   The value of the combined portfolio at the end of the six-month holding period is:

$978.40 + $46.30 = $1,024.70

The change in the value of the combined portfolio during this six-month period is $24.70

The value of the combined portfolio is the sum of the market value of the bond and the value of the *short* position in the forward contract. At the start of the six-month holding period, the bond is worth $1,000 and the forward contract has a value of zero (because this is not an off-market forward contract, no money changes hands at initiation). Six months later, the bond value is $978.40 and the value of the *short* position in the forward contract is $46.30, as calculated in part (b).

The fact that the combined value of the long position in the bond and the short position in the forward contract at the forward contract's maturity date is equal to the forward price on the forward contract at its initiation date is not a coincidence. By taking a long position in the underlying asset and a short position in the forward contract, the investor has created a fully hedged (and hence risk-free) position and should earn the risk-free rate of return. The six-month risk-free rate of return is 5% (annualized), which produces a return of $24.70 over a six-month period:

$$(\$1,000 \times 1.05^{(1/2)}) - \$1,000 = \$24.70$$

These results support VanHusen's statement that selling a forward contract on the underlying bond protects the portfolio during a period of rising interest rates. The loss in the value of the underlying bond during the six-month holding period is offset by the cash payment made at expiration date to the holder of the short position in the forward contract; that is, a short position in the forward contract protects (hedges) the long position in the underlying asset.

5.   a.   Accurate. Futures contracts are marked to the market daily. Holding a short position on a bond futures contract during a period of rising interest rates (declining bond prices) generates positive cash inflow from the daily mark to market. If an investor in a futures contract has a long position when the price of the underlying asset increases, then the daily mark to market generates a positive cash inflow that can be reinvested. Forward contracts settle only at expiration date and do not generate any cash flow prior to expiration.

b.   Inaccurate. According to the cost-of-carry model, the futures contract price is adjusted upward by the cost of carry for the underlying asset. Bonds (and other financial instruments), however, do not have any significant storage costs. Moreover, the cost of carry is reduced by any coupon payments paid to the bondholder during the life of the futures contract. Any "convenience yield" from holding the underlying bond also reduces the cost of carry. As a result, the cost of carry for a bond is likely to be negative.

CHAPTER 23: FUTURES, SWAPS, AND RISK MANAGEMENT

PROBLEM SETS

1. In formulating a hedge position, a stock's beta and a bond's duration are used similarly to determine the expected percentage gain or loss in the value of the underlying asset for a given change in market conditions. Then, in each of these markets, the expected percentage change in value is used to calculate the expected dollar change in value of the stock or bond portfolios, respectively. Finally, the dollar change in value of the underlying asset, along with the dollar change in the value of the futures contract, determines the hedge ratio.

    The major difference in the calculations necessary to formulate a hedge position in each market lies in the manner in which the first step identified above is computed. For a hedge in the equity market, the product of the equity portfolio's beta with respect to the given market index and the expected percentage change in the index for the futures contract equals the expected percentage change in the value of the portfolio. Clearly, if the portfolio has a positive beta and the investor is concerned about hedging against a decline in the index, the result of this calculation is a decrease in the value of the portfolio. For a hedge in the fixed income market, the product of the bond's modified duration and the expected change in the bond's yield equals the expected percentage change in the value of the bond. Here, the investor who has a long position in a bond (or a bond portfolio) is concerned about the possibility of an increase in yield, and the resulting change in the bond's value is a loss.

    A secondary difference in the calculations necessary to formulate a hedge position in each market arises in the calculation of the hedge ratio. In the equity market, the hedge ratio is typically calculated by dividing the total expected dollar change in the value of the portfolio (for a given change in the index) by the profit (i.e., the dollar change in value) on one futures contract (for the given change in the index). In the bond market, the comparable calculation is generally thought of in terms of the price value of a basis point (PVBP) for the bond and the PVBP for the futures contract, rather than in terms of the total dollar change in both the value of the portfolio and the value of a single futures contract.

2. One of the considerations that would enter into the hedging strategy for a U.S. exporting firm with outstanding bills to its customers denominated in foreign currency is whether the U.S. firm also has outstanding payables denominated in the same foreign currency. Since the firm receives foreign currency when its customers' bills are paid, the firm hedges by taking a short position in the foreign currency. The U.S. firm would reduce its short position in futures to the extent that outstanding payables offset outstanding receivables with the same maturity because the outstanding payables effectively hedge the exchange rate risk of the outstanding receivables. Equivalently, if the U.S. firm expects to incur ongoing obligations denominated in the same foreign currency in order to meet expenses required to deliver additional products to its customers, then the firm would reduce its short position in the foreign currency futures. In general, if the U.S. firm incurs expenses in the

same foreign currency, then the firm would take a short position in the currency futures to hedge its profits measured in the foreign currency. If the U.S. firm incurs all of its expenses in U.S. dollars, but bills its customers in the foreign currency, then the firm would take a position to hedge the outstanding receivables, not just the profit. Another consideration that affects the U.S. exporting firm's willingness to hedge its exchange rate risk is the impact of depreciation of the foreign currency on the firm's prices for its products. For a U.S. firm that sets its prices in the foreign currency, the dollar-equivalent price of the firm's products is reduced when the foreign currency depreciates, so that the firm is likely to find it desirable to increase its short position in currency futures to hedge against this risk. If the U.S. firm is not able to increase the price of its products in the foreign currency due to competition, the depreciation of the foreign currency has an impact on profits similar to the impact of foreign currency depreciation on the U.S. firm's receivables.

3. The hedge will be much more effective for the gold-producing firm. Prices for distant maturity oil futures contracts have surprisingly low correlation with current prices because convenience yields and storage costs for oil can change dramatically over time. When near-term oil prices fall, there may be little or no change in longer-term prices, since oil prices for very distant delivery generally respond only slightly to changes in the current market for short-horizon oil. Because the correlation between short- and long-maturity oil futures is so low, hedging long-term commitments with short-maturity contracts does little to eliminate risk; that is, such a hedge eliminates very little of the variance entailed in uncertain future oil prices.

    In contrast, both convenience yields and storage costs for gold are substantially smaller and more stable; the result is that the correlation between short-term and more distant gold futures prices is substantially greater. In other words, the basis between near and distant maturity gold futures prices is far less variable, so hedging long-term prices with short-term gold contracts results in a substantially greater percentage reduction in volatility.

4. Municipal bond yields, which are below T-bond yields (tax-exempt status), are expected to close in on Treasury yields. Because yields and prices are inversely related, municipal bond prices will perform poorly compared to Treasuries. Establish a spread position, buying Treasury-bond futures and selling municipal bond futures. The net bet on the general level of interest rates is approximately zero. You have made a bet on relative performances in the two sectors.

5. a. $S_0 \times (1 + r_M) - D = (1,425 \times 1.06) - 15 = 1,495.50$

    b. $S_0 \times (1 + r_f) - D = (1,425 \times 1.03) - 15 = 1,452.75$

c. The futures price is too low. Buy futures, short the index, and invest the proceeds of the short sale in T-bills:

	CF Now	CF in 6 months
Buy futures	0	$S_T - 1,422$
Short index	1,425	$-S_T - 15$
Buy T-bills	−1,425	1,467.75
Total	0	30.75

6. a. The value of the underlying stock is:

$$\$250 \times 1,600 = \$400,000$$
$$\$25/\$400,000 = 0.0000625 = 0.0063\% \text{ of the value of the stock}$$

b. $\$40 \times 0.000063 = \$0.00250$

c. $\$0.10/\$0.0025 = 40.00$

The transaction cost in the stock market is 40.00 times the transaction cost in the futures market.

7. a. You should be short the index futures contracts. If the stock value falls, you need futures profits to offset the loss.

b. Each contract is for $250 times the index, currently valued at 1,650. Therefore, each contract controls stock worth: $\$250 \times 1,650 = \$412,500$
In order to hedge a $16.5 million portfolio, you need:

$$\frac{16,500,000}{412,500} = 40 \text{ contracts}$$

c. Now, your stock swings only 0.6 as much as the market index. Hence, you need 0.6 as many contracts as in (b): $0.6 \times 40 = 24$ contracts.

8. If the beta of the portfolio were 1.0, she would sell $1 million of the index. Because beta is 1.25, she should sell $1.25 million of the index.

9. You would short $0.50 of the market index contract and $0.75 of the computer industry contract for each dollar held in IBM.

10. The dollar is depreciating relative to the euro. To induce investors to invest in the U.S., the U.S. interest rate must be higher.

11. a. From parity: $F_0 = E_0 \times \dfrac{1+r_{US}}{1+r_{UK}} = 2.00 \times \dfrac{1.04}{1.06} = 1.962$

  b. Let $F_0 = \$2.03/£$. Dollars are relatively too cheap in the forward market $\leftrightarrow$ pounds are too expensive. Borrow the present value of £1, use the proceeds to buy pound-denominated bills in the spot market, and sell £1 forward:

Action Now	CF in $	Action at period-end	CF in $
Sell £1 forward for $2.03	0	Collect $2.03, deliver £1	$2.03 – E_1
Buy £1/1.06 in spot market; invest at the British risk-free rate	–2.00/1.06 = –$1.887	Exchange £1 for E_1	E_1
Borrow $1.887	$1.887	Repay loan; U.S. interest rate = 4%	–$1.962
Total	0	Total	$0.068

12. a. Lend in the U.K.

  b. Borrow in the U.S.

  c. Lending in the U.S. offers a 4% rate of return. Lending in the U.K. and covering interest rate risk with futures or forwards offers a rate of return of

$$r_{US} = \left[(1+r_{UK}) \times \frac{F_0}{E_0} \right] - 1 = \left[1.07 \times \frac{1.98}{2.00} \right] - 1 = 0.0593 = 5.93\%$$

An arbitrage strategy involves simultaneous lending (UK) and borrowing (US) with the covering of interest rate risk:

Action Now	CF in $	Action at period-end	CF in $
Borrow $2.00 in U.S.	$2.00	Repay loan	–$2.00 × 1.04
Convert borrowed dollars to pounds; lend £1 pound in U.K.	–$2.00	Collect repayment; exchange proceeds for dollars	1.07 × E_1
Sell forward £1.07 at F_0 =	0	Unwind forward	1.07 × ($1.98 – E_1)
Total	0	Total	$0.0386

13. The farmer must sell forward

  100,000 × (1/0.90) = 111,111 bushels of yellow corn

  This requires selling 111,111/5,000 = 22.2 contracts

14. The closing futures price will be: $100 - 0.40 = 99.60$

    The initial futures price was 99.7400, so the loss to the long side is 14 basis points or

    14 basis points $\times$ \$25 per basis point = \$350

    The loss can also be computed as

    $0.0014 \times \frac{1}{4} \times \$1,000,000 = \$350$

15. Suppose the yield on your portfolio increases by 1.5 basis points. Then the yield on the T-bond contract is likely to increase by 1 basis point. The loss on your portfolio will be

    \$1 million $\times \Delta y \times D^* = \$1,000,000 \times 0.00015 \times 4 = \$600$

    The change in the futures price (per \$100 par value) will be

    $\$95 \times 0.0001 \times 9 = \$0.0855$

    This is a change of \$85.50 on a \$100,000 par value contract. Therefore you should sell:

    $\$600/\$85.50 = 7$ contracts

16. She must sell: $\$1 \text{ million} \times \frac{8}{10} = \$0.8 \text{ million of T-bonds}$

17. If yield changes on the bond and the contracts are each 1 basis point, then the bond value will change by

    $\$10,000,000 \times 0.0001 \times 8 = \$8,000$

    The contract will result in a cash flow of

    $\$100,000 \times 0.0001 \times 6 = \$60$

    Therefore, the firm should sell: $8,000/60 = 133$ contracts

    The firm sells the contracts because you need profits on the contract to offset losses as a bond issuer if interest rates increase.

18. $F_0 = S_0(1 + r_f)^T = 1500 \times 1.02 = 1530$

    If $F_0 = 1545$, you could earn arbitrage profits as follows:

	CF Now	CF in 1 year
Buy gold	−1500	S_T
Short futures	0	$1545 - S_T$
Borrow \$980	1500	−1530
Total	0	15

    The forward price must be 1530 in order for this strategy to yield no profit.

19. If a poor harvest today indicates a worse than average harvest in future years, then the futures prices will rise in response to today's harvest, although presumably the two-year price will change by less than the one-year price. The same reasoning holds if corn is stored across the harvest. Next year's price is determined by the available supply at harvest time, which is the actual harvest plus the stored corn. A smaller harvest today means less stored corn for next year which can lead to higher prices.

Suppose first that corn is never stored across a harvest, and second that the quality of a harvest is not related to the quality of past harvests. Under these circumstances, there is no link between the current price of corn and the expected future price of corn. The quantity of corn stored will fall to zero before the next harvest, and thus the quantity of corn and the price in one year will depend solely on the quantity of next year's harvest, which has nothing to do with this year's harvest.

20. The required rate of return on an asset with the same risk as corn is

$$.5\% + 0.5(.9\% - .5\%) = .7\% \text{ per month}$$

Thus, in the absence of storage costs, three months from now corn would sell for

$$\$5.50 \times 1.007^3 = \$5.616$$

The future value of three month's storage costs is

$$\$0.03 \times FA(.5\%, 3) = \$0.090 \text{ (PMT} = \$0.03; N = 3; I = 0.5; PV = \$0; \text{ Solve for } FV = \$0.09).$$

where FA stands for the future value factor for a level annuity with a given interest rate and number of payments. Thus, in order to induce storage, the expected price would have to be

$$\$5.616 + \$0.090 = \$5.707$$

Because the expected spot price is $5.88, you would store corn.

21. If the exchange of currencies were structured as three separate forward contracts, the forward prices would be determined as follows:

Forward exchange rate × $1 million euros = Dollars to be delivered

Year 1: $1.50 \times (1.04/1.03) \times 1$ million euros = $1.5146 million

Year 2: $1.50 \times (1.04/1.03)^2 \times 1$ million euros = $1.5293 million

Year 3: $1.50 \times (1.04/1.03)^3 \times 1$ million euros = $1.5441 million

Instead, we deliver the same number of dollars (F^*) each year. The value of F^* is determined by first computing the present value of this obligation:

$$\frac{F^*}{1.04^1} + \frac{F^*}{1.04^2} + \frac{F^*}{1.04^3} = \frac{1.5146}{1.04^1} + \frac{1.5293}{1.04^2} + \frac{1.5441}{1.04^3} = 4.2430$$

F^* equals $1.5290 million per year (PV = 4.243; N = 3; I = 4; FV = $0; Solve for PMT = 1.529).

22. The firm's overall cost of the fund will equal the spread between the LIBOR rate and the fixed rate on debt times the notional principal. In this case $(0.06-0.07) \times \$100,000,000 = -\$1,000,000$.

23. a. The swap rate moved in favor of firm ABC. ABC should have received 1% more per year than it could receive in the current swap market. Based on notional principal of $10 million, the loss is

    $0.01 \times \$10$ million $= \$100,000$ per year.

    b. The market value of the fixed annual loss is obtained by discounting at the current 5% rate on three-year swaps. The loss is

    $\$100,000 \times$ Annuity factor (5%, 3) $= \$272,325$
    (PMT $= \$100,000$; N $= 3$; I $= 5$; FV $= \$0$; Solve for PV $= \$272,325$)

    c. If ABC had become insolvent, XYZ would not be harmed. XYZ would be happy to see the swap agreement canceled. However, the swap agreement ought to be treated as an asset of ABC when the firm is reorganized.

24. The firm receives a fixed rate that is 2% higher than the market rate. The extra payment of $(0.02 \times \$10$ million) has present value equal to
    $\$200,000 \times$ Annuity factor (8%, 5) $= \$798,542$
    (PMT $= \$200,000$; N $= 5$; I $= 8$; FV $= \$0$; Solve for PV $= \$798,542$)

25. a. From parity: $F_0 = 1,600 \times (1 + 0.03) - 20 = 1,628$

    Actual F_0 is 1,624; so the futures price is 4 below the "proper" level.

    b. Buy the relatively cheap futures, sell the relatively expensive stock and lend the proceeds of the short sale:

	CF Now	CF in 6 months
Buy futures	0	$S_T - 1,624$
Sell shares	1,600	$-S_T - 20$
Lend $1,600	−1,600	1,648
Total	0	4

c. If you do not receive interest on the proceeds of the short sales, then the $1,600 you receive will not be invested but will simply be returned to you. The proceeds from the strategy in part (b) are now negative: an arbitrage opportunity no longer exists.

	CF Now	CF in 6 months
Buy futures	0	$S_T - 1{,}624$
Sell shares	1,600	$-S_T - 20$
Place $1,200 in margin account	−1,600	1,600
Total	0	−44

d. If we call the original futures price F_0, then the proceeds from the long-futures, short-stock strategy are

	CF Now	CF in 6 months
Buy futures	0	$S_T - F_0$
Sell shares	1,600	$-S_T - 20$
Place $1,200 in margin account	−1,600	1,600
Total	0	$1{,}580 - F_0$

F_0 can be as low as 1,580 without giving rise to an arbitrage opportunity.

On the other hand, if F_0 is higher than the parity value (1,628), then an arbitrage opportunity (buy stocks, sell futures) will exist.

	CF Now	CF in 6 months
Sell futures	0	$F_0 - S_T$
Buy shares	−1,600	$S_T + 20$
Borrow $1,200	1,600	−1,648
Total	0	$F_0 - 1{,}628$

Therefore, the no-arbitrage range is

$$1{,}580 \leq F_0 \leq 1{,}628$$

26. a. Call p the fraction of proceeds from the short sale to which we have access. Ignoring transaction costs, the lower bound on the futures price that precludes arbitrage is the following usual parity value (except for the factor p):

$$S_0(1 + r_f p) - D$$

The dividend (D) equals: $0.012 \times 1{,}350 = \$16.20$

The factor p arises because only this fraction of the proceeds from the short sale can be invested in the risk-free asset. We can solve for p as follows:

$$1{,}350 \times (1 + 0.022p) - 16.20 = 1{,}351 \Rightarrow p = 0.579$$

b. With $p = 0.9$, the no-arbitrage lower bound on the futures price is
$$1,350 \times [1 + (0.022 \times 0.9)] - 16.20 = 1,360.53$$

The actual futures price is 1,351. The departure from the bound is therefore 9.53. This departure also equals the potential profit from an arbitrage strategy. The strategy is to short the stock, which currently sells at 1,350. The investor receives 90% of the proceeds (1,215) and the remainder (135) remains in the margin account until the short position is covered in six months. The investor buys futures and lends 1,215:

	CF Now	CF in 6 months
Buy futures	0	$S_T - 1,351$
Sell shares	1350 − 135	$135 - S_T - 16.20$
Lend	−1,215	$1,215 \times 1.022 = 1,241.73$
Total	0	9.53

The profit is: $9.53 \times \$250$ per contract = $2,382.50

CFA PROBLEMS

1. a. By spot-futures parity:
$$F_0 = S_0 \times (1 + r_f) = 185 \times [1 + (0.06/2)] = 190.55$$

b. The lower bound is based on the reverse cash-and-carry strategy.

Action Now	CF in $	Action at period-end	CF in $
Buy one TOBEC index futures contract	0	Sell one TOBEC index futures contract	$100 \times (F_1 - F_0)$
Sell spot TOBEC index	+$18,500	Buy spot TOBEC index	$-\$100 \times S_1$
Lend $18,500	−$18,500	Collect loan repayment	$18,500 \times 1.03 = +\$19,055$
		Pay transaction costs	−$15.00
Total	0	Total	$-\$100 F_0 + \$19,040$

(Note that $F_1 = S_1$ at expiration.)
$-\$100 F_0 + \$19,040 = 0 \rightarrow$
The lower bound for F_0 is: $19,040/100 = 190.40$

2. a. The strategy would be to sell Japanese stock index futures to hedge the market risk of Japanese stocks, and to sell yen futures to hedge the currency exposure.

b. Some possible practical difficulties with this strategy include
- Contract size on futures may not match size of portfolio.
- Stock portfolio may not closely track index portfolios on which futures trade.
- Cash flow management issues from marking to market.
- Potential mispricing of futures contracts (violations of parity).

3. a. The hedged investment involves converting the $1 million to foreign currency, investing in that country, and selling forward the foreign currency in order to lock in the dollar value of the investment. Because the interest rates are for 90-day periods, we assume they are quoted as bond equivalent yields, annualized using simple interest. Therefore, to express rates on a per quarter basis, we divide these rates by 4:

	Japanese government	Swiss government
Convert $1 million to local currency	$1,000,000 × 133.05 = ¥133,050,000	$1,000,000 × 1.5260 = SF1,526,000
Invest in local currency for 90 days	¥133,050,000 × [1 + (0.076/4)] = ¥135,577,950	SF1,526,000 × [1 + (0.086/4)] = SF1,558,809
Convert to $ at 90-day forward rate	135,577,950/133.47 = $1,015,793	1,558,809/1.5348 = $1,015,643

b. The results in the two currencies are nearly identical. This near-equality reflects the interest rate parity theorem. This theory asserts that the pricing relationships between interest rates and spot and forward exchange rates must make covered (that is, fully hedged and riskless) investments in any currency equally attractive.

c. The 90-day return in Japan is 1.5793%, which represents a bond-equivalent yield of 1.5793% × 365/90 = 6.405%. The 90-day return in Switzerland is 1.5643%, which represents a bond-equivalent yield of 1.5643% × 365/90 = 6.344%. The estimate for the 90-day risk-free U.S. government money market yield is in this range.

4. The investor can buy X amount of pesos at the (indirect) spot exchange rate and invest the pesos in the Mexican bond market. Then, in one year, the investor will have

$$X \times (1 + r_{MEX}) \text{ pesos}$$

These pesos can then be converted back into dollars using the (indirect) forward exchange rate. Interest rate parity asserts that the two holding period returns must be equal, which can be represented by the formula:

$$(1 + r_{US}) = E_0 \times (1 + r_{MEX}) \times (1/F_0)$$

The left side of the equation represents the holding-period return for a U.S. dollar-denominated bond. If interest rate parity holds, then this term also corresponds to the U.S. dollar holding-period return for the currency-hedged Mexican one-year bond. The right side of the equation is the holding-period return, in dollar terms, for a currency-hedged peso-denominated bond. Solving for r_{US}:

$$(1 + r_{US}) = 9.5000 \times (1 + 0.065) \times (1/9.8707)$$

$$(1 + r_{US}) = 1.0250$$

$$r_{US} = 2.50\%$$

Thus $r_{US} = 2.50\%$, which is the same as the yield for the one-year U.S. bond.

5.   a.   From parity: $F_0 = E_0 \times \left(\dfrac{1+r_{Japan}}{1+r_{US}}\right)^{0.5} = 124.30 \times \left(\dfrac{1.0010}{1.0380}\right)^{0.5} = 122.06453$

b.

Action Now	CF in $	Action at Period-end	CF in ¥
Borrow $1,000,000 in U.S.	$1,000,000	Repay loan	$-(\$1,000,000 \times 1.035^{0.25}) =$ $-\$1,008,637.446$
Sell forward $1,008,637.446 at $F_0 = ¥123.2605$	0	Unwind forward	$-(1,008,637.446 \times ¥123.2605) =$ $-¥124,325,155.9127$
Convert borrowed dollars to yen; lend ¥124,300,000 in Japan	$-\$1,000,000$	Collect repayment in yen	$¥124,300,000 \times 1.005^{0.25} =$ $¥124,455,084.5187$
Total	0	Total	¥129,928.61

The arbitrage profit is ¥129,928.61

6.   a.   Delsing should sell stock index futures contracts and buy bond futures contracts. This strategy is justified because buying the bond futures and selling the stock index futures provides the same exposure as buying the bonds and selling the stocks. This strategy assumes high correlation between the bond futures and the bond portfolio, as well as high correlation between the stock index futures and the stock portfolio.

b.   The number of contracts in each case is:

i. $5 \times \$200,000,000 \times 0.0001 = \$100,000$

$\$100,000/97.85 = 1022$ contracts

ii. $\$200,000,000/(\$1,378 \times 250) = 581$ contracts

7.   <u>Situation A.</u> The market value of the portfolio to be hedged is $20 million. The market value of the bonds controlled by one futures contract is $63,330. If we were to equate the market values of the portfolio and the futures contract, we would sell

$20,000,000/$63,330 = 315.806 contracts

However, we must adjust this "naive" hedge for the price volatility of the bond portfolio relative to the futures contract. Price volatilities differ according to both the duration and the yield volatility of the bonds. In this case, the yield volatilities may be assumed equal, because any yield spread between the Treasury portfolio and the Treasury bond underlying the futures contract is likely to be stable. However, the duration of the Treasury portfolio is less than that of the futures contract. Adjusting the naive hedge for relative duration and relative yield volatility, we obtain the adjusted hedge position

$$315.806 \times \frac{7.6}{8.0} \times 1.0 = 300 \text{ contracts}$$

<u>Situation B.</u> Here, the treasurer seeks to hedge the purchase price of the bonds; this requires a long hedge. The market value of the bonds to be purchased is

$20 million \times 0.93 = $18.6 million

The duration ratio is 7.2/8.0, and the relative yield volatility is 1.25. Therefore, the hedge requires the treasurer to take a long position in

$$\frac{18,600,000}{63,330} \times \frac{7.2}{8.0} \times 1.25 = 330 \text{ contracts}$$

8.   a.   % change in T-bond price = Modified duration × Change in YTM

$$= 7.0 \times 0.50\% = 3.5\%$$

     b.   When the YTM of the T-bond changes by 50 basis points, the predicted change in the yield on the KC bond is $1.22 \times 50 = 61$ basis points. Therefore

% change in KC price = Modified duration × Change in YTM

$$= 6.93 \times 0.61\% = 4.23\%$$

CHAPTER 24: PORTFOLIO PERFORMANCE EVALUATION

PROBLEM SETS

1. The dollar-weighted average will be the internal rate of return between the initial and final value of the account, including additions and withdrawals. Using Excel's XIRR function, utilizing the given dates and values, the dollar-weighted average return is as follows:

Date	Account
1/1/2010	−$148,000.00
1/3/2010	$2,500.00
3/20/2010	$4,000.00
7/5/2010	$1,500.00
12/2/2010	$14,360.00
3/10/2011	−$23,000.00
4/7/2011	$3,000.00
5/3/2011	$198,000.00
	26.99%

=XIRR(C13:C20,B13:B20)

Since the dates of additions and withdrawals are not equally spaced, there really is no way to solve this problem using a financial calculator. Excel can solve this very quickly.

2. As established in the following result from the text, the Sharpe ratio depends on both alpha for the portfolio (α_P) and the correlation between the portfolio and the market index (ρ):

$$\frac{E(r_P - r_f)}{\sigma_P} = \frac{\alpha_P}{\sigma_P} + \rho S_M$$

Specifically, this result demonstrates that a lower correlation with the market index reduces the Sharpe ratio. Hence, if alpha is not sufficiently large, the portfolio is inferior to the index. Another way to think about this conclusion is to note that, even for a portfolio with a positive alpha, if its diversifiable risk is sufficiently large, thereby reducing the correlation with the market index, this can result in a lower Sharpe ratio.

3. The IRR (i.e., the dollar-weighted return) cannot be ranked relative to either the geometric average return (i.e., the time-weighted return) or the arithmetic average return. Under some conditions, the IRR is greater than each of the other two averages, and similarly, under other conditions, the IRR can also be less than each of the other averages. A number of scenarios can be developed to illustrate this conclusion. For example, consider a scenario where the rate of return each period consistently increases over several time periods. If the amount invested also increases each period, and then all of the proceeds are withdrawn at the end of several periods, the IRR is greater than either the geometric or the

arithmetic average because more money is invested at the higher rates than at the lower rates. On the other hand, if withdrawals gradually reduce the amount invested as the rate of return increases, then the IRR is less than each of the other averages. (Similar scenarios are illustrated with numerical examples in the text, where the IRR is shown to be less than the geometric average, and in Concept Check 1, where the IRR is greater than the geometric average.)

4. It is not necessarily wise to shift resources to timing at the expense of security selection. There is also tremendous potential value in security analysis. The decision as to whether to shift resources has to be made on the basis of the macro, compared to the micro, forecasting ability of the portfolio management team.

5. a. Arithmetic average: $\bar{r}_{ABC} = 10\%$; $\bar{r}_{XYZ} = 10\%$

   b. Dispersion: $\sigma_{ABC} = 7.07\%$; $\sigma_{XYZ} = 13.91\%$

      Stock XYZ has greater dispersion.
      (Note: We used 5 degrees of freedom in calculating standard deviations.)

   c. Geometric average:
      $$r_{ABC} = (1.20 \times 1.12 \times 1.14 \times 1.03 \times 1.01)^{1/5} - 1 = 0.0977 = 9.77\%$$
      $$r_{XYZ} = (1.30 \times 1.12 \times 1.18 \times 1.00 \times 0.90)^{1/5} - 1 = 0.0911 = 9.11\%$$

      Despite the fact that the two stocks have the same arithmetic average, the geometric average for XYZ is less than the geometric average for ABC. The reason for this result is the fact that the greater variance of XYZ drives the geometric average further below the arithmetic average.

   d. In terms of "forward-looking" statistics, the arithmetic average is the better estimate of expected rate of return. Therefore, if the data reflect the probabilities of future returns, 10 percent is the expected rate of return for both stocks.

6. a. Time-weighted average returns are based on year-by-year rates of return:

Year	Return = (Capital gains + Dividend)/Price
2013 – 2014	[($120 – $100) + $4]/$100 = 24.00%
2014 – 2015	[($90 – $120) + $4]/$120 = –21.67%
2015 – 2016	[($100 – $90) + $4]/$90 = 15.56%

Arithmetic mean: (24% – 21.67% + 15.56%)/3 = 5.96%

Geometric mean: $(1.24 \times 0.7833 \times 1.1556)^{1/3} - 1 = 0.0392 = 3.92\%$

b.

Date	Cash Flow	Explanation
1/1/13	–$300	Purchase of three shares at $100 each
1/1/14	–$228	Purchase of two shares at $120 less dividend income on three shares held
1/1/15	$110	Dividends on five shares plus sale of one share at $90
1/1/16	$416	Dividends on four shares plus sale of four shares at $100 each

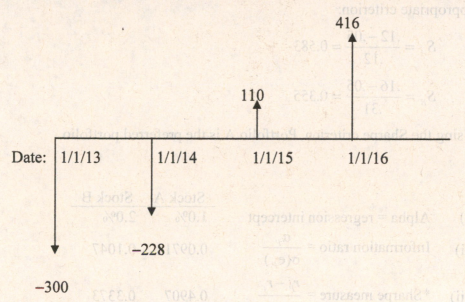

Dollar-weighted return = Internal rate of return = –0.1607%
(CF 0 = –$300; CF 1 = –$228; CF 2 = $110; CF 3 = $416; Solve for IRR = 16.07%.)

7.

Time	Cash Flow	Holding Period Return
0	3×(–$90) = –$270	
1	$100	(100–90)/90 = 11.11%
2	$100	0%
3	$100	0%

a.   Time-weighted geometric average rate of return =

$$(1.1111 \times 1.0 \times 1.0)^{1/3} - 1 = 0.0357 = 3.57\%$$

b.   Time-weighted arithmetic average rate of return = (11.11% + 0 + 0)/3 = 3.70%

The arithmetic average is always greater than or equal to the geometric average; the greater the dispersion, the greater the difference.

c.   Dollar-weighted average rate of return = IRR = 5.46%
[Using a financial calculator, enter: $n = 3$, PV = –270, FV = 0, PMT = 100. Then compute the interest rate, or use the $CF_0 = -300$, $CF_1 = 100$, $F_1 = 3$, then compute IRR]. The IRR exceeds the other averages because the investment fund was the largest when the highest return occurred.

8.   a.   The alphas for the two portfolios are:

$$\alpha_A = 12\% - [5\% + 0.7 \times (13\% - 5\%)] = 1.4\%$$

$$\alpha_B = 16\% - [5\% + 1.4 \times (13\% - 5\%)] = -0.2\%$$

Ideally, you would want to take a long position in Portfolio A and a short position in Portfolio B.

b.   If you will hold only one of the two portfolios, then the Sharpe measure is the appropriate criterion:

$$S_A = \frac{.12 - .05}{.12} = 0.583$$

$$S_B = \frac{.16 - .05}{.31} = 0.355$$

Using the Sharpe criterion, Portfolio A is the preferred portfolio.

9.

a.

		Stock A	Stock B
(i)	Alpha = regression intercept	1.0%	2.0%
(ii)	Information ratio = $\dfrac{\alpha_P}{\sigma(e_P)}$	0.0971	0.1047
(iii)	*Sharpe measure = $\dfrac{r_P - r_f}{\sigma_P}$	0.4907	0.3373
(iv)	†Treynor measure = $\dfrac{r_P - r_f}{\beta_P}$	8.833	10.500

* To compute the Sharpe measure, note that for each stock, $(r_P - r_f)$ can be computed from the right-hand side of the regression equation, using the assumed parameters r_M = 14% and r_f = 6%. The standard deviation of each stock's returns is given in the problem.

† The beta to use for the Treynor measure is the slope coefficient of the regression equation presented in the problem.

b.   (i)   If this is the only risky asset held by the investor, then Sharpe's measure is the appropriate measure. Since the Sharpe measure is higher for Stock A, then A is the best choice.

(ii)   If the stock is mixed with the market index fund, then the contribution to the overall Sharpe measure is determined by the appraisal ratio; therefore, Stock B is preferred.

(iii) If the stock is one of many stocks, then Treynor's measure is the appropriate measure, and Stock B is preferred.

10. We need to distinguish between market timing and security selection abilities. The intercept of the scatter diagram is a measure of stock selection ability. If the manager tends to have a positive excess return even when the market's performance is merely "neutral" (i.e., has zero excess return), then we conclude that the manager has on average made good stock picks. Stock selection must be the source of the positive excess returns.

Timing ability is indicated by the curvature of the plotted line. Lines that become steeper as you move to the right along the horizontal axis show good timing ability. The steeper slope shows that the manager maintained higher portfolio sensitivity to market swings (i.e., a higher beta) in periods when the market performed well. This ability to choose more market-sensitive securities in anticipation of market upturns is the essence of good timing. In contrast, a declining slope as you move to the right means that the portfolio was more sensitive to the market when the market did poorly and less sensitive when the market did well. This indicates poor timing.

We can therefore classify performance for the four managers as follows:

	Selection Ability	Timing Ability
A.	Bad	Good
B.	Good	Good
C.	Good	Bad
D.	Bad	Bad

11. a. Bogey: $(0.60 \times 2.5\%) + (0.30 \times 1.2\%) + (0.10 \times 0.5\%) = 1.91\%$
Actual: $(0.70 \times 2.0\%) + (0.20 \times 1.0\%) + (0.10 \times 0.5\%) = \underline{1.65}$
*Under*performance: 0.26%

b. Security Selection:

Market	(1) Differential Return within Market (Manager – Index)	(2) Manager's Portfolio Weight	(3) = (1) × (2) Contribution to Performance
Equity	−0.5%	0.70	−0.35%
Bonds	−0.2	0.20	−0.04
Cash	0.0	0.10	0.00
Contribution of security selection:			−0.39%

c. Asset Allocation:

Market	(1) Excess Weight (Manager – Benchmark)	(2) Index Return	(3) = (1) × (2) Contribution to Performance
Equity	0.10%	2.5%	0.25%
Bonds	−0.10	1.2	−0.12
Cash	0.00	0.5	0.00
	Contribution of asset allocation:		0.13%

Summary:

Security selection	−0.39%
Asset allocation	0.13
Excess performance	−0.26%

12. a. Manager: $(0.30 \times 20\%) + (0.10 \times 15\%) + (0.40 \times 10\%) + (0.20 \times 5\%) = 12.50\%$
Bogey: $(0.15 \times 12\%) + (0.30 \times 15\%) + (0.45 \times 14\%) + (0.10 \times 12\%) = \underline{13.80}$

Added value: −1.30%

b. Added value from country allocation:

Country	(1) Excess Weight (Manager – Benchmark)	(2) Index Return minus Bogey	(3) = (1) × (2) Contribution to Performance
U.K.	0.15	−1.8%	−0.27%
Japan	−0.20	1.2	−0.24
U.S.	−0.05	0.2	−0.01
Germany	0.10	−1.8	−0.18
	Contribution of country allocation:		−0.70%

c. Added value from stock selection:

Country	(1) Differential Return within Country (Manager – Index)	(2) Manager's Country weight	(3) = (1) × (2) Contribution to Performance
U.K.	0.08	0.30%	2.4%
Japan	0.00	0.10	0.0
U.S.	−0.04	0.40	−1.6
Germany	−0.07	0.20	−1.4
	Contribution of stock selection:		−0.6%

Summary:

Country allocation	−0.70%
Stock selection	−0.60
Excess performance	−1.30%

13. *Support*: A manager could be a better performer in one type of circumstance than in another. For example, a manager who does no timing but simply maintains a high beta, will do better in up markets and worse in down markets. Therefore, we should observe performance over an entire cycle. Also, to the extent that observing a manager over an entire cycle increases the number of observations, it would improve the reliability of the measurement.

Contradict: If we adequately control for exposure to the market (i.e., adjust for beta), then market performance should not affect the relative performance of individual managers. It is therefore not necessary to wait for an entire market cycle to pass before evaluating a manager.

14. The use of universes of managers to evaluate relative investment performance does, to some extent, overcome statistical problems, as long as those manager groups can be made sufficiently homogeneous with respect to style.

15. a. The manager's alpha is 10% – [6% + 0.5 × (14% – 6%)] = 0

    b. From Black-Jensen-Scholes and others, we know that, on average, portfolios with low beta have historically had positive alphas. (The slope of the empirical security market line is shallower than predicted by the CAPM.) Therefore, given the manager's low beta, performance might actually be subpar despite the estimated alpha of zero.

16. a. The most likely reason for a difference in ranking is due to the absence of diversification in Fund A. The Sharpe ratio measures excess return per unit of total risk, while the Treynor ratio measures excess return per unit of systematic risk. Since Fund A performed well on the Treynor measure and so poorly on the Sharpe Measure, it seems that the fund carries a greater amount of unsystematic risk, meaning it is not well-diversified and systematic risk is not the relevant risk measure.

17. The within sector selection calculates the return according to security selection. This is done by summing the weight of the security in the portfolio multiplied by the return of the security in the portfolio minus the return of the security in the benchmark:

    Large Cap Sector: 0.6×(.17 – .16)= 0.6%

    Mid Cap Sector: 0.15×(.24 – .26) = –0.3%

    Small Cap Sector: 0.25×(.20 – .18)= 0.5%

    Total Within-Sector Selection = 0.6% – 0.3% + 0.5% = 0.8%

18. Primo Return $= 0.6 \times 17\% + 0.15 \times 24\% + 0.25 \times 20\% = 18.8\%$
     Benchmark Return $= 0.5 \times 16\% + 0.4 \times 26\% + 0.1 \times 18\% = 20.2\%$
     Primo − Benchmark $= 18.8\% - 20.2\% = -1.4\%$ (Primo underperformed benchmark)

To isolate the impact of Primo's pure sector allocation decision relative to the benchmark, multiply the weight difference between Primo and the benchmark portfolio in each sector by the benchmark sector returns:

$$(0.6 - 0.5) \times (.16) + (0.15 - 0.4) \times (.26) + (0.25 - 0.1) \times (.18) = -2.2\%$$

To isolate the impact of Primo's pure security selection decisions relative to the benchmark, multiply the return differences between Primo and the benchmark for each sector by Primo's weightings:

$$(.17 - .16) \times (.6) + (.24 - .26) \times (.15) + (.2 - 0.18) \times (.25) = 0.8\%$$

19. Because the passively managed fund is mimicking the benchmark, the R^2 of the regression should be very high (and thus probably higher than the actively managed fund).

20. a. The euro appreciated while the pound depreciated. Primo had a greater stake in the euro-denominated assets relative to the benchmark, resulting in a positive currency allocation effect. British stocks outperformed Dutch stocks resulting in a negative market allocation effect for Primo. Finally, within the Dutch and British investments, Primo outperformed with the Dutch investments and under-performed with the British investments. Since they had a greater proportion invested in Dutch stocks relative to the benchmark, we assume that they had a positive security allocation effect in total. However, this cannot be known for certain with this information. It is the best choice, however.

21. a. $\dfrac{r_P - r_f}{\sigma_P} \rightarrow S_{\text{Miranda}} = \dfrac{.102 - .02}{.37} = .2216 \qquad S_{\text{S\&P}} = \dfrac{-.225 - .02}{.44} = .5568$

     b. To compute M^2 measure, blend the Miranda Fund with a position in T-bills such that the adjusted portfolio has the same volatility as the market index. Using the data, the position in the Miranda Fund should be $.44/.37 = 1.1892$ and the position in T-bills should be $1 - 1.1892 = -0.1892$ (assuming borrowing at the risk-free rate).

     The adjusted return is: $r_{p^*} = (1.1892) \times 10.2\% - (.1892) \times 2\% = .1175 = 11.75\%$

     Calculate the difference in the adjusted Miranda Fund return and the benchmark:
     $$M^2 = r_{p^*} - r_M = 11.75\% - (-22.50\%) = 34.25\%$$
     [Note: The adjusted Miranda Fund is now 59.46% equity and 40.54% cash.]

c. $\dfrac{r_P - r_f}{\beta_P} \rightarrow T_{\text{Miranda}} = \dfrac{.102 - .02}{1.10} = .0745 \quad T_{\text{S\&P}} = \dfrac{-.225 - .02}{1.00} = -.245$

d. $\alpha_P = r_P - [r_f + \beta_P(r_M - r_f)]$

$\qquad = 0.102 - [0.02 + 1.10 \times (-0.225 - 0.02)]$

$\qquad = .3515 = 35.15\%$

22. This exercise is left to the student; answers will vary.

CFA PROBLEMS

1. a. <u>Manager A</u>

   Strength. Although Manager A's one-year total return was somewhat below the international index return (–6.0 percent versus –5.0 percent), this manager apparently has some country/security return expertise. This large local market return advantage of 2.0 percent exceeds the 0.2 percent return for the international index.

   Weakness. Manager A has an obvious weakness in the currency management area. This manager experienced a marked currency return shortfall, with a return of –8.0 percent versus –5.2 percent for the index.

   <u>Manager B</u>

   Strength. Manager B's total return exceeded that of the index, with a marked positive increment apparent in the currency return. Manager B had a –1.0 percent currency return compared to a –5.2 percent currency return on the international index. Based on this outcome, Manager B's strength appears to be expertise in the currency selection area.

   Weakness. Manager B had a marked shortfall in local market return. Therefore, Manager B appears to be weak in security/market selection ability.

   b. The following strategies would enable the fund to take advantage of the strengths of each of the two managers while minimizing their weaknesses.

      1. *Recommendation:* One strategy would be to direct Manager A to make no currency bets relative to the international index and to direct Manager B to make only currency decisions, and no active country or security selection bets.

      Justification: This strategy would mitigate Manager A's weakness by hedging all currency exposures into index-like weights. This would allow capture of Manager A's country and stock selection skills while avoiding losses from poor currency management. This strategy would also mitigate Manager B's weakness, leaving an index-like portfolio construct and capitalizing on the apparent skill in currency management.

2. *Recommendation:* Another strategy would be to combine the portfolios of Manager A and Manager B, with Manager A making country exposure and security selection decisions and Manager B managing the currency exposures created by Manager A's decisions (providing a "currency overlay").

Justification: This recommendation would capture the strengths of both Manager A and Manager B and would minimize their collective weaknesses.

2. a. Indeed, the one year results were terrible, but one year is a poor statistical base from which to draw inferences. Moreover, the board of trustees had directed Karl to adopt a long-term horizon. The board specifically instructed the investment manager to give priority to long-term results.

b. The sample of pension funds had a much larger share invested in equities than did Alpine. Equities performed much better than bonds. Yet the trustees told Alpine to hold down risk, investing not more than 25 percent of the plan's assets in common stocks. (Alpine's beta was also somewhat defensive.) Alpine should not be held responsible for an asset allocation policy dictated by the client.

c. Alpine's alpha measures its risk-adjusted performance compared to the market:

$$\alpha = 13.3\% - [7.5\% + 0.90 \times (13.8\% - 7.5\%)] = 0.13\% \text{ (actually above zero)}$$

d. Note that the last five years, and particularly the most recent year, have been bad for bonds, the asset class that Alpine had been encouraged to hold. Within this asset class, however, Alpine did much better than the index fund. Moreover, despite the fact that the bond index underperformed both the actuarial return and T-bills, Alpine outperformed both. Alpine's performance *within* each asset class has been superior on a risk-adjusted basis. Its overall disappointing returns were due to a heavy asset allocation weighting towards bonds which was the board's, not Alpine's, choice.

e. A trustee may not care about the time-weighted return, but that return is more indicative of the manager's performance. After all, the manager has no control over the cash inflows and outflows of the fund.

3. a. Method I does nothing to separately identify the effects of market timing and security selection decisions. It also uses a questionable "neutral position," the composition of the portfolio at the beginning of the year.

b. Method II is not perfect but is the best of the three techniques. It at least attempts to focus on market timing by examining the returns for portfolios constructed from bond market *indexes* using actual weights in various indexes versus year-average weights. The problem with this method is that the year-average weights need not correspond to a client's "neutral" weights. For example, what if the manager were optimistic over the entire year regarding long-term bonds? Her average weighting could reflect her optimism, and not a neutral position.

c.   Method III uses net purchases of bonds as a signal of bond manager optimism. But such net purchases can be motivated by withdrawals from or contributions to the fund rather than the manager's decisions. (Note that this is an open-ended mutual fund.) Therefore, it is inappropriate to evaluate the manager based on whether net purchases turn out to be reliable bullish or bearish signals.

4.   Treynor measure = $\dfrac{17-8}{1.1} = 8.182$

5.   Sharpe measure = $\dfrac{(.24-.08)}{.18} = 0.888$

6.   a.   **Treynor measures**

Portfolio X: $\dfrac{(10-6)}{0.6} = 6.67$ S&P 500: $\dfrac{(12-6)}{1.0} = 6.00$

Sharpe measures

Portfolio X: $\dfrac{(.10-.06)}{0.18} = 0.222$ S&P 500: $\dfrac{(.12-.06)}{.13} = 0.462$

Portfolio X outperforms the market based on the Treynor measure, but underperforms based on the Sharpe measure.

b.   The two measures of performance are in conflict because they use different measures of risk. Portfolio X has less systematic risk than the market, as measured by its lower beta, but more total risk (volatility), as measured by its higher standard deviation. Therefore, the portfolio outperforms the market based on the Treynor measure but underperforms based on the Sharpe measure.

7.   Geometric average = $(1.15 \times 0.90)^{1/2} - 1 = 0.0173 = 1.73\%$

8.   Geometric average = $(0.91 \times 1.23 \times 1.17)^{1/3} - 1 = 0.0941 = 9.41\%$

9.   Internal rate of return = 7.5%
(CF 0 = –$2,000; CF 1 = $150; CF 2 = $2,150; Solve for IRR = 7.5%)

10. d.

11. Time-weighted average return $= (1.15 \times 1.1)^{1/2} - 1 = 12.47\%$

[The arithmetic mean is: $\dfrac{15\% + 10\%}{2} = 12.5\%$]

To compute dollar-weighted rate of return, cash flows are:

$CF_0 = -\$500,000$

$CF_1 = -\$500,000$

$CF_2 = (\$500,000 \times 1.15 \times 1.10) + (\$500,000 \times 1.10) = \$1,182,500$

Dollar-weighted rate of return $= 11.71\%$ (Solve for IRR in financial calculator).

12. a. Each of these benchmarks has several deficiencies, as described below.

Market index:

- A market index may exhibit survivorship bias. Firms that have gone out of business are removed from the index, resulting in a performance measure that overstates actual performance had the failed firms been included.
- A market index may exhibit double counting that arises because of companies owning other companies and both being represented in the index.
- It is often difficult to exactly and continually replicate the holdings in the market index without incurring substantial trading costs.
- The chosen index may not be an appropriate proxy for the management style of the managers.
- The chosen index may not represent the entire universe of securities. For example, the S&P 500 Index represents 65 to 70 percent of U.S. equity market capitalization.
- The chosen index (e.g., the S&P 500) may have a large capitalization bias.
- The chosen index may not be investable. There may be securities in the index that cannot be held in the portfolio.

Benchmark normal portfolio:

- This is the most difficult performance measurement method to develop and calculate.
- The normal portfolio must be continually updated, requiring substantial resources.
- Consultants and clients are concerned that managers who are involved in developing and calculating their benchmark portfolio may produce an easily-beaten normal portfolio, making their performance appear better than it actually is.

Median of the manager universe:

- It can be difficult to identify a universe of managers appropriate for the investment style of the plan's managers.
- Selection of a manager universe for comparison involves some, perhaps much, subjective judgment.
- Comparison with a manager universe does not take into account the risk taken in the portfolio.

- The median of a manager universe does not represent an "investable" portfolio; that is, a portfolio manager may not be able to invest in the median manager portfolio.
- Such a benchmark may be ambiguous. The names and weights of the securities constituting the benchmark are not clearly delineated.
- The benchmark is not constructed prior to the start of an evaluation period; it is not specified in advance.
- A manager universe may exhibit survivorship bias; managers who have gone out of business are removed from the universe, resulting in a performance measure that overstates the actual performance had those managers been included.

b. i. The Sharpe ratio is calculated by dividing the portfolio risk premium (i.e., actual portfolio return minus the risk-free return) by the portfolio standard deviation:

$$\text{Sharpe ratio} = \frac{r_P - r_f}{\sigma_P}$$

The Treynor measure is calculated by dividing the portfolio risk premium (i.e., actual portfolio return minus the risk-free return) by the portfolio beta:

$$\text{Treynor measure} = \frac{r_P - r_f}{\beta_P}$$

Jensen's alpha is calculated by subtracting the market risk premium, adjusted for risk by the portfolio's beta, from the actual portfolio excess return (risk premium). It can be described as the difference in return earned by the portfolio compared to the return implied by the Capital Asset Pricing Model or Security Market Line:

$$\alpha_P = r_P - [r_f + \beta_P(r_M - r_f)]$$

ii. The Sharpe ratio assumes that the relevant risk is total risk, and it measures excess return per unit of total risk. The Treynor measure assumes that the relevant risk is systematic risk, and it measures excess return per unit of systematic risk. Jensen's alpha assumes that the relevant risk is systematic risk, and it measures excess return at a given level of systematic risk.

13. i. Incorrect. Valid benchmarks are unbiased. Median manager benchmarks, however, are subject to significant survivorship bias, which results in several drawbacks, including the following:

- The performance of median manager benchmarks is biased upwards.
- The upward bias increases with time.
- Survivor bias introduces uncertainty with regard to manager rankings.
- Survivor bias skews the shape of the distribution curve.

    ii.   Incorrect. Valid benchmarks are unambiguous and can be replicated. The median manager benchmark is ambiguous because the weights of the individual securities in the benchmark are not known. The portfolio's composition cannot be known before the conclusion of a measurement period because identification as a median manager can occur only after performance is measured.

            Valid benchmarks are also investable. The median manager benchmark is not investable—a manager using a median manager benchmark cannot forgo active management and simply hold the benchmark. This is a result of the fact that the weights of individual securities in the benchmark are not known.

    iii.   The statement is correct. The median manager benchmark may be inappropriate because the median manager universe encompasses many investment styles and, therefore, may not be consistent with a given manager's style.

14.   a.   Sharpe ratio $= \dfrac{r_P - r_f}{\sigma_P}$

$$S_{Williamson}: \frac{22.1\% - 5.0\%}{16.8\%} = 1.02 \quad S_{Joyner}: \frac{24.2\% - 5.0\%}{20.2\%} = 0.95$$

            Treynor measure $= \dfrac{r_P - r_f}{\beta_P}$

$$T_{Williamson}: \frac{22.1\% - 5.0\%}{1.2} = 14.25 \quad T_{Joyner}: \frac{24.2\% - 5.0\%}{0.8} = 24.00$$

   b.   The difference in the rankings of Williamson and Joyner results directly from the difference in diversification of the portfolios. Joyner has a higher Treynor measure (24.00) and a lower Sharpe ratio (0.95) than does Williamson (14.25 and 1.202, respectively), so Joyner must be less diversified than Williamson. The Treynor measure indicates that Joyner has a higher return per unit of systematic risk than does Williamson, while the Sharpe ratio indicates that Joyner has a lower return per unit of total risk than does Williamson.

CHAPTER 25: INTERNATIONAL DIVERSIFICATION

PROBLEM SETS

1. "International Investing Raises Questions" was published in *The Wall Street Journal* in 1997. Some of the arguments presented in the article may no longer be compelling more than a decade later. For example, the following statement from the article is no longer true for many U.S. multinationals: "When you look at these multinationals, the factor that drives their performance is their home market." The same can also be said of the assertion that "… most of their costs—especially labor costs—will be incurred in the U.S." However, the following argument from the article is still valid: "U.S. multinationals tend to be owned by U.S. investors, who will be swayed by the ups and downs of the U.S. market." An additional argument that is not mentioned in the piece is the fact that, when investing in U.S. multinationals, it is essentially impossible to determine the degree of one's international exposure. A portfolio of foreign stocks provides an investor a better understanding of this exposure. The correlation between portfolios of foreign stocks and the U.S. equity market is likely to be less than the correlation of a portfolio of U.S. multinationals with the U.S. market.

2. Which of the returns is more relevant to an investor depends on whether the investor hedges the local currency. If the foreign exchange risk has been hedged, then the relevant figure is the stock market returns measured in the local currency. If the foreign exchange risk is not hedged, then the relevant returns are the dollar-denominated returns.

3. a. $10,000/2 = £5,000

   £5,000/£40 = 125 shares

   b. To fill in the table, we use the relation:

   $$1 + r(\text{US}) = [(1 + r(\text{UK})]\frac{E_1}{E_0}$$

Price per Share (£)	Pound-Denominated Return (%)	Dollar-Denominated Return (%) for Year-End Exchange Rate		
		$1.80/£	$2.00/£	$2.20/£
£35	−12.5%	−21.25%	−12.5%	−3.75%
40	0.0	−10.00	0.0	10.00
45	12.5	1.25	12.5	23.75

   c. The dollar-denominated return equals the pound-denominated return when the exchange rate is unchanged over the year.

4. The standard deviation of the pound-denominated return (using 3 degrees of freedom) is 10.21%. The dollar-denominated return has a standard deviation of 13.10% (using 9 degrees of freedom), greater than the pound-denominated standard deviation. This is due to the addition of exchange rate risk.

5. a. First we calculate the dollar value of the 125 shares of stock in each scenario. Then we add the profits from the forward contract in each scenario.

Price per Share (£)		Dollar Value of Stock at Given Exchange Rate		
	Exchange Rate:	$1.80/£	$2.00/£	$2.20/£
£35		7,875	8,750	9,625
£40		9,000	10,000	11,000
£45		10,125	11,250	12,375
Profits on Forward Exchange:		1,500	500	–500
$[= 5000(2.10 - E_1)]$				

Price per Share (£)		Total Dollar Proceeds at Given Exchange Rate		
	Exchange Rate:	$1.80/£	$2.00/£	$2.20/£
£35		9,375	9,250	9,125
40		10,500	10,500	10,500
45		11,625	11,750	11,875

Finally, calculate the dollar-denominated rate of return, recalling that the initial investment was $10,000:

Price per Share (£)		Rate of return (%) at Given Exchange Rate		
	Exchange Rate:	$1.80/£	$2.00/£	$2.20/£
£35		–6.25%	–7.50%	–8.75%
0		5.00	5.00	5.00
45		16.25	17.50	18.75

b. The standard deviation is now 10.24%. This is lower than the unhedged dollar-denominated standard deviation and is only slightly higher than the standard deviation of the pound-denominated return.

6. **Currency Selection**
EAFE: $[0.30 \times (-10\%)] + (0.10 \times 0\%) + (0.60 \times 10\%) = 3.0\%$
Manager: $[0.35 \times (-10\%)] + (0.15 \times 0\%) + (0.50 \times 10\%) = 1.5\%$

Loss of 1.5% relative to EAFE.

Country Selection
EAFE: $(0.30 \times 20\%) + (0.10 \times 15\%) + (0.60 \times 25\%) = 22.50\%$
Manager: $(0.35 \times 20\%) + (0.15 \times 15\%) + (0.50 \times 25\%) = 21.75\%$

Loss of 0.75% relative to EAFE.

Stock Selection

$[(18\% - 20\%) \times 0.35] + [(20\% - 15\%) \times 0.15] + [(20\% - 25\%) \times 0.50] = -2.45\%$

Loss of 2.45% relative to EAFE.

7. $1 + r(US) = [1 + r_f(UK)] \times (F_0/E_0) = 1.08 \times (1.85/1.75) = 1.1417 \Rightarrow r(US) = 14.17\%$

8. You can now purchase: $\$10,000/\$1.75 = £5,714.29$

   This will grow with 8% interest to $£5,714.29 \times (1.08) = £6,171.43$. Therefore, to lock in your return, you would sell forward £6,171.43 at the forward exchange rate.

9. A naïve investment by an investor who resides in Foreign Country A might include only a small fraction of the portfolio invested in the home country, and a relatively greater weight invested in U.S. securities. This might not be an appropriate approach for a foreign investor who is likely to be comfortable with a home bias, just as American investors seem to be. A reasonable way to scale down the weight invested in foreign countries (for example, the portfolio weight maintained by the investor from Foreign Country A in U.S. securities) is to focus on the weight of U.S. imports in the entire consumption basket of the investor (including durable goods) rather than emphasizing market capitalization. Since this consumption basket includes health care, for example, as well as other substantial items that have no import component, the resultant desired weight in U.S. securities will be smaller than market capitalization would suggest.

CFA PROBLEMS

1. Initial investment = $2,000 \times \$1.50 = \$3,000$

   Final value = $2,400 \times \$1.75 = \$4,200$

   Rate of return = $(\$4,200/\$3,000) - 1 = 0.40 = 40\%$

2. a.

3. c.

4. a. The primary rationale is the opportunity for diversification. Factors that contribute to low correlations of stock returns across national boundaries are
   i. Imperfect correlation of business cycles.
   ii. Imperfect correlation of interest rates.
   iii. Imperfect correlation of inflation rates.
   iv. Exchange rate volatility.

b. Obstacles to international investing are

  i. *Availability of information*, including insufficient data on which to base investment decisions. Interpreting and evaluating data that is different in form and/or content than the routinely available and widely understood U.S. data is difficult. Also, much foreign data is reported with a considerable lag.

  ii. *Liquidity*, in terms of the ability to buy or sell, in size and in a timely manner, without affecting the market price. Most foreign exchanges offer (relative to U.S. norms) limited trading, and experience greater price volatility. Moreover, only a (relatively) small number of individual foreign stocks enjoy liquidity comparable to that in the U.S., although this situation is improving steadily.

  iii. *Transaction costs*, particularly when viewed as a combination of commission plus spread plus market impact costs, are well above U.S. levels in most foreign markets. This, of course, adversely affects return realization.

  iv. *Political risk*, including the extreme case of expropriation and the more common case of blocked funds.

  v. *Foreign currency risk*, although to a great extent, this can be hedged.

c. The asset-class performance data for this particular period reveal that non-U.S. dollar bonds provided a small incremental return advantage over U.S. dollar bonds, but at a considerably higher level of risk. Each category of fixed income assets outperformed the S&P 500 Index measure of U.S. equity results with regard to both risk and return, which is certainly an unexpected outcome. Within the equity area, non-U.S. stocks, represented by the EAFE Index, outperformed U.S. stocks by a considerable margin with only slightly more risk. In contrast to U.S. equities, this asset category performed as it should relative to fixed income assets, providing more return for the higher risk involved.

  Concerning the Account Performance Index, its position on the graph reveals an aggregate outcome that is superior to the sum of its component parts. To some extent, this is due to the beneficial effect on performance resulting from multi-market diversification and the differential covariances involved. In this case, the portfolio manager(s) (apparently) achieved an on-balance positive alpha, adding to total portfolio return by their actions. The addition of international (i.e., non-U.S.) securities to a portfolio that would otherwise have held only domestic (U.S.) securities clearly worked to the advantage of this fund over this time period.

5. The return on the Canadian bond is equal to the sum of
   Coupon income +
   Gain or loss from the premium or discount in the forward rate relative to the spot exchange rate +
   Capital gain or loss on the bond.
   Over the six-month period, the return is

   Coupon + Forward premium/Discount + Capital gain =

   $$\frac{7.50\%}{2} + (-0.75\%) + \text{Price change in \%} = 3.00\% + \% \text{ capital gain}$$

The expected semiannual return on the U.S. bond is 3.25%. Since the U.S. bond is selling at par and its yield is expected to remain unchanged, there is no expected capital gain or loss on the U.S. bond. Therefore, in order to provide the same return, the Canadian bond must provide a capital gain of 0.25% (i.e., 1/4 point relative to par value of 100) over and above any expected capital gain on the U.S. bond.

6. a. We exchange $1 million for foreign currency at the current exchange rate and sell forward the amount of foreign currency we will accumulate 90 days from now. For the yen investment, we initially receive:

$$1 \text{ million}/0.0119 = ¥84.034 \text{ million}$$

Invest for 90 days to accumulate:

$$¥84.034 \times [1 + (0.0252/4)] = ¥84.563 \text{ million}$$

(Note that we divide the quoted 90-day rate by 4 because quoted money market interest rates typically are annualized using simple interest, assuming a 360-day year.)

If we sell this number of yen forward at the forward exchange rate of 0.0120¥/dollar, we will end up with

$$84.563 \text{ million} \times 0.0120 = \$1.0148 \text{ million}$$

The 90-day dollar interest rate is 1.48%.

Similarly, the dollar proceeds from the 90-day Canadian dollar investment will be

$$\frac{\$1 \text{ million}}{0.7284} \times \left(1 + \frac{0.0674}{4}\right) \times 0.7269 = \$1.0148 \text{ million}$$

The 90-day dollar interest rate is 1.48%, the same as that in the yen investment.

   b. The dollar-hedged rate of return on default-free government securities in both Japan and Canada is 1.48%. Therefore, the 90-day interest rate available on U.S. government securities must also be 1.48%. This corresponds to an APR of 5.92%, which is greater than the APR in Japan and less than the APR in Canada. This result makes sense, as the relationship between forward and spot exchange rates indicates that the U.S. dollar is expected to depreciate against the yen and appreciate against the Canadian dollar.

7. a. Incorrect. There have been periods of strong performance despite weak currencies. It is also possible that an appreciating currency could enhance performance.

   b. Correct.

   c. Correct.

   d. Incorrect. Correlations are not stable over time. Also, the portfolio can move dramatically away from the efficient frontier from one period to the next.

8. a.   The following arguments could be made in favor of active management:

     Economic diversity: the diversity of the Otunian economy across various sectors may offer the opportunity for the active investor to employ "top-down" sector timing strategies.

     High transaction costs: very high transaction costs may discourage trading activity by international investors and lead to inefficiencies that may be exploited successfully by active investors.

     Good financial disclosure and detailed accounting standards: good financial disclosure and detailed accounting standards may provide the well-trained analyst an opportunity to perform fundamental research analysis in order to identify inefficiently priced securities.

     Capital restrictions: restrictions on capital flows may discourage foreign investor participation and serve to segment the Otunian market, thus creating exploitable market inefficiencies for the active investor.

     Developing economy and securities market: developing economies and markets are often characterized by inefficiently priced securities and by rapid economic change and growth. The active investor may exploit these characteristics.

     Settlement problems: long delays in settling trades by nonresidents may serve to discourage international investors, leading to inefficiently priced securities which may be exploited by active management.

     The following arguments could be made in favor of indexing:

     Economic diversity: economic diversity across a broad sector of industries implies that indexing may provide a diverse representative portfolio that is not subject to the risks associated with concentrated sectors.

     High transaction costs: indexing would be favored by the implied lower levels of trading activity and costs.

     Settlement problems: indexing would be favored by the implied lower levels of trading activity and settlement requirements.

     Financial disclosure and accounting standards: wide public availability of reliable financial information presumably leads to greater market efficiency, reducing the value of both fundamental analysis and active management, and favoring indexing.

     Restrictions of capital flows: indexing would be favored by the implied lower levels of trading activity and thus smaller opportunity for regulatory interference.

     b.   A recommendation for active management would focus on short-term inefficiencies in, and long-term prospects for, the developing Otunian markets and economy, inefficiencies and prospects which would not generally be found in more developed markets.

     A recommendation for indexing would focus on the factors of economic diversity, high transaction costs, settlement delays, capital flow restrictions, and lower management fees.

CHAPTER 26: HEDGE FUNDS

PROBLEM SETS

1. No, a market-neutral hedge fund would not be a good candidate for an investor's entire retirement portfolio because such a fund is not a diversified portfolio. The term *market-neutral* refers to a portfolio position with respect to a specified market inefficiency. However, there could be a role for a market-neutral hedge fund in the investor's overall portfolio; the market-neutral hedge fund can be thought of as an approach for the investor to add alpha to a more passive investment position such as an index mutual fund.

2. The incentive fee of a hedge fund is part of the hedge fund compensation structure; the incentive fee is typically equal to 20% of the hedge fund's profits beyond a particular benchmark rate of return. Therefore, the incentive fee resembles the payoff to a call option, which is more valuable when volatility is higher. Consequently, the hedge fund portfolio manager is motivated to take on high-risk assets in the portfolio, thereby increasing volatility and the value of the incentive fee.

3. There are a number of factors that make it harder to assess the performance of a hedge fund portfolio manager than a typical mutual fund manager. Some of these factors are

    - Hedge funds tend to invest in more illiquid assets so that an apparent alpha may be in fact simply compensation for illiquidity.
    - Hedge funds' valuation of less liquid assets is questionable.
    - Survivorship bias and backfill bias result in hedge fund databases that report performance only for more successful hedge funds.
    - Hedge funds typically have unstable risk characteristics making performance evaluation that depends on a consistent risk profile problematic.
    - Tail events skew the distribution of hedge fund outcomes, making it difficult to obtain a representative sample of returns over relatively short periods of time.

4. The problem of survivorship bias is that only the returns for survivors will be reported and the index return will be biased upwards. Backfill bias results when a new hedge fund is added to an index and the fund's historical performance is added to the index's historical performance. The problem is that only funds that survived will have their performance added to the index, resulting in upward bias in index returns.

5. The Merrill Lynch High Yield index may be the best individual market index for fixed income hedge funds and the Russell 3000 may be the individual market index for equity hedge funds. However, a combination of indexes may be the best market index, as it has been found that multifactor model do the best in explaining hedge fund returns. Of equity hedge funds, market neutral strategies should have a return that is closest to risk-free, but they are not risk free.

6. Funds of funds are usually considered good choices for individual investors because they offer diversification and usually more liquidity. One problem with funds of funds is that they usually have lower returns. This is a result from both the additional layer of fees and cash drag (resulting from the desire for liquidity).

7. Of the equity hedge funds, market neutral strategies should have a return that is closest to risk-free; however, they are not completely risk-free and typically have exposure to both systematic and unsystematic risks.

8. No, statistical arbitrage is not true arbitrage because it does not involve establishing risk-free positions based on security mispricing. Statistical arbitrage is essentially a portfolio of risky bets. The hedge fund takes a large number of small positions based on apparent small, temporary market inefficiencies, relying on the probability that the expected return for the totality of these bets is positive.

9. Management fee = $0.02 \times \$1$ billion = $20 million

	Portfolio Rate of Return (%)	Incentive Fee (%)	Incentive Fee ($ million)	Total Fee ($ million)	Total Fee (%)
a.	−5	0	0	20	2
b.	0	0	0	20	2
c.	5	0	0	20	2
d.	10	20	10	30	3

10. The incentive fee is typically equal to 20 percent of the hedge fund's profits beyond a particular benchmark rate of return. However, if a fund has experienced losses in the past, then the fund may not be able to charge the incentive fee unless the fund exceeds its previous high-water mark. The incentive fee is less valuable if the high-water mark is $67, rather than $66. With a high-water mark of $67, the net asset value of the fund must reach $67 before the hedge fund can assess the incentive fee. The high-water mark for a hedge fund is equivalent to the exercise price for a call option on an asset with a current market value equal to the net asset value of the fund.

11. a.   First, compute the Black Scholes value of a call option with the following parameters:

$$S_0 = 62$$
$$X = 66$$
$$R = 0.04$$
$$\sigma = 0.50$$
$$T = 1 \text{ year}$$

Therefore: $C = \$11.685$

The value of the annual incentive fee is:

$$0.20 \times C = 0.20 \times \$11.685 = \$2.337$$

b.   Here we use the same parameters used in the Black-Scholes model in part (a) with the exception that $X = 62$

Now: $C = \$13.253$

The value of the annual incentive fee is

$$0.20 \times C = 0.20 \times \$13.253 = \$2.651$$

c.   Here we use the same parameters used in the Black-Scholes model in part (a) with the exception that:

$$X = S_0 \times e^{0.04} = 62 \times e^{0.04} = 64.5303$$

Now: $C = \$12.240$

The value of the annual incentive fee is

$$0.20 \times C = 0.20 \times \$12.240 = \$2.448$$

d.   Here we use the same parameters used in the Black-Scholes model in part (a) with the exception that $X = 62$ and $\sigma = 0.60$

Now: $C = \$15.581$

The value of the annual incentive fee is

$$0.20 \times C = 0.20 \times \$15.581 = \$3.116$$

12. a.   The spreadsheet indicates that the end-of-month value for the S&P 500 in September 1977 was 96.53, so the exercise price of the put written at the beginning of October 1977 would have been

$$0.95 \times 96.53 = 91.7035$$

At the end of October, the value of the index was 92.34, so the put would have expired out of the money and the put writer's payout was zero. Since it is unusual for the S&P 500 to fall by more than 5 percent in one month, all but 10 of the 120 months between October 1977 and September 1987 would have a payout of zero. The first month with a positive payout would have been January 1978. The exercise price of the put written at the beginning of January 1978 would have been

$$0.95 \times 95.10 = 90.3450$$

At the end of January, the value of the index was 89.25 (more than a 6% decline), so the option writer's payout would have been:

90.3450 − 89.25 = 1.0950

The average gross monthly payout for the period would have been 0.2437 and the standard deviation would have been 1.0951.

b. In October 1987, the S&P 500 decreased by more than 21 percent, from 321.83 to 251.79. The exercise price of the put written at the beginning of October 1987 would have been

0.95 × 321.83 = 305.7385

At the end of October, the option writer's payout would have been:

305.7385 − 251.79 = 53.9485

The average gross monthly payout for the period October 1977 through October 1987 would have been 0.6875 and the standard deviation would have been 5.0026. Apparently, tail risk in naked put writing is substantial.

13. a. In order to calculate the Sharpe ratio, we first calculate the rate of return for each month in the period October 1982—September 1987. The end of month value for the S&P 500 in September 1982 was 120.42, so the exercise price for the October put is

0.95 × 120.42 = 114.3990

Since the October end of month value for the index was 133.72, the put expired out of the money so that there is no payout for the writer of the option. The rate of return the hedge fund earns on the index is therefore equal to

(133.72/120.42) − 1 = 0.11045 = 11.045%

Assuming that the hedge fund invests the $0.25 million premium along with the $100 million beginning of month value, then the end of month value of the fund is

$100.25 million × 1.11045 = $111.322 million

The rate of return for the month is

($111.322/$100.00) − 1 = 0.11322 = 11.322%

The first month that the put expires in the money is May 1984. The end of month value for the S&P 500 in April 1984 was 160.05, so the exercise price for the May put is

0.95 × 160.05 = 152.0475

The May end of month value for the index was 150.55, and therefore the payout for the writer of a put option on one unit of the index is

152.0475 − 150.55 = 1.4975

The rate of return the hedge fund earns on the index is equal to

(150.55/160.05) − 1 = −0.05936 = −5.936%

The payout of 1.4975 per unit of the index reduces the hedge fund's rate of return by

$$1.4975/160.05 = 0.00936 = 0.936\%$$

The rate of return the hedge fund earns is therefore equal to

$$-5.936\% - 0.936\% = -6.872\%$$

The end of month value of the fund is

$$\$100.25 \text{ million} \times 0.93128 = \$93.361 \text{ million}$$

The rate of return for the month is

$$(\$93.361/\$100.00) - 1 = -0.06639 = -6.639\%$$

For the period October 1982—September 1987

Mean monthly return = 1.898%

Standard deviation = 4.353%

Sharpe ratio = (1.898% − 0.7%)/4.353% = 0.275

b. For the period October 1982—October 1987

Mean monthly return = 1.238%

Standard deviation = 6.724%

Sharpe ratio = (1.238% − 0.7%)/6.724% = 0.080

14. a. Since the hedge fund manager has a long position in the Waterworks stock, he should sell six contracts, computed as follows:

$$\frac{\$2,000,000 \times 0.75}{\$250 \times 1,000} = 6 \text{ contracts}$$

b. The standard deviation of the monthly return of the hedged portfolio is equal to the standard deviation of the residuals, which is 6 percent. The standard deviation of the residuals for the stock is the volatility that cannot be hedged away. For a market-neutral (zero-beta) position, this is also the total standard deviation.

c. The expected rate of return of the market-neutral position is equal to the risk-free rate plus the alpha:

$$0.5\% + 2.0\% = 2.5\%$$

We assume that monthly returns are approximately normally distributed. The z-value for a rate of return of zero is

$$-2.5\%/6.0\% = -0.4167$$

Therefore, the probability of a negative return is $N(-0.4167) = 0.3385$

15. a. The residual standard deviation of the portfolio is smaller than each stock's standard deviation by a factor of $\sqrt{100} = 10$ or, equivalently, the residual variance of the portfolio is smaller by a factor of 100. So, instead of a residual standard deviation of 6 percent, residual standard deviation is now 0.6 percent.

   b. The expected return of the market-neutral position is still equal to the risk-free rate plus the alpha:

   $$0.5\% + 2.0\% = 2.5\%$$

   Now the z-value for a rate of return of zero is

   $$-2.5\%/0.6\% = -4.1667$$

   Therefore, the probability of a negative return is $N(-4.1667) = 0.0000155$
   A negative return is very unlikely.

16. a. For the (now improperly) hedged portfolio:

   $$\text{Variance} = (0.25^2 \times 5^2) + 6^2 = 37.5625$$

   $$\text{Standard deviation} = 6.129\%$$

   b. Since the manager has misestimated the beta of Waterworks, the manager will sell four S&P 500 contracts (rather than the six contracts in Problem 6):

   $$\frac{\$2,000,000 \times 0.50}{\$250 \times 1,000} = 4 \text{ contracts}$$

   The portfolio is not completely hedged so the expected rate of return is no longer 2.5 percent. We can determine the expected rate of return by first computing the total dollar value of the stock plus futures position.

   The dollar value of the stock portfolio is

   $$\$2,000,000 \times (1 + r_{portfolio}) = \$2,000,000 \times [1 + 0.005 + 0.75 \times (r_M - 0.005) + 0.02 + e]$$
   $$= \$2,042,500 + \$1,500,000 \times r_M + \$2,000,000 \times e$$

   The dollar proceeds from the futures position equal

   $$4 \times \$250 \times (F_0 - F_1) = \$1,000 \times [(S_0 \times 1.005) - S_1]$$
   $$= \$1,000 \times S_0 \times [1.005 - (1 + r_M)]$$
   $$= \$1,000 \times 1,000 \times [0.005 - r_M]$$
   $$= \$5,000 - \$1,000,000 \times r_M$$

   The total value of the stock plus futures position at the end of the month is

   $$\$2,047,500 + (\$1,500,000 - \$1,000,000) \times r_M + \$2,000,000 \times e$$
   $$= \$2,047,500 + \$500,000 \times (0.01) + \$2,000,000 \times e$$
   $$= \$2,052,500 + \$2,000,000 \times e$$

The expected rate of return for the (improperly) hedged portfolio is

$$(\$,2052,500 / \$2,000,000) - 1 = .02625 = 2.625\%$$

Now the z-value for a rate of return of zero is:

$$-2.625\%/6.129\% = -0.4283$$

The probability of a negative return is $N(-0.4283) = 0.3342$
Here, the probability of a negative return is similar to the probability computed in Problem 14.

c. The variance for the diversified (but improperly hedged) portfolio is

$$(0.25^2 \times 5^2) + 0.6^2 = 1.9225$$

Standard deviation = 1.3865%

The z-value for a rate of return of zero is:

$$-2.625\%/1.3865\% = -1.8933$$

The probability of a negative return is $N(-1.8933) = 0.0292$

The probability of a negative return is now far greater than the result with proper hedging in Problem 15.

d. The market exposure from improper hedging is far more important in contributing to total volatility (and risk of losses) in the case of the 100-stock portfolio because the idiosyncratic risk of the diversified portfolio is so small.

17. a., b., c.

	Hedge Fund 1	Hedge Fund 2	Hedge Fund 3	Fund of Funds	Stand-Alone Fund
Start of year value (millions)	$100.0	$100.0	$100.0	$300.0	$300.0
Gross portfolio rate of return	20%	10%	30%		
End of year value (before fee)	$120.0	$110.0	$130.0		$360.0
Incentive fee (Individual funds)	$ 4.0	$ 2.0	$ 6.0		$ 12.0
End of year value (after fee)	$116.0	$108.0	$124.0	$348.0	$348.0
Incentive fee (Fund of Funds)				$ 9.6	
End of year value (Fund of Funds)				$338.4	
Rate of return (after fee)	16.0%	8.0%	24.0%	12.8%	16.0%

Note that the end-of-year value (after-fee) for the Stand-Alone (SA) Fund is the same as the end-of-year value for the Fund of Funds (FF) before FF charges its extra layer of incentive fees. Therefore, the investor's rate of return in SA (16.0%) is higher than in FF (12.8%) by an amount equal to the extra layer of fees ($9.6 million, or 3.2%) charged by the Fund of Funds.

d.

	Hedge Fund 1	Hedge Fund 2	Hedge Fund 3	Fund of Funds	Stand-Alone Fund
Start-of-year value (millions)	$100.0	$100.0	$100.0	$300.0	$300.0
Gross portfolio rate of return	20%	10%	−30%		
End-of-year value (before fee)	$120.0	$110.0	$ 70.0		$300.0
Incentive fee (Individual funds)	$ 4.0	$ 2.0	$ 0.0		$ 0.0
End-of-year value (after fee)	$116.0	$108.0	$ 70.0	$294.0	$300.0
Incentive fee (Fund of Funds)				$ 0.0	
End-of-year value (Fund of Funds)				$294.0	
Rate of return (after fee)	16.0%	8.0%	−30.0%	−2.0%	0.0%

Now, the end-of-year value (after fee) for SA is $300, while the end-of-year value for FF is only $294, despite the fact that neither SA nor FF charge an incentive fee. The reason for the difference is the fact that the Fund of Funds pays an incentive fee to each of the component portfolios. If even one of these portfolios does well, there will be an incentive fee charged. In contrast, SA charges an incentive fee only if the aggregate portfolio does well (at least better than a 0% return). The fund of funds structure therefore results in total fees at least as great as (and usually greater than) the stand-alone structure.

CHAPTER 27: THE THEORY OF
ACTIVE PORTFOLIO MANAGEMENT

PROBLEM SETS

1. Views about the relative performance of bonds compared to stocks can have a significant impact on how security analysis is conducted. For example, as a result of a predicted decrease in interest rates, bonds are now expected to perform better than previously expected. This performance forecast may also reflect forecasts about the quality (credit) spreads for bonds. In addition to the implications of macro forecasts, the play on yields can have important implications for corporations in financial distress with high leverage. The hierarchy of use of the model suggests a top-down analysis, starting with the BL model inputs. This does not rule out feedback in the opposite direction if, for example, the preponderance of security analysis suggests an unexpectedly good (or bad) economy (or economic sector).

2. The specific tasks for the econometrics unit might entail the following:
    a. Help the macro forecasters with their forecasts for asset allocation and in setting up views for the BL model.
    b. Help the quality control unit estimate forecasting records.
    c. Provide a resource to handle statistics problems that other units may encounter.

3. Exercise left to student; answers will vary.

4. Exercise left to student; answers will vary.

5. To assign a dollar value to an improvement in performance, we would start with the expected value of M^2. This is the expected incremental return (risk adjusted) from active management. Apply this incremental M^2 to the dollar value of the portfolio over future periods and compute the present value of these dollar increments to determine the dollar value of the activity. Proceed to obtain the incremental M^2 in a top-down manner. Estimate the improvement in the Sharpe ratio which comes from an increase in the information ratio (IR) of the active portfolio.

    The activity envisioned in this problem amounts to an improvement in the forecasting accuracy of an analyst who examines a set number of securities. This limits the improvement of the overall IR to that of those securities. (Recall that the overall squared IR is the sum of squared IRs of the individual securities.) Improved accuracy means greater weight given to the analyst's forecasts. This constitutes an increment to the *expected* IR of the analyst. The expected IR of securities covered by the analyst (that may arise from either positive or negative alpha forecasts) may be obtained in two ways: (1) directly from the analyst's past forecasts or (2) from estimates of the distribution of past abnormal returns of the stock in question.

CHAPTER 28: INVESTMENT POLICY AND
THE FRAMEWORK OF THE CFA INSTITUTE

PROBLEM SETS

1. You would advise them to exploit all available retirement tax shelters, such as 403b, 401k, Keogh plans, and IRAs. Since they will not be taxed on the income earned from these accounts until they withdraw the funds, they should avoid investing in tax-preferred instruments like municipal bonds. If they are very risk-averse, they should consider investing a large proportion of their funds in inflation-indexed CDs, which offer a riskless real rate of return.

2. a. The least risky asset for a person investing for her child's college tuition is an account denominated in units of college tuition. Such an account is the College Sure CD offered by the College Savings Bank of Princeton, New Jersey. A unit of this CD pays, at maturity, an amount guaranteed to equal or exceed the average cost of a year of undergraduate tuition, as measured by an index prepared by the College Board.

   b. The least risky asset for a defined benefit pension fund with benefit obligations that have an average duration of 10 years is a bond portfolio with a duration of 10 years and a present value equal to the present value of the pension obligation. This is an immunization strategy that provides a future value equal to (or greater than) the pension obligation, regardless of the direction of change in interest rates. Note that immunization requires periodic rebalancing of the bond portfolio.

   c. The least risky asset for a defined benefit pension fund that pays inflation-protected benefits is a portfolio of immunized Treasury inflation-indexed securities with a duration equal to the duration of the pension obligation (i.e., in this scenario, a duration of 10 years). (Note: These securities are also referred to as Treasury inflation-protected securities, or TIPS.)

3. a. George More's expected accumulation at age 65:

	n	i	PV	PMT		FV
Fixed income	25	3%	$100,000	$1,500	$\Rightarrow$	FV = $264,067
Common stocks	25	6%	$100,000	$1,500	$\Rightarrow$	FV = $511,484

   b. Expected retirement annuity:

	n	i	PV	FV		PMT
Fixed income	15	3%	$264,067	0	$\Rightarrow$	PMT = $22,120
Common stocks	15	6%	$511,484	0	$\Rightarrow$	PMT = $52,664

c. In order to get a fixed-income annuity of $30,000 per year, his accumulation at age 65 would have to be:

	n	i	PMT	FV		PV
Fixed income	15	3%	$30,000	0	⇒	PV = $358,138

His annual contribution would have to be:

	n	i	PV	FV		PMT
Fixed income	25	3%	$100,000	−$358,138	⇒	PMT = $4,080

This is $2,580 more per year than the $1,500 current contribution.

4. a. The answer depends on the assumptions made about the investor's effective income tax rates for the period of accumulation and for the period of withdrawals. First, we assume that (i) tax rates remain constant throughout the entire time horizon; and (ii) the investor's taxable income remains relatively constant throughout. Consequently, the investor's effective tax rate does not change, and we find that the Roth IRA and the conventional IRA provide the same after-tax benefits.

Alternatively, we might consider a scenario in which a household has a low income early in the accumulation period and higher income later in the accumulation period and during the withdrawal period. If tax rates are constant throughout the time horizon, then the investor's effective tax rate would be lower throughout the accumulation period than during the withdrawal period, and as a result, the Roth IRA would provide higher after-tax benefits. This is a consequence of the fact that an investor's Roth IRA contributions during the accumulation period are taxed at the lower rate, while withdrawals from a conventional IRA would be taxed at the higher rate. Similarly, the conventional IRA provides higher after-tax benefits in the event that the effective tax rate is higher during the accumulation period than it is during the period of withdrawals.

Clearly, each of the scenarios described here represents an extremely unrealistic simplification. The issue becomes more complex if we consider the many possible changes, both in tax law and in the investor's individual circumstances, that can have an impact on the effective tax rate.

b. For the Roth IRA, contributions are made with after-tax dollars, so the tax rate is known (and taxes are paid) during the accumulation period; the tax rate for withdrawals at retirement from a Roth IRA is zero and is therefore also known with certainty, assuming the US Congress does not change the law. Contributions to a conventional IRA during the accumulation period are tax-free, but the tax rate for withdrawals is not known until the withdrawals are made at retirement. This tax rate uncertainty for a conventional IRA has two sources. First, the investor is unable to anticipate legislated changes in future tax rates. Second, even if tax rates were to remain constant, the investor cannot determine her future tax bracket because she cannot accurately forecast her taxable income at retirement. Consequently, the Roth IRA provides protection against tax-rate uncertainty, while the conventional IRA subjects the investor to substantial tax rate uncertainty.

CFA PROBLEMS

1. a. (i) Return requirement: IPS Y has the appropriate language. Since the plan is currently underfunded, the primary objective should be to make the pension fund financially stronger. The risk inherent in attempting to maximize total returns would be inappropriate.

   (ii) Risk tolerance: IPS Y has the appropriate language. Because of the fund's underfunded status, the plan has limited risk tolerance; should the fund incur a substantial loss, payments to beneficiaries could be jeopardized.

   (iii) Time horizon: IPS Y has the appropriate language. Although going-concern pension plans usually have a long time horizon, the Acme plan has a shorter time horizon because of the reduced retirement age and the relatively high median age of the workforce.

   (iv) Liquidity: IPS X has the appropriate language. Because of the early retirement feature starting next month and the age of the workforce (which indicates an increasing number of retirees in the near future), the pan needs a moderate level of liquidity in order to fund monthly benefit payments.

   b. The current portfolio is the most appropriate choice for the pension plan's asset allocation. The current portfolio offers:

   (i) An expected return that exceeds the plan's return requirement.

   (ii) An expected standard deviation that only slightly exceeds the plan's target.

   (iii) A level of liquidity that should be sufficient for future needs.

   The higher expected return will ameliorate the plan's underfunded status somewhat, and the change in the fund's risk profile will be minimal. The portfolio has significant allocations to U.K. bonds (42 percent) and large-cap equities (13 percent) in addition to cash (5 percent). The availability of these highly liquid assets should be sufficient to fund monthly benefit payments when the early retirement feature takes effect next month, particularly in view of the stable income flows from these investments.

   The Graham portfolio offers:

   (i) An expected return that is slightly below the plan's requirement.

   (ii) An expected standard deviation that is substantially below the plan's target.

   (iii) A level of liquidity that should be more than sufficient for future needs.

   Given the plan's underfunded status, the portfolio's expected return is unacceptable.

   The Michael portfolio offers:

   (i) An expected return that is substantially above the plan's requirement.

   (ii) An expected standard deviation that far exceeds the plan's target.

   (iii) A level of liquidity that should be sufficient for future needs.

   Given the plan's underfunded status, the portfolio's level of risk is unacceptable.

2. c. Liquidity

3. b. Organizing the management process itself.

4. a. An approach to asset allocation that GSS could use is the one detailed in the chapter. It consists of the following steps:

   1. Specify asset classes to be included in the portfolio. The major classes usually considered are:
      Money market instruments (usually called cash)
      Fixed income securities (usually called bonds)
      Stocks
      Real estate
      Precious metals
      Other

   2. Specify capital market expectations. This step consists of using both historical data and economic analysis to determine your expectations of future rates of return over the relevant holding period on the assets to be considered for inclusion in the portfolio. This step typically involves macroeconomic analysis to provide some insight regarding the current state of the economy.

   3. Derive the efficient portfolio frontier. This step consists of finding portfolios that achieve the maximum expected return for any given degree of risk.

   4. Find the optimal asset mix. This step consists of selecting the efficient portfolio that best meets your risk and return objectives while satisfying the constraints you face.

   b. A guardian investor typically is an individual who wishes to preserve the purchasing power of his assets. Extreme guardians would be exclusively in AAA short-term credits. GSS should first determine how long the time horizon is and how high the return expectations are. Assuming a long time horizon and 8–10 percent return (pretax) expectations, the portfolio could be allocated 30–40 percent bonds, 30–40 percent stocks, and modest allocations to each of the other asset groups.

5. a. OBJECTIVES

   1. *Return*
      The required total rate of return for the JU endowment fund is the sum of the spending rate and the expected long-term increase in educational costs:

      Spending rate = $126 million (current spending need) / ($2,000 million current fund balance less $200 million library payment)

      = $126 million/$1,800 million = 7 percent

      The expected educational cost increase is 3 percent. The sum of the two components is 10 percent. Achieving this relatively high return would ensure that the endowment's real value is maintained.

2. *Risk*

Evaluation of risk tolerance requires an assessment of both the ability and the willingness of the endowment to take risk.

Ability: Average risk

- Endowment funds are long term in nature, having infinite lives. This long time horizon by itself would allow for above-average risk.
- However, creative tension exists between the JU endowment's demand for high current income to meet immediate spending requirements and the need for long-term growth to meet future requirements. This need for a spending rate (in excess of
  5 percent) and the university's heavy dependence on those funds allow for only average risk.

Willingness: Above average risk

- University leaders and endowment directors have set a spending rate in excess of 5 percent. To achieve their 7 percent real rate of return, the fund must be invested in above-average risk securities. Thus, the 7 percent spending rate indicates a willingness to take above-average risk.
- In addition, the current portfolio allocation, with its large allocations to direct real estate and venture capital, indicates a willingness to take above-average risk.

  Taking both ability and willingness into consideration, the endowment's risk tolerance is best characterized as above average.

CONSTRAINTS

1. *Time Horizon*.
   A two-stage time horizon is needed. The first stage recognizes short-term liquidity constraints ($200 million library payment in eight months). The second stage is an infinite time horizon (endowment funds are established to provide permanent support).

2. *Liquidity*.
   Generally, endowment funds have long time horizons, and little liquidity is needed in excess of annual distribution requirements. However, the JU endowment requires liquidity for the upcoming library payment in addition to the current year's contribution to the operating budget. Liquidity needs for the next year are

Library payment	+$200 million
Operating budget contribution	+ 126 million
Annual portfolio income	− 29 million
Total	+$297 million

   Annual portfolio income =

   $(0.04 \times \$40 \text{ million}) + (0.05 \times \$60 \text{ million}) + (0.01 \times \$300 \text{ million})$
   $+ (0.001 \times \$400 \text{ million}) + (0.03 \times \$700 \text{ million}) = \$29 \text{ million}$

3. *Taxes*. U.S. endowment funds are tax-exempt.

4. *Legal/Regulatory.*

   U.S. endowment funds are subject to predominantly state (but some federal) regulatory and legal constraints, and standards of prudence generally apply. Restrictions imposed by Bremner may pose a legal constraint on the fund (no more than 25 percent of the initial Bertocchi Oil and Gas shares may be sold in any one-year period).

5. *Unique Circumstances.*

   Only 25 percent of donated Bertocchi Oil and Gas shares may be sold in any one-year period (constraint imposed by donor). This constraint reinforces the need for diversification of the portfolio. A secondary consideration is the need to budget the one-time $200 million library payment in eight months.

b. (Answers may vary)

U.S. money market fund: 15% (Range: 14% – 17%)
Liquidity needs for the next year are

Library payment	+$200 million
Operating budget contribution	+ 126 million
Annual portfolio income	– 29 million
Total	+$297 million

Total liquidity of at least $297 million is required (14.85 percent of current endowment assets). Additional allocations (more than 2 percent above the suggested 15 percent) would be overly conservative. This cushion should be sufficient for any transaction needs (i.e., mismatch of cash inflows/outflows).

Intermediate global bond fund: 10% (Range: 10% – 20%)
To achieve a 10 percent portfolio return, the fund needs to take above average risk (e.g., 10% in global bond fund and 20% venture capital). An allocation below 10 percent would involve taking unnecessary risk that would put the safety and preservation of the endowment fund in jeopardy. An allocation in the 11% to 20% range could still be tolerated because the slight reduction in portfolio expected return would be partially compensated by the reduction in portfolio risk. An allocation above 20% would not satisfy the endowment fund return requirements.

Global equity fund: 15% (Range: 15% – 25%)

Bertocchi Oil and Gas common stock: 15%

There is a single issuer concentration risk associated with the current allocation, and a 25% reduction ($100 million), which is the maximum reduction allowed by the donor, is required ($400 million – $100 million = $300 million remaining).

Direct real estate: 25% (20 – 30%)
To help fund short-term outflows, exposure to real estate will be decreased. This is a moderate decrease since divesting more than 2/5 (35% → 25%) of the $700 million allocated to direct real estate would be difficult given general illiquidity of the direct real estate market.

Venture capital: 20% (15%–25%)

To help fund short-term cash outflows, exposure to venture capital will be reduced. This will be a modest decrease since divesting more than 1/5 (25% → 20%) of the $500 million venture capital allocation would be difficult given lock-up periods, contractual agreements and general illiquidity. An allocation above 25 percent would involve taking unnecessary risk that would put the safety and preservation of the endowment fund in jeopardy. An allocation below 25 percent would not satisfy the endowment fund return requirements.

The suggested allocations (point estimates) would allow the JU endowment fund to meet the 10 percent return requirement, calculated as follows:

Asset	Suggested Allocation	Expected Return	Weighted Return
U.S. money market fund	0.15	4.0%	0.600%
Intermediate global bond fund	0.10	5.0	0.500
Global equity fund	0.15	10.0	1.500
Bertocchi common stock	0.15	15.0	2.250
Direct real estate	0.25	11.5	2.875
Venture capital	0.20	20.0	4.000
Total	1.00		11.725%

The allowable allocation ranges, taken in proper combination, would surpass the 10 percent return requirement, maintaining a long-run, above average risk approach to its portfolio.

6. a. *Overview.* Fairfax is 58 years old and has seven years until a planned retirement. She has a fairly lavish lifestyle but few money worries. Her large salary pays all current expenses, and she has accumulated $2 million in cash equivalents from savings in previous years. Her health is excellent, and her health insurance coverage will continue after retirement and is employer paid. She is not well versed in investment matters and has had the good sense to connect with professional counsel to start planning for her investment future, a future that is complicated by ownership of a $10 million block of company stock that, while listed on the NYSE, pays no dividends and has a zero-cost basis for tax purposes. All salary, investment income (except interest on municipal bonds) and realized capital gains are taxed to Fairfax at a 35 percent rate; this and a 4 percent inflation rate are expected to continue into the future. Fairfax would accept a 3 percent real, after-tax return from the investment portfolio to be formed from her $2 million in savings (the savings portfolio) if that return could be obtained with only modest portfolio volatility (i.e., less than a 10% annual decline). She is described as being conservative in all things.

OBJECTIVES

- *Return Requirement.* Fairfax's need for portfolio income begins seven years from now, at the date of retirement. The investment focus for her savings portfolio should be on growing the portfolio's value in the interim in a way that provides protection against loss of purchasing power. Her 3 percent real, after-tax return preference implies a gross total return requirement of at least 10.8 percent, assuming her investments are fully taxable (as is the case now) and assuming 4 percent inflation and a 35 percent tax rate. For Fairfax to maintain her current lifestyle, then, at retirement, she would have to generate inflation-adjusted annual income of

$$\$500,000 \times 1.04^7 = \$658,000$$

If the market value of Reston's stock does not change, and if she is able to earn a 10.8 percent return on the savings portfolio (or 7% nominal after-tax return), then, by retirement age, she should accumulate:

$$\$10,000,000 + (\$2,000,000 \times 1.07^7) = \$13,211,500$$

To generate \$658,000 per year, a 5.0 percent return on the \$13,211,500 would be needed.

$$\$658,000/\$13,211,500 = 0.0498$$

- *Risk Tolerance.* The information provided indicates that Fairfax is quite risk averse; she is unwilling to experience a decline of more than 10 percent in the value of the savings portfolio in any given year. This would indicate that the portfolio should have below average risk exposure in order to minimize its downside volatility. In terms of overall wealth, Fairfax is able to take more than average risk, but because of her preferences and the nondiversified nature of the total portfolio, a below-average risk objective is appropriate for the savings portfolio. It should be noted, however, that truly meaningful statements about the risk of Fairfax's total portfolio are tied to assumptions regarding both the volatility of Reston's stock (if it is retained) and when and at what price the Reston stock will be sold. Because the Reston holding constitutes 83 percent of Fairfax's total portfolio, it will largely determine the risk she actually experiences as long as this holding remains intact.

CONSTRAINTS

- *Time Horizon.* Two-time horizons are applicable to Fairfax's life. The first time horizon represents the period during which Fairfax should set up her financial situation in preparation for the balance of the second time horizon, her retirement period of indefinite length. Of the two horizons, the longer term to the expected end of her life is the dominant horizon because it is over this period that the assets must fulfill their primary function of funding her expenses, as an annuity, in retirement.

- *Liquidity.* With liquidity defined either as income needs or as cash reserves to meet emergency needs, Fairfax's liquidity requirement is minimal. Five hundred thousand dollars of salary is available annually, health cost concerns are nonexistent, and we know of no planned needs for cash from the portfolio.

- *Taxes*. Fairfax's taxable income (salary, taxable investment income, and realized capital gains on securities) is taxed at a 35 percent rate. Careful tax planning and coordination with investment planning is required. Investment strategy should include seeking income that is sheltered from taxes and holding securities for lengthy time periods in order to produce larger after-tax returns. Sale of the Reston stock will have sizeable tax consequences because Fairfax's cost basis is zero; special planning will be needed for this eventuality. Fairfax may want to consider some form of charitable giving, either during her lifetime or at death. She has no immediate family, and we know of no other potential gift or bequest recipients.

- *Laws and Regulations*. Fairfax should be aware of, and abide by, any securities (or other) laws or regulations relating to her insider status at Reston and her holding of Reston stock. Although there is no trust instrument in place, if Fairfax's future investing is handled by an investment advisor, the responsibilities associated with the Prudent Person Rule will come into play, including the responsibility for investing in a diversified portfolio. Also, she has a need to seek estate planning legal assistance, even though there are no apparent recipients for gifts or bequests.

- *Unique Circumstances and/or Preferences*. The value of the Reston stock dominates the value of Fairfax's portfolio. A well-defined exit strategy needs to be developed for the stock as soon as is practical and appropriate. If the value of the stock increases, or at least does not decline before it is liquidated, Fairfax's present lifestyle can be maintained after retirement with the combined portfolio. A significant and prolonged setback for Reston Industries, however, could have disastrous consequences. Such circumstances would require a dramatic downscaling of Fairfax's lifestyle or generation of alternate sources of income in order to maintain her current lifestyle. A worst-case scenario might be characterized by a 50 percent drop in the market value of Reston's stock and sale of that stock to diversify the portfolio, where the sale proceeds would be subject to a 35 percent tax rate. In this scenario, the net proceeds of the Reston part of the portfolio would be

$$\$10,000,000 \times 0.5 \times (1 - 0.35) = \$3,250,000$$

When added to the savings portfolio, total portfolio value would be $5,250,000. For this portfolio to generate $658,000 in income, a 12.5 percent return would be required.

$$\$658,000 \div \$5,250,000 = 0.1253$$

Synopsis. The policy governing investment in Fairfax's Savings Portfolio will put emphasis on realizing a 3 percent real, after-tax return from a mix of high-quality assets with less than average risk. Ongoing attention will be given to Fairfax's tax planning and legal needs, her progress toward retirement, and the value of her Reston stock. The Reston stock holding is a unique circumstance of decisive significance in this situation. Developments should be monitored closely, and protection against the effects of a worst-case scenario should be implemented as soon as possible.

b. *Critique.* The Coastal proposal produces a real, after-tax expected return of approximately 5.18 percent, which exceeds the 3 percent level sought by Fairfax. The expected return for this proposal can be calculated by first subtracting the tax-exempt yield from the total current yield: 4.9% − 0.55% = 4.35%

Next, convert this to an after-tax yield: 4.35% × (1 − 0.35) = 2.83%

The tax-exempt income is then added back to the total: 2.83% + 0.55% = 3.38%

The appreciation portion of the return (5.8%) is then added to the after-tax yield to get the nominal portfolio return: 3.38% + 5.80% = 9.18%

The 4 percent inflation rate is subtracted to produce the expected real after-tax return: 9.18% − 4.0% = 5.18%

This result can also be obtained by computing these returns for each of the individual holdings, weighting each result by the portfolio percentage and then adding to derive a total portfolio result.

From the data available, it is not possible to determine specifically the inherent degree of portfolio volatility. Despite meeting the return criterion, the allocation is neither realistic nor, in its detail, appropriate to Fairfax's situation in the context of an investment policy usefully applicable to her. The primary weaknesses are the following:

- Allocation of equity assets. Exposure to equity assets will be necessary in order to achieve the return requirements specified by Fairfax; however, greater diversification of these assets among other equity classes is needed to produce a more efficient, potentially less volatile portfolio that would meet both her risk tolerance parameters and her return requirements. An allocation that focuses equity investments in U.S. large-cap and/or small-cap holdings and also includes smaller international and real estate investment trust exposure is more likely to achieve the return and risk tolerance goals. If more information were available concerning the returns and volatility of the Reston stock, an argument could be made that this holding is the U.S. equity component of her portfolio. But the lack of information on this issue precludes taking it into account for the savings portfolio allocation and creates the need for broader equity diversification.

  - Cash allocation. Within the proposed fixed-income component, the 15 percent allocation to cash is excessive given the limited liquidity requirement and the low return for this asset class.

  - Corporate/municipal bond allocation. The corporate bond allocation (10 percent) is inappropriate given Fairfax's tax situation and the superior after-tax yield on municipal bonds relative to corporate (5.5 percent vs. 4.9 percent after-tax return).

  - Venture capital allocation. The allocation to venture capital is questionable given Fairfax's policy statement indicating that she is quite risk averse. Although venture capital may provide diversification benefits, venture capital returns historically have been more volatile than other risky assets such as U.S. large- and small-cap stocks. Hence, even a small percentage allocation to venture capital may be inappropriate.

- Lack of risk/volatility information. The proposal concentrates on return expectations and ignores risk/volatility implications. Specifically, the proposal should have addressed the expected volatility of the entire portfolio to determine whether it falls within the risk tolerance parameters specified by Fairfax.

c.   (i)   Fairfax has stated that she is seeking a 3 percent real, after-tax return. Table 28G provides nominal, pretax figures, which must be adjusted for both taxes and inflation in order to ascertain which portfolios meet Fairfax's return objective. A simple solution is to subtract the municipal bond return component from the stated return, then subject the resulting figure to a 35 percent tax rate, and then add back tax-exempt municipal bond income. This produces a nominal, after-tax return. Finally, subtract 4 percent inflation to arrive at the real, after-tax return. For example, Allocation A has a real after-tax return of 3.4%, calculated as follows:

$$\{[0.099 - (0.072 \times 0.4)] \times (1-0.35)\} + (0.072 \times 0.4) - 0.04 = 3.44\%$$

Alternatively, this can be calculated as follows: multiply the taxable returns by their respective allocations, sum these products, adjust for the tax rate, add the result to the product of the nontaxable (municipal bond) return and its allocation, and deduct the inflation rate from this sum. For Allocation A:

$$[(0.045 \times 0.10) + (0.13 \times 0.20) + (0.15 \times 0.10) + (0.15 \times 0.10) + (0.10 \times 0.10)] \times$$
$$(1 - 0.35) + [(0.072 \times 0.4)] - 0.04 = 3.46\%$$

	Allocation				
Return Measure	A	B	C	D	E
Nominal return	9.9%	11.0%	8.8%	14.4%	10.3%
Real after-tax return	3.5	3.1	2.5	5.3	3.5

Table 28G also provides after-tax returns that could be adjusted for inflation and then used to identify those portfolios that meet Fairfax's return guidelines.

Allocations A, B, D, and E meet Fairfax's real, after-tax return objectives.

(ii)   Fairfax has stated that a worst case return of −10 percent in any 12-month period would be acceptable. The expected return less two times the portfolio risk (expected standard deviation) is the relevant risk tolerance measure. In this case, three allocations meet the criterion: A, C, and E.

	Allocation				
Parameter	A	B	C	D	E
Expected return	9.9%	11.0%	8.8%	14.4%	10.3%
Exp. std. deviation	9.4	12.4	8.5	18.1	10.1
Worst-case return	−8.9	−13.8	−8.2	−21.8	−9.9

d.   (i)   The Sharpe Ratio for Allocation D, using the cash equivalent rate of 4.5 percent as the risk-free rate, is: $(0.144 - 0.045)/0.181 = 0.547$

(ii)   The two allocations with the best Sharpe Ratios are A and E; the ratio for each of these allocations is 0.574.

e.   The recommended allocation is A. The allocations that meet both the minimum real, after-tax objective and the maximum risk tolerance objective are A and E. These allocations have identical Sharpe Ratios and both of these allocations have large positions in municipal bonds. However, Allocation E also has a large position in REITs, whereas the comparable equity position for Allocation A is a diversified portfolio of large and small cap domestic stocks. Because of the diversification value of the large and small stock positions in Allocation A, as opposed to the specialized or nondiversified nature of REIT stocks and their limited data history, one would have greater confidence that the expected return data for the large- and small-cap stock portfolios will be realized than for the REIT portfolio.

7.   a.   The key elements that should determine the foundation's grant-making (spending) policy are

   (i)   Average expected inflation over a long time horizon;

   (ii) Average expected nominal return on the endowment portfolio over the same long horizon; and,

   (iii) The 5 percent -of-asset-value payout requirement imposed by tax authorities as a condition for ongoing U.S. tax exemption, a requirement that is expected to continue indefinitely.

   To preserve the real value of its assets and to maintain its spending in real terms, the foundation cannot pay out more, on average over time, than the real return it earns from its investment portfolio, since no fund-raising activities are contemplated. In effect, the portion of the total return representing the inflation rate must be retained and reinvested if the foundation's principal is to grow with inflation and, thus, maintain its real value and the real value of future grants.

   b.   **OBJECTIVES**

   Return Requirement: Production of current income, the committee's focus before Mr. Franklin's gift, is no longer a primary objective, given the increase in the asset base and the committee's understanding that investment policy must accommodate long-term as well as short-term goals. The need for a minimum annual payout equal to 5 percent of assets must be considered, as well as the need to maintain the real value of these assets. A total return objective (roughly equal to the grant rate plus the inflation rate, but not less than the 5 percent required for maintenance of the foundation's tax-exempt status) is appropriate.

   Risk Tolerance: The increase in the foundation's financial flexibility arising from Mr. Franklin's gift and the change in the committee's spending policy have increased the foundation's ability to assume risk. The organization has a more or less infinite expected life span and, in the context of this long-term horizon, has the ability to accept the consequences of short-term fluctuations in asset values. Moreover, adoption of a clear-cut spending rule will permit cash flows to be planned with some precision, adding stability to annual budgeting and reducing the need for precautionary liquidity. Overall, the foundation's risk tolerance is above average and oriented to long-term considerations.

CONSTRAINTS

Liquidity Requirements: Liquidity needs are low, with little likelihood of unforeseen demands requiring either forced asset sales or immense cash. Such needs as exist, principally for annual grant-making, are known in advance and relatively easy to plan for in a systematic way.

Time Horizon: The foundation has a virtually infinite life; the need to plan for future as well as current financial demands justifies a long-term horizon with perhaps a five-year cycle of planning and review.

Taxes: Tax-exempt under present U.S. law if the annual minimum payout requirement (currently 5 percent of asset value) is met.

Legal and Regulatory: Governed by state law and prudent person standards; ongoing attention must be paid to maintaining the tax-exempt status by strict observance of IRS and any related Federal regulations.

Unique Circumstances: The need to maintain real value after grants is a key consideration, as is the 5 percent of assets requirement for tax exemption. The real return achieved must meet or exceed the grant rate, with the 5 percent level a minimum requirement.

Narrative: Investment actions shall take place in a long-term, tax-exempt context, reflect above-average risk tolerance, and emphasize production of real total returns, but with at least a 5 percent nominal return.

c. To meet requirements of this scenario, it is first necessary to identify a spending rate that is both sufficient (i.e., 5 percent or higher in nominal terms) and feasible (i.e., prudent and attainable under the circumstances represented by the Table 26H data and the empirical evidence of historical risk and return for the various asset classes). The real return from the recommended allocation should be shown to equal or exceed the minimum payout requirement (i.e., equal to or greater than 5 percent in nominal terms).

The allocation philosophy will reflect the foundation's need for real returns at or above the grant rate, its total return orientation, its above-average risk tolerance, its low liquidity requirements, and its tax exempt status. While the Table 26H data and historical experience provide needed inputs to the process, several generalizations are also appropriate:

1. Allocations to fixed income instruments will be less than 50 percent as bonds have provided inferior real returns in the past, and while forecasted real returns from 1993 to 2000 are higher, they are still lower than for stocks. Real return needs are high and liquidity needs are low. Bonds will be included primarily for diversification and risk reduction purposes. The ongoing cash flow from bond portfolios of this size should easily provide for all normal working capital needs.

2. Allocations to equities will be greater than 50 percent, and this asset class will be the portfolio's "work horse asset." Expected and historical real returns are high, the horizon is long, risk tolerance is above average, and taxes are not a consideration.

3. Within the equity universe there is room in this situation for small-cap as well as large-cap issues, for international as well as domestic issues, and perhaps, for venture capital investment as well. Diversification will contribute to risk reduction, and total return could be enhanced. All could be included.

4. Given its value as an alternative to stocks and bonds as a way to maintain real return and provide diversification benefits, real estate could be included in this portfolio. In a long-term context, real estate has provided good inflation protection, helping to protect real return production.

An example of an appropriate, modestly aggressive allocation is shown below. Table 28H contains an array of historical and expected return data which was used to develop real return forecasts. In this case, the objective was to reach a spending level in real terms as close to 6 percent as possible, a level appearing to meet the dual goals of the committee and that is also feasible. The actual expected real portfolio return is 5.8 percent.

	Intermediate Term Forecast of Real Returns	Recommended Allocation	Real Return Contribution
Cash (U.S.) T-bills	0.7%	*0%	
Bonds:			
Intermediate	2.3	5	0.115%
Long Treasury	4.2	10	0.420
Corporate	5.3	10	0.530
International	4.9	10	0.490
Stocks:			
Large cap	5.5	30	1.650
Small cap	8.5	10	0.850
International	6.6	10	0.660
Venture capital	12.0	5	0.600
Real estate	5.0	10	0.500
Total expected return		100%	5.815%

*Cash is excluded— ongoing cash flow from the portfolio should be sufficient to meet all normal working capital needs.

8. a. The Maclins' overall risk objective must consider both willingness and ability to take risk.

Willingness: The Maclins have a below-average willingness to take risk, based on their unhappiness with the portfolio volatility in recent years and their desire to avoid shortfall risk in excess of −12 percent return in any one year in the value of the investment portfolio.

Ability: The Maclins have an average ability to take risk. While their large asset base and a long time horizon would otherwise suggest an above-average ability to take risk, their living expenses (£74,000) are significantly greater than Christopher's after-tax salary (£48,000), causing them to be very dependent on projected portfolio returns to cover the difference, and thereby reducing their ability to take risk.

Overall: The Maclins' overall risk tolerance is below average, as their below-average willingness to take risk dominates their average ability to take risk in determining their overall risk tolerance.

b. The Maclins' return objective is to grow the portfolio to meet their educational and retirement needs as well as to provide for ongoing net expenses. The Maclins will require annual after-tax cash flows of £26,000 (calculated below) to cover ongoing net expenses, and they will need £2 million in 18 years to fund their children's education and their own retirement. To meet this objective, the Maclins' pretax required return is 7.38 percent, which is calculated below.

The after-tax return required to accumulate £2 million in 18 years, beginning with an investable base of £1,235,000 (calculated below) and with annual outflows of £26,000, is 4.427 percent. When adjusted for the 40 percent tax rate, this results in a 7.38 percent pretax return: $4.427\%/(1 - 0.40) = 7.38\%$

Annual cash flow = –£26,000

Christopher's annual salary	80,000
Less: Taxes (40%)	–32,000
Living expenses	–74,000
Net annual cash flow	–£26,000

Asset base = £1,235,000	
Inheritance	900,000
Barnett Co. common stock	220,000
Stocks and bonds	160,000
Cash	5,000
Subtotal	£1,285,000
Less one-time needs:	
Down payment on house	–30,000
Charitable donation	–20,000
Total assets	£1,235,000

Note: No inflation adjustment is required in the return calculation because increases in living expenses will be offset by increases in Christopher's salary.

c. The Maclins' investment policy statement should include the following constraints:

(i) Time horizon: The Maclins have a two-stage time horizon because of their changing cash flow and resource needs. The first stage is the next 18 years. The second stage begins with their retirement and the university education years for their children.

(ii) Liquidity requirements: The Maclins have one-time immediate expenses (£50,000) that include the deposit on the house they are purchasing and the charitable donation in honor of Louise's father.

(iii) Tax concerns: The U.K. has a 40 percent marginal tax rate on both ordinary income and capital gains. Therefore there is no preference for investment returns from taxable dividends or interest over capital gains. Taxes will be a drag on investment performance because all expenditures will be after tax.

(iv) Unique circumstances: The large holding of the Barnett Co. common stock (representing 18 percent of the Maclins' total portfolio) and the resulting lack of diversification is a key factor to be included in evaluating the risk of the Maclins' portfolio and in the future management of the Maclins' assets. The Maclins' desire not to invest in alcohol and tobacco stocks is another constraining factor, especially in the selection of any future investment style or manager.

9. a. 1. The cash reserve is too high.
The 15 percent (or £185,250) cash allocation is not consistent with the liquidity constraint.
- The large allocation to a low-return asset contributes to a shortfall in return relative to required return.

2. The 15 percent allocation to Barnett Co. common stock is too high.
- The risk of holding a 15 percent position in Barnett stock, with a standard deviation of 48, is not appropriate for the Maclins' below-average risk tolerance and −12 percent shortfall risk limitation.
- The large holding in Barnett stock is inconsistent with adequate portfolio diversification.

3. Shortfall risk exceeds the limitation of −12 percent return in any one year.
- The Maclins have stated that their shortfall risk limitation is −12 percent return in any one year. Subtracting 2 times the standard deviation from the portfolio's expected return, we find:

$$6.70\% - (2 \times 12.40\%) = -18.10\%$$

This is below their shortfall risk limitation.

4. The expected return is too low (the allocation between stocks and bonds is not consistent with return objective).
- The portfolio's expected return of 6.70 percent is less than the return objective of 7.38 percent.

b.   Note: The Maclins have purchased their home and made their charitable contribution.
Cash: 0% to 3%
The Maclins do not have an ongoing need for a specific cash reserve fund. Liquidity
needs are low and only a small allocation for emergencies need be considered.
Portfolio income will cover the annual shortfall in living expenses. Therefore the
lowest allocation to cash is most appropriate.

U.K. corporate bonds: 50% to 60%
The Maclins need significant exposure to this less volatile asset class, given their
below-average risk tolerance. Stable return, derived from current income, will also be
needed to offset the annual cash flow shortfall. Therefore the highest allocation to
U.K. corporate bonds is most appropriate.

U.S. equities: 20% to 25%
The Maclins must meet their return objective while addressing their risk tolerance.
U.S. equities offer higher expected returns than bonds and also offer international
diversification benefits. The risk/return profile is also relatively more favorable than
it is for either U.K. bonds or Barnett stock. Therefore the highest allocation to U.S.
equities is most appropriate.

Barnett Co. common stock: 0% to 5%

The Maclins' below-average risk tolerance includes a shortfall risk limitation of -12
percent return in any one year, and the Barnett stock is very volatile. There is too
much stock-specific (nonsystematic) risk in this concentrated position for such an
investor. They also have employment risk with Barnett. Therefore the lowest
allocation to Barnett stock is most appropriate.

The following sample allocations are provided to illustrate that selected ranges meet
the return objective.

Sample allocation 1:

Asset Class	Weight (%)	Return (%)	Weighted Return (%)
Cash	1	1.0	0.01
U.K. corporate bonds	55	5.0	2.75
U.K. small-capitalization	10	11.0	1.10
U.K. large-capitalization	10	9.0	0.90
U.S. equities	20	10.0	2.00
Barnett Co. common stock	4	16.0	0.64
Portfolio expected return			7.40

Sample allocation 2:

Asset Class	Weight (%)	Return (%)	Weighted Return (%)
Cash	1	1.0	0.01
U.K. corporate bonds	50	5.0	2.50
U.K. small-capitalization	10	11.0	1.10
U.K. large-capitalization	10	9.0	0.90
U.S. equities	24	10.0	2.40
Barnett Co. common stock	5	16.0	0.80
Portfolio expected return			7.71